Bowhunters' Digest

4th EDITION

FROM THE PUBLISHERS OF

DEER &
DEER HUNTING.
MAGAZINE

Edited by Kevin Michalowski

Published by

**krause
publications**

700 E. State Street • Iola, WI 54990-0001
Telephone: 715/445-2214

Please call or write for our free catalog of publications.
Our toll-free number to place an order or obtain a free catalog is 800-258-0929
or please use our regular business telephone 715-445-2214
for editorial comment and further information.

Library of Congress Catalog Number: 83-91589
ISBN: 0-87341-758-5

Printed in the United States of America

Dedication

This book is offered to the first primitive hunter who thought to launch an arrow from a stick bent with a piece of sinew and to all those who have looked at a bow and said, "That would work better if..."

The sport of bowhunting will continue to flourish as long as those who hear music in the strings continue to seek the perfect tune.

Foreword

Hunting with a bow is an ancient art that pulls at the strings of the most primal human feelings. Paradoxically, bowhunting is also a thoroughly modern sport complete with space-age technology and benefiting from all the power of modern computers and industrial manufacturing techniques.

Somewhere in the mix the modern-day bowhunter has found balance. But this fulcrum is dynamic, shifting with the whims of popularity and advances of technology. The bows of today are technological marvels when compared to those produced just two decades ago. They shoot arrows faster and flatter than most archers ever thought possible. That may also be a function of the modern arrow. This most basic projectile has also seen its share of technological advances.

Changes in technology have also spawned changes in hunting tactics. Archers now employ all manner of calls, decoys and scents in an effort to bring deer within range of a razor-sharp broadhead. Tree stands are lighter and stronger. Attachments and archery accessories are today an industry unto themselves and no one can tell what the future will bring.

At the same time, archery's sub-groups continue to grow, pushing the bowhunting industry this way and that as manufacturers tailor their product offerings to serve those who make bowhunting a growth industry. The dynamic nature of the sport can perhaps best be seen in the dramatic growth in traditional archery. While technology is carrying arrows farther and faster, there is growing group that leans toward a simpler, more basic form. Custom bowyers are facing back order as demand for top-quality recurves and longbows forces consumers to pay a premium for these implements once thought obsolete by the technology-loving compound bow crowd.

Bowhunters' Digest brings these elements together, providing bowhunters of all skill levels a look at what's happening in the sport. This is a compilation, recording the voices of several of today's top archers. They offer tips, tricks, hunting tactics and general information with one goal in mind: Increasing the enjoyment of the bowhunters who page through this text.

The beauty of bowhunting, indeed one of the aspects that draws many to the sport, is the individuality it offers. Bowhunters may pick and choose which elements they wish to incorporate into their hunt. Aside from the game laws, there are no rules. The material presented here does not pretend to be the last word on bowhunting. Instead, it is offered up in small pieces, each filled with information and opinions presented by those who have achieved success using their chosen methods and equipment. This is done to allow hunters to build on their individual hunting programs.

Use this book to improve your hunting success and increase your enjoyment of the sport. Use it as a reference to explain tactics and technology—both old and new—that you've not yet tried, but don't expect this book to be the last word on the sport. Those who love bowhunting should hope they never see the "last word" on the sport for that would surely mean the sport has reached the end of its grand existence.

Kevin Michalowski
Editor, Bowhunters' Digest

Acknowledgments

While it wouldn't be possible to name each individual who helped create this book, I want to thank the authors who diligently pursued their stories and the archery and accessory manufacturers who offered technical assistance and information as Bowhunters' Digest came together.

Hunting and storytelling have gone hand-in-hand since the dawn of time. All of us who hunt, stop to listen when others talk about the sport. We are always looking for more information, a new tactic or a new piece of gear that will increase our enjoyment and improve our chances of success.

Writers live with the spirit of the storyteller. Manufacturers are the driving force that pushes continued expansion of this grand hunting opportunity. As we continue to work together our sport will grow and thrive, bringing the wonders of the natural world to the attention of a new generation of participants.

Kevin Michalowski
Editor, Bowhunters' Digest

Table of Contents

The Deer

CHAPTER 1

Four Factors That Influence Deer Movement

By John L. Sloan

My cameraman, Gary Holmes, turned off the power and set the camera down. "Now," he said, "if the deer just do what you said they will, we're in business."

I had just hung a portable tree stand and done a standup for a television episode explaining why I had put it where I did. The tree stand was placed on the basis of how I felt four factors would influence the deer movement in the area.

In most instances, there are only four factors that influence deer movement. They are:

Food, Cover, Terrain, Structure.

Except in arid regions or in severe drought, water plays little in the scheme of things, except where it serves as a structure.

The site for this particular tree stand had all four factors coming together at one place. And it worked. We waited two days to hunt the location and a nine-point, 225-pound buck, offered a 20-yard broadside shot during our first outing.

Bowhunting is a game of yards. Tree stand placement must be perfect within a couple yards of where the deer will pass. Unlike the gun hunter, archers can not compensate for a stand that's 30 yards out of position. Success depends on hanging the stand correctly the first time. Everything I do regarding stand placement is done based on the four factors. Always.

Each time I make the statement that everything is related to these four factors, I offer to bet on it. I'll bet that nobody can come up with a situation that I can't relate to one of the factors. Then I'll show that person how the factors affect the deer movement. Think about it. Deer move in accordance with food, cover, terrain and structure under every circumstance. These factors may be modified by things such as the rut or hunting pressure or even a change in one of the factors. It's really very simple.

Deer, like all animals, simply react to their surroundings. They don't do things because they think about it. For instance, deer will not react to hunting pressure before the pressure is applied. They will not move to feed on acorns before the acorns fall. They will not cross a fence at a certain spot because they think it will be easier than some other spot. They look for a low spot. Deer do what they do according to what is happening now.

It all starts with a food source. Scanning trees for likely areas of acorn production is a great way to start scouting new territory.

s the food source changes, a deer's feeding patterns change. Don't look for deer in the beans when the white ak acorns start dropping.

Food

How many times have you heard it? "I atched this buck all summer in the bean elds. Then I never saw him during hunting eason." Sound familiar? What happened? Vell, let's take a look.

Food is the catalyst. Food is what makes deer nove. Without a food source, we have no deer. .nd it is dynamics of the food supply that auses deer movement. Food is the most important of the four factors. Deer must have food. If he food source changes, deer movement hanges. When the buck feeding in the bean eld finds the white oak acorns have started ropping, he moves. Simple? I'll come back to his buck later with another factor change.

Consider this scenario. We are in the Midvest. The crops are still in the fields. It is early ow season, Oct. 5, and you have just five days o hunt. You know better than to try to hunt leer in standing corn fields. Unless you set the ield on fire you won't have much luck, and armers do not like their fields on fire. So you it the woods.

The ridge tops are covered with white oak trees and they are raining acorns. Deer sign is everywhere. This is where I would hang stands. After two days, I've seen some does, plenty of them and a few small bucks. On the night of the second day, a massive storm hits with high winds and heavy rain. On day three I see no deer and I notice a sound is gone from the woods. I no longer hear any acorns dropping. At midday, I explore a deep, sheltered creek bottom. Acorns are dropping everywhere. I move my stands.

Things can change that quickly. As one food source emerges or as a preferred food source becomes ripe, the deer alter their patterns. They react to what is happening right now.

The more abundant a food source is, the more difficult it becomes to hunt white-tailed deer. The more abundant a food source is, the less a deer must travel to reach that food source. It is the travel that is the undoing of a deer from the hunter's viewpoint. The traveling deer is the vulnerable deer, the huntable deer. If deer don't move, we don't see them.

Finding a food source before it becomes ripe is a key to hanging a productive stand.

But where do deer travel and why? Deer travel according to the three remaining factors: cover, terrain and structure. Cover and terrain guide travel. Structure alters travel routes. Deer spend their entire lives going from point A to point B. How they choose their routes is what we must understand.

Cover

Next to a food source, nothing is more important to a deer than cover. As deer move, cover is the most important factor in determining the route they choose. In open country, it is not unusual to find that big bucks are nocturnal.

What better cover can you have than the cover of darkness? In more wooded areas, cover can take odd forms. Hunters need to pay attention to cover in order to choose a good ambush site.

I never did really figure out what it was. Maybe an old road. Maybe a firebreak. Maybe an old irrigation ditch. The path was lower than the rest of the swamp and when deer walked in it, they were hard to see. Once I figured it out, it was obvious. Terrain had become cover and deer were using it. Sometimes, cover can be too thick. Deer, just as you and I, usually take the path of least resistance. For a deer, that path must have some cover but it

Hay bales, properly used can become structure. They can also become blinds.

need not be impenetrable. Huge bucks sometimes head for impenetrable stuff, but for the average deer just being close to the thick stuff is good enough.

Add a little hunting pressure and the deer are likely to move to thicker cover. They move to more secure food sources during daylight and come to the fields well after dark. Remember the buck that vanished from the bean field back at the start of this story? Could he have reacted to pressure, scouting pressure, by simply using more cover?

If you examine the places deer enter or leave a field, they may not appear much different from any place else. That's because you are likely looking at it from the field. What's on the other side? Does that trail lead to thick cover or up or down a ridge or to a bedding area? Maybe it is a path that offers some cover in relatively open country. Deer are using the path for a reason. That reason is usually because the trail provides some type of cover that's a little bit better than other cover in the area. Two examples come to

mind. In Pike County, Illinois, a small thicket of black locust was the only cover leading to a picked corn field. The field was on one side of the locust, a high-grown CRP field was on the other. To get from the CRP to the corn, the deer must go through the locust thicket. Even in the rain and heavy cover the site provided a good shot. No deer would have considered walking through open ground to move between fields when there was cover handy.

Another time, I found deer feeding in a bean field. They were coming in after dark. About 50 yards short of the field was an island in a shallow creek. The island was as thick as my hair once was. I hung a stand and crept in via the creek about 3:30 in the afternoon. By 5 P.M. I was back at the truck, doe in tow. Thick cover close to a food source. That's a staging area. That's a hunting site.

So cover is a constant consideration in choosing stand locations. In bowhunting, you don't need to see 300 yards. Many of the best stands provide less than 30 yards of view in any direction. But these stands key on a particular factor that I feel will almost force deer to come past those stands. With the cover issue, well, covered, I next turn to terrain.

Terrain

We've already established that deer will take the path of least resistance. It's especially true in hill country. For me, nothing is more difficult than patterning deer in flat country. I love varied terrain features. I love sloping ridge fingers and bowls and saddles and gaps and high creek banks. Don't you? You should. These features sure make choosing a stand location easier.

The first time you scout some new territory, have you ever noticed that before you realize it, you are walking on a deer trail? Think about this: A land owner has 500 acres of hardwood or mixed hardwood/pine timber. He wants to sell some. Comes the dozers and skidders. The dozer roads go up the sloping points. They cross the ridges at intersections or saddles. They cross the creeks at low banks. They go around the edge of the bowls. The timbering is done, the woods are quiet. The roads, still raw dirt, begin to show deer tracks and new growth begins and still the deer sign is in the roads; increasing. Deer use the path of least resistance. It is here the first rubs and scrapes often appear. New growth provides a food source and cover. Now you have food, cover and terrain in one place. The features of the terrain, will dictate which areas of cover deer will use to travel to and from a food source. That's a deer travel pattern. Any time cover, terrain and structure intersect, hang a stand.

The bucks, once the rut begins, travel constantly. As they travel, they rub and scrape. They move from one family unit to another searching for the first estrus doe. They move from one ridge system to another. They go up and down and they follow easy-to-understand, easy-to-find travel routes. If the cover is sufficient, they travel just as you and I would. Give them an overgrown logging road and they are in business. If there is no such road in the area just look for the easiest way to get from A to B. That is the route deer will be using. Set up your stand where the elements of cover, terrain and food meet and it will be a winner. With this basic understanding of food, cover and terrain, it is time to look at the most dynamic factor.

Structure

If food and cover and terrain are the factors that cause and dictate deer movement, then structure is the factor that may alter deer movement patterns. Because of that and because we can often alter structure to suit our purposes, it becomes an important factor to understand thoroughly. First lets examine some common types of structure. Structure is something a deer must deal with as he travels.

Deer cross fences. Deer cross roads. Deer cross streams. Deer enter fields. Deer enter woodlots. Deer go around open pastures and fields. Deer follow trails up and down ridges. What are the pieces of structure here? Fence, road, stream, fields, woodlots and one that is a sleeper. The trail itself can be structure at times. To pick a good spot for a stand, it's important to be aware of how deer respond to changes in structure. All of the items listed above are things deer have to go over, under, around or through. Knowing which choice a deer will make leads you to choosing the right stand.

A few years ago, following hurricane Hugo, many of the deer trails where I was hunting in Alabama, were abandoned. Why? Trees fell down across them. Structure. Something deer had to deal with. It altered their travel. Getting an idea here? Let's start with my favorite structure, a fence row.

Deer have no trouble crossing a fence. But the truth is, they would much rather go under it or at least cross at a low place. Especially bucks, concerned about their running gear, don't you see. What they really like is a place where the fence is down. Remember when I was talking about the stand I hung and killed the nine pointer. Here is what I dealt with.

There was a picked cornfield on one side and a thick, overgrown fence row bordering the field. Next to the thicket was a shallow slough with a woods road on the other side of the slough. There was a long strip of high grass leading into the slough on one end. My guess was, the deer would bed in the tall grass and at some point move to the field to check for hot does. He could go any way if he wanted to jump the fence or be exposed to prying eyes. But if he followed the overgrown fence row to where the fence was down, he would be exposed at only one point, there at the shallow slough 20 yards in front of my stand. He came down the fence row at 5:10 p.m. and stepped into the opening broadside exactly where I said I thought he would. In that case, I had no need to alter the structure. The fence was already down.

Providing you have permission, you can alter structure to funnel deer where you want them. Lower a strand of wire or raise a strand of wire. If it is your fence or an old one with no livestock to worry about, take the fence down between two posts. Do it where a deer would likely cross.

Stream crossings can't usually be altered but they can be easily recognized and make great stand locations because they, as it is with the fence, form funnels. Deer may travel some distance to cross at a shallow place with a sloping bank.

Anytime a field is fenced, you have structure in the form of the fence but hay bales can also be structure. Some land I once leased was composed mainly of hay fields. They were not fenced and deer could and did enter them at will. A

Water, in the form of structure, is something deer have to deal with. Understanding this is a key to finding a good stand location.

A fence certainly qualifies as structure and deer would rather go under one than over it. Now, that's a funnel!

In another instance, I cut-down a pair of big, worthless, sweetgum trees. I dropped them both across the trail leading to a creek crossing. After that, the deer had to go around the ends and approached within range of my stand.

Mr. Horace liked to play cattle rancher. Since it was his property, there wasn't much I could say. But there was one small woodlot that was fenced. It was bordered on three sides by open pasture. The fourth side was a bunch of weeds and small cedar trees. Since the cattle couldn't get into the weed field and since it didn't belong to Mr. Horace, he didn't mind if I cut a gap in the old fence that separated it from the woodlot, which was full of white oak trees. That turned out to be the most effective funnel I've ever seen and I made it by simply opening a hole in the fence.

Ever notice how deer seem to cross the road in the curves? Could it be that a curve provides the most cover in each direction? A road is structure. Deer must deal with it. They cross it in the same place much of the time. Find that place, hang a stand.

There are only four factors that influence deer movement. Prove me wrong. Better yet, understand them and use them to place perfect stands.

talk with the landowner resulted in big, round bales of hay placed end to end, around the end of the field next to the woods. Now the deer had to deal with that structure. I had a one-bale gap, 15 yards from a stand in a bushy cedar tree.

Four factors influence everything. Know them, make them work for you and you'll know success as a bowhunter.

CHAPTER 2

They Are Where They Eat

By Bob Humphrey

Throughout the year deer devote most of their time and energy to feeding. As the autumn days grow shorter and colder feeding takes on greater significance.

The race is on to put on a layer of fat for the winter and deer begin to gather in areas that offer preferred foods. Even the bucks, who take a brief respite from feeding during the rut, will follow does to these areas. By learning to recognize and locate the deer's favorite autumn foods, and hunting in the areas where they are found, hunters can significantly increase their odds of success.

In order to predict where deer will concentrate in their relentless search for food it is helpful to have a basic understanding of their feeding ecology. Deer are ruminants. They feed for brief periods of time then bed down. Partially chewed food ingested while feeding is stored in the rumen—the first of four chambers in their stomach. Once in the security of bedding cover, they regurgitate a wad or cud of food from the rumen and chew it more thoroughly. This adaptation allows them to mini-

Deer are ruminants. After feeding they will retire to the security of bedding cover to chew their cud of partially digested food. Finding a food source and setting a stand location between the food and bedding cover is a great way to tag a whitetail.

Apples are a favorite soft mast of deer. If you can locate an apple tree, particularly on an old farmstead with cover near by, chances are good you'll see plenty of deer in the area.

mize the time they are exposed to potential danger while obtaining food. They can also reduce their time of exposure by selecting more nutritious foods.

Deer are almost exclusively vegetarians, and their four-chambered stomach is designed to efficiently process plant foods, which are often difficult to digest. Because of this, they can feed on a greater variety of plants than other species with simple stomachs. This is especially important during the winter when only low-quality food is available. Deer can even digest highly lignified foods like woody browse.

Though they can choose from a broad range of foods, deer are actually quite selective in their feeding. Evolution has instilled in them the ability to discriminate foods that best meet their nutritional needs. The level of preference deer exhibit toward a particular food is termed palatability. When applied to humans, this term usually refers to some relative measure of

the flavor, while in deer it is more a function of nutritional quality.

If afforded the opportunity, deer will choose foods that best meet their nutritional requirements at a given time of the year. Throughout the year, a deer's diet changes as a response to both changing nutritional requirements and food availability. In the spring and summer, does are seeking foods that will provide maximum nutrition to themselves and their offspring. Bucks, meanwhile, are seeking out foods high in minerals to support antler growth. Later, the emphasis for both sexes changes to putting on a layer of fat for the winter and they seek out high-calorie foods. By year's end, their diet is more a function of availability than preference.

As hunters, we are most interested in a deer's fall and early winter diet. What do deer eat from September through December. This is the time of greatest transition, in terms of both behavior and food selection. There is also a great deal of variability in food selection between geographic areas, even on a somewhat localized level. Still, there are general patterns.

Herbs

Throughout the summer and into early fall, deer graze on herbaceous vegetation such as leaves, grasses, and forbs, which provide minerals and other nutrients important for growth. These are both abundant and well distributed, but deer do show preferences. One example is cover crops such as clover and alfalfa.

Not all fields are created equal. A fair amount of my preseason scouting consists of driving roads at twilight and glassing fields for deer. Over the years I have noticed deer seem to prefer one field over another when, to my eyes, both fields seem the same. After talking to landowners I discovered the difference. Crop fields require treatment with mineral fertilizers, which the plants then take up as they grow. The more fertilizer applied, the more palatable the clover or alfalfa will be to the deer. The animals quickly learn the difference. These are often the first concentration areas of the fall. The next are grain crops.

Crops

Deer will eat a variety of grains but research has shown that where they occur, corn and soybeans are at the top of the preferred foods list. Though deer feed on them throughout the growing season, the two periods of greatest utilization occur during the first few weeks of the growing season, when herbaceous growth is most palatable, and in late summer when the grains have ripened. This is when deer are beginning to lay on their winter fat and their diet is shifting to foods high in calories. In southern states waste grains may remain important food sources throughout the winter, while in the north, there is usually a much narrower window of opportunity. Here, the best time to hunt is just before harvest.

Any farmer, or local wildlife damage control agent will tell you that truck crops are also relished by deer. They seem to be somewhat less finicky here, eating a variety of fruits and vegetables including melons, squash, broccoli, cauliflower, cabbage, and potatoes. Still, there always seems to be a few local favorites, which vary between geographic areas. Your best bet is to talk to local farmers or wildlife agents and find out which plants deer are hitting the hardest. These folks may even be able to direct you to a specific parcel of land.

Surrounding land use can also influence the extent to which deer will use a particular crop field. Research has shown heaviest crop damage occurs in fields bordered by woodlands, and the larger the surrounding wooded areas, the heavier the damage. In Midwestern states, where croplands dominate the landscape, it is important to take note of crop rotations. An active crop field amidst fallow fields will be a local hot spot.

Waste grains will be used by deer well into the winter. Corn, soybeans and oats really attract deer to the area. Stubble fields are often prime feeding areas.

Most hunters know deer love acorns. It pays to keep track of the oak trees in your hunting area. If you know when the acorns are ripe and falling, you'll know when to go looking for the deer.

Woody Browse

Woody browse is the single most important type of winter food across much of the white-tailed deer's range. A major shift in diet occurs in the fall. As herbaceous vegetation dies off and loses its nutritional value, or becomes unavailable because of snow, deer change from grazers to browsers. In the northeastern and north-central United States and southern Canada, they feed almost exclusively on woody browse in winter, while in central and southern states they may supplement their diet with mast or crops.

With little exception, hardwoods are preferred over softwoods and within hardwoods deer show strong preferences. Among the preferred species in northern forests are maple, beaked hazelnut, viburnum, and dogwood. Deer will browse on other species like birch, aspen, oak, and even alder, but only if the others are in short supply. In southern areas where these species don't occur, they're replaced with species like black gum, redbud, and honeysuckle.

The key to finding deer concentrations in these areas is to find concentrations of preferred browse species. A prime example is cutovers. These are the "grainfields" of the hardwood forest. Young growth is the most palatable to deer and recent cuts areas are usually choked with saplings and stump sprouts.

Even if you can't identify the young woody vegetation by species, a quick look at it will tell you whether or not deer are utilizing it. Unlike rabbits, deer have no top incisors. Thus, the tips of branches and twigs they have browsed have a ragged, torn appearance rather than the neat cut left by a rabbit.

The extent to which individual plants have been browsed is also an important clue to the level of use an area is receiving. Deer tend to move as they feed and seldom take more than a couple of bites from a single plant. Thus, a heavily-browsed shrub is an indication of repeated use. Over several seasons, heavily browsed shrubs begin to acquire a "broomed" appearance. Once you learn to recognize it, you can spot it from a distance.

Interestingly, while deer show strong preferences for a number of tree and shrub species, one of their favorite types of woody browse is a vine—greenbriar. This species appears at or near the top of the list in nearly all of the studies on preferred browse species. Even better, it occurs across much of the eastern half of the U.S. It is most useful to deer hunters where it occurs in pockets of local abundance.

In regions where deep snows and cold temperatures force deer into yards, they must rely much more on softwoods. Most provide little nutritional value and are merely filler foods. Two notable exceptions are northern white cedar and American yew. Both are highly digestible. Unfortunately, because they are so strongly preferred, they are often absent from traditional winter range. However, where wintering conditions do not occur every year, these plants have a chance to regenerate. Then, when a bad winter does hit, deer converge on these areas, providing a boon to late-season bowhunters.

There is another, quite unexpected habitat in which these two species are heavily utilized by deer—suburbia. Both northern white cedar (arbor vitae) and yew are popular ornamental shrubs. In winter, deer browsing on them is one of the most common sources of damage

Heavily browsed shrubs will take on a "broomed" appearance. It's easy to see which shrubs the deer prefer. Then, all you have to do is hunt near the food.

complaints. Bowhunters can take advantage of this. Many states like Pennsylvania, Connecticut, Ohio, and Delaware have late seasons that allow archers to hunt where firearms hunters cannot.

Mast

Most hunters are familiar with the relationship between acorns and deer. High in calories, acorns are an ideal fall/winter food. Research has also demonstrated that where available, they are the most preferred whitetail food. However, their usefulness for attracting concentrations of deer varies with their relative abundance.

Obviously, in good years deer will be in the oaks. But in areas of oak-dominated hardwood forests, they can find food just about anywhere. Consequently, they don't need to travel far to feed and don't concentrate in any particular area.

Annual pre-season scouting is critical to hunting oaks for several reasons. Mast crop failures can be highly localized. For example a spring cold snap could result in poor mast production from oaks in low-lying areas where cold air is trapped, or on higher areas exposed to winds. Conversely, trees on south-facing slopes may have been spared. Come fall, the deer will be zeroing in on those few areas where trees are dropping acorns.

There are a couple of important differences between white and red oaks that are worth noting. The acorns of white oaks mature in one season while those of red oaks take two years to mature. Because they can produce acorns every year under favorable conditions, white oaks are a reliable food source and in areas where both species occur, whites become relatively more important when red oaks have a poor nut drop. There is also some evidence that deer show a preference for white oaks early in the fall. The theory is that white oaks have fewer tannins and are less bitter when they first drop.

Because the red oak has a two-year acorn cycle, most hunters assume that a good mast crop will occur only every other year. This oversimplification can be misleading. First, while individual trees tend to produce acorns only every other year, not all the trees in an area are synchronized. This means that in a poor production year there may still be a few trees producing nuts. Secondly, red oaks can produce acorns annually by having both one- and two-year-old acorns. They'll usually produce a bumper crop in good years but still drop a few nuts in poor years. These are most often the oldest, and biggest trees. Over the years, deer have learned these trees and will return to them faithfully. Once you find such a tree, you'll return as well. In either case, the out-of-sync trees or the big annual producers are major concentrators of feeding deer.

Acorns aren't the only form of hard mast. In fact, where or when acorns are scarce, other types of mast can be of relatively greater importance in concentrating deer. Unlike oaks, which often occur in large groves, species like butternut, hickory, and walnut tend to occur in patches or as individual trees. Their nuts may be the only mast for miles around.

Though not as important, soft mast also makes up part of a deer's early fall diet. They'll consume the fruit of a variety of species including dogwood, sumac, viburnum, parsley haw, blueberry hawthorn, American beautyberry, cherry, and persimmon. Among their favorites are brambles like raspberry and blackberry. They feed not only on the succulent berries but also on the leaves, which tend to persist later than the leaves of other forbs and deciduous shrubs.

Other

Mushrooms are a deer favorite but seldom concentrate deer as they are normally relatively scarce and randomly located. There is one notable exception. Within a day or two after a heavy rain, mushrooms will suddenly appear in numbers. My experience has shown they are most numerous under a dense softwood canopy. Areas such as pine plantations, which usually function only as travel-through areas, suddenly become feeding hot spots for a few days.

One of the deer's all-time favorite fall foods, apples, can alternately be considered a crop, mast, or browse, depending on how, when, and where they are utilized. In the orchards, deer begin feeding on the apple crop as soon as the fruits begin to ripen and fall, that's after the first frost in northern climes. Much to the chagrin of orchard owners, apple branches are also a particularly palatable browse; deer can devastate a young orchard. While orchard owners would probably welcome the assistance in controlling deer, working orchards are tough to hunt. Deer tend to be skittish because of all the human activity. A large orchard also allows deer to feed over a larger area.

A much better situation is to find an area with a few isolated wild trees. Here, apples represent soft mast that is a deer magnet and the relative scarcity of these trees serves to concentrate deer. Old farmsteads are a great place to find wild apples trees. These locations usually have several abandoned apple trees that still produce fruit and the dense surrounding cover of reverting old fields offers deer more security.

Old topographic maps are very helpful in locating abandoned orchards or overgrown farmsteads. Orchards appear on the maps as green dots on a white background. Fields and open areas around homesteads are white. If you see that this pattern has changed on a newer map, or if you can visit the area, and see that it is now wooded, strike out on foot for a closer look. Topography is also helpful in locating wild apples. They often occur growing along the edges of drainage-ways and ravines, where seeds, washed down from orchards or farmsteads have taken root and grown.

Because deer spend most of their active time feeding, your best chance of finding them is by finding their favorite foods. Across their range and throughout the year, deer eat a broad variety of foods but it is the preferred foods of autumn that are of greatest importance to the hunter. The relative importance of a preferred food species is inversely related to its abundance; the scarcer it is, the more likely it will be to attract concentrations of deer where it does occur. Its importance also increases later in the year as this is the time when food is least abundant and at its lowest nutritive value.

CHAPTER 3

Learning Is Key To Bagging More Deer

By Bruce Ingram

Glance through the pages of most bowhunting magazines. Sit in on the conversations at many archery shops. Peruse the pages of a favorite stick and string catalog, and the major topic of interest typically is big bucks. But examine the bowhunter success rates in your home state, and you'll likely see that in any given year only 15 to 30 percent of archers kill a whitetail at all, much less a big buck.

When it comes to bowhunting, the difference between perception and reality is obviously great. If the truth be known, the vast majority of American bowhunters won't kill a deer this coming season. Just what are some strategies we can implement that will help us become more successful? They start with the basics.

Learn When to Shoot

Bowhunters have very little margin for error when they decide to draw on a whitetail. No matter how great an individual's upper body strength, if a hunter underestimates the distance from himself to his quarry, he will likely not be able to remain at full draw until the animal moves to within range. Not surprisingly, Jim Crumley, inventor of Trebark, says that determining a deer's distance is a prime consideration for him.

"The best time to determine where a deer will have to be before you will shoot is right after you have put up a stand," said Crumley. "For example, I know that my effective range is a maximum of 20 to 30 yards, depending on the terrain and vegetation.

"So I mark off trees, stumps, and other landmarks that fall within that range, and others that fall just beyond it. When a deer comes into view, I know when I should get ready to shoot and when I should actually draw back on my bow."

The next step, said Crumley, comes when a bowhunter sees a deer. The hunter often has to

Jim Crumley glassing for deer on a Virginia mountain. Crumley says that proper tree stand placement is crucial to his success.

Learn when to shoot, says Jim Crumley who is pictured here, and you will become a more efficient bowhunter.

determine quickly the direction the deer will take so the hunter can position himself properly in his tree stand. Admittedly, this is a difficult task because whitetails often seem inclined to amble any number of directions instead of walking right into a good shooting lane. However, if an archer has already considered such factors as food sources, game trails, and wind currents, he should have a fairly good idea of which way a deer will pass.

Finally, says Crumley, a hunter must figure out what a deer's body language is telling him.

"Obviously, there are many more situations that say 'don't shoot' than there are ones that say 'go ahead'," said Crumley. "If a deer is looking directly toward you, if his head and tail are erect, if he is stomping the ground, these are all situations that should tell a hunter to remain still. Sometimes an animal will just look nervous or continue moving along at a good pace. Both are situations where a shot is very risky.

"But if a deer is just walking along, stopping and eating, or looking away from you, then by all means prepare to shoot. Bowhunters do a

lot of talking about deer 'jumping the string.' But, in truth, generally only highly nervous deer do that. If a hunter reads a deer's body language correctly and that animal appears at ease, there is very little chance that it will jump the string."

Even if a hunter makes all the right decisions, he still may not be able to let fly an arrow. Crumley relates that this past season he had a buck come down a mountain toward his stand. The Virginian watched the whitetail approach his stand from beyond 40 yards, walk directly under the portable, and meander slowly and unconcernedly away. Crumley did not have a shot the entire time, some five minutes, that the deer was within range. Such is the nature of bowhunting.

Learn to Make Stand Placements

Several days last October, I hunted a prime woodlot that was dominated by white oaks which were dripping acorns like a hyperactive leaky faucet. Deer traffic was intense, but I was never able to loose an arrow. The reason: I could never quite determine exactly

Jim Crumley checking out the distance between a food plot and his treestand. Learn the distances from your stand to a deer's foods before you enter the woods to hunt.

where to situate my portable. This is a common problem for both veteran and novice archers emphasizes Jimmy Johnson, director of public relations for Ol' Man Treestands in Mississippi.

"I would say that bowhunters make three major errors in terms of stand placement: Failure to take into account wind direction, deer food sources, and bedding sites," said Johnson. "Of the three, wind is by far the number one factor that causes hunters to be unsuccessful.

"For example, if the wind is blowing so that it hits you in the back and carries your scent in the direction you are facing and anticipating the deer will be coming from, you are busted."

Even if the wind direction is favorable, Johnson says archers still will not be successful unless they understand the big picture of the area they are hunting. For instance, come evening, every hunter knows that whitetails will travel from bedding to feeding areas. But what secondary food sources lie along the way? Where do major trails intersect and how close are they to the major menu item? How

far is the bedding site from the forage grounds? Do deer typically arrive at the latter during daylight?

Determine the answers and you are only part of the way toward knowing where you should place a stand. For the next question a bowhunter must solve is the exact location of the major funnel between the bedding and feeding locales. Johnson maintains that once hunters learn to identify and analyze funnels, they will be able to kill deer that dwell in the three primary habitat forms in America: lowlands, hill country, and mountains.

"In lowlands, the major habitat feature is a swamp or some other form of water," said Johnson. "So I look for high ground between two swamps, a place where a creek meanders between two different forest types, or an opening with thick timber on one side and water on the other.

"In hill country, the hot spot is where one ridge ends and another begins. The space between those ridges will likely be a feeding, bedding, or travel lane. For mountain hunting,

Deer grazing on honeysuckle. Learn the various forms of deer foods and you likely become a better hunter not only for whitetails but also for other game animals.

nothing beats a saddle, that is a dip in a ridge. Deer will always use a saddle to move from one hollow to the next."

In any kind of habitat, Johnson concludes, deer will travel the "path with the least resistance." Every funnel will have such a trail.

Learn to Avoid Scent-Related Mistakes

If in the afterlife, Saint Peter has kept a tally of how many deer spooked because they winded us before they arrived within our shooting range, and if our admission through the proverbial pearly gates depends on that number being in the low double digits, then surely most of us bowhunters should plan now for a life of eternal damnation.

Larry Richard, president of Pete Richard, Inc., a manufacturer of scent products, maintains that archers commit a number of blunders regarding scent control.

"The number one mistake made is that too many bowhunters don't pay enough attention to detail," said Richard. "Take, for example, hunting boots. I bet the average hunter stores his hunting boots in a clothes closet for most of the year. Boots pick up all kinds of odors there as they do when a hunter walks to his car, stops for gas, or goes to a fast food place before he enters the woods.

"Another major error involves clothes storage. Hunting clothes should be stored in a hard plastic tub that can be sealed tight. Many

archer searches for deer sign along a creek bottom. Bowhunters must be keen observers of all aspects of a itetail's world.

whunters place their clothes in a black plas- bag, which is better than leaving them out, course. But a plastic bag can 'breathe' and sorb odors that later could alert deer."

Of course, before hunting garb ever enters a rage device, it should be washed with a nt eliminator product. Proper clothes care es not end there, either, insists Richard. He ys that in order to decrease the chance that r attire will alarm deer, we should take great ins to avoid traveling to our stands on the me paths that deer use to make their way rough the forest.

"I recently talked to a bowhunter who had a ke buck cross his scent trail as it was near- g his stand," said Richard. "The spike put its se down to the trail, next looked directly vard the stand where the hunter was, and en bolted. If a small buck has that good a se, imagine what a mature doe or buck can tect."

Another major scent snafu, continues Rich- d, is not following the directions for cover

or attractant scent bottles. Companies in these fields typically place detailed directions on the containers, and those directions should be strictly followed. Many hunters mistak- enly believe that they can not go wrong by dousing themselves with cover scent that is natural to an area. But if that odor is too strong, it may well alert a whitetail that something is amiss.

Similarly, archers often misunderstand how attractants work; so claims Brian Johansen, marketing director of Buck Stop Lure Com- pany in Michigan.

"Many hunters, not just bowhunters, suffer from the belief that attractants are some sort of magic cure-all," said Johansen. "If they put that scent on, a big buck will come charging in on them. Sometimes, events do really work out that way, but most of the time they do not.

"To trigger a response from a deer, a hunter usually will have to stimulate two of its three most important senses: sight, hearing, and smell. If a deer hears or sees something that arouses its curiosity or sexual interest, it will use its sense of smell to confirm that interest. That is one reason why combining calling with attractants is so effective."

Interestingly, Johansen states that archers often do not maximize the potential of sexual attractants. For example, doe-in-heat concoctions can be applied any time after a buck rubs the velvet from his antlers. In fact, the pre-rut period is often the best time to lure in a buck with an estrous scent. Among the least likely times to entice a buck is when the does are actually in heat. Then there is very little reason for a buck to leave a hot doe to check out a scent trail that a hunter has laid down.

Another error that archers make concerns their failure to realize that curiosity scents (with apple imitations being a prime example) can work in unusual places.

"There don't have to be apples growing naturally in an area for a deer to be drawn to their odor," said Johansen. "A curiosity scent, like apples, will draw deer any time, anywhere. Whitetails won't turn down what they think is a meal of apples, just because there are no apples on area trees."

Learn the Proper Mental Attitude

Killing a deer with a bow is rarely an easy task. How, then, do we archers keep our spirits up when we know that day after day we will go afield and very likely be unsuccessful? Robin Stublen, president of Buckskin Industries in Florida, acknowledges that bowhunters become easily frustrated.

"We become discouraged because the deer don't act the way we think they should," said Stublen. "Deer are on no one's schedule except their own, and they react to a host of environmental factors.

"For example, a tree may fall across a portion of trail that is a hundred yards or more from our stand. For years, that stand has been productive, and then suddenly it no longer is. Bowhunters are forced to learn an entire area because of little things like that fallen tree, whereas gun hunters don't often have to pay such attention to detail."

After a bowhunter acknowledges that his form of hunting demands more of him, he then can go about developing a positive mental idea says Stublen. First, we should enter the woods with a positive mindset each day, and realize

that even if we do not kill a deer that day, we have learned some things that will help us eventually do so.

Second, archers should realize that they will make many more mistakes afield than gun hunters will. Don't expect to kill every whitetail that comes to within 20 yards of a tree stand. Many of these deer, because of a wide spectrum of possible errors on our part or just plain good fortune for the animal, will walk away.

Third, hunters should understand that bowhunting is extremely hard work. Real, in-the-woods, bowhunting, insists Stublen, is nothing like what is portrayed on videos where the celebrity athlete always kills the big buck.

Revel in Your Pastime.

"Too many times society stresses that hard statistical results must be presented before someone has succeeded in something," said Stublen. "Bowhunters shouldn't feel that way. Sometimes it is better for us to fail and learn than to kill something and not learn anything. I am just thankful that I live in a country where I can bowhunt. Remember that, keep a positive attitude, and good things will eventually happen."

Finally, Learn What Deer Can Teach Us

One of the biggest advantages of being a bowhunter is that we are able to observe whitetails in a very intimate setting. Indeed, deer can teach us a great deal says Harold Knight of Knight & Hale Game Calls in Kentucky.

"Since bow seasons last three months or more in many states, bowhunters get to observe deer and learn from them from almost late summer through early winter," said Knight. "First, we learn how the whitetail changes his habitat and habits from season to season. Where and why does he bed? Where does he go when he feels pressured? Why does he travel on certain trails at certain times.

"Second, I think we learn a great respect for the deer's major senses: hearing, smell, and sight. But I also think that we learn that whitetails have a sixth sense. A mature doe or buck that is within 20 to 30 yards of you acts like a totally different creature from one that is 100 yards away. They almost seem to sense that something is not quite right."

Last, continues Knight, whitetails can teach us much about the food chain that exists in the outdoors. Although deer generally prefer hard mast foods such as acorns, they also consume a variety of soft mast menu items as well as various kinds of forbs. If we learn these foods by observing whitetails, we will become much better woodsman and hunters when we pursue other game animals from squirrels to turkeys. We will also more likely become better deer hunters.

Becoming a better deer hunter is bound to help you improve your success rate. Implement the strategies suggested here and you'll likely become more successful this fall.

CHAPTER 4

Finding Those Big Bottomland Bucks

By C.D. Denmon

The word bottomlands to many brings a dreamy vision of big, wide-racked bucks. To others the word brings visions of nightmarish tangles of scrub oaks or wet, dense swamps.

Regardless of what image the word conjures up, bottomlands are found in every region of the whitetail's range. In the bottomlands of Montana you may find dense hardwood thickets or brush 4 feet high. In Maine you'll find dense cedar swamps. No matter where you hunt, the things you will always find in the bottomlands are big bucks.

Granted, not all bottomlands are made up of dense cover. But dense cover is where I always go looking for big deer. Many of the oldest and biggest bucks and does will head for this heavy cover during the hunting season. Some of the more reclusive deer will spend a majority of their time in these areas all year long.

One more thing that may draw you to the deepest, darkest, wettest cover around is the lack of hunting pressure. Only diehard bowhunters will venture into such areas. Other hunters have plenty of excuses: lack of viewing distance, trophy-sized mosquitoes, the lack of food for deer in that particular vicinity. Still, when it comes right down to it, the real reason is accessibility. Most archery hunters head for the easy access of crop fields

Close range encounters are common in and around dense bottomland areas at any time of the year. Scout as if you are still hunting so you don't spook the deer into the next county. Move slowly and cautiously and always pay attention to the wind and your scent. Photo by C.D. Denmon

and the big hardwoods and their acorns. These areas usually offer excellent vantage points to observe deer at longer ranges. Although I hunt these areas too, I most often head for the bottomlands when the pressure is on. That's where the deer are, why should I be hunting elsewhere?

Think about it. How many times have you been out spotlighting and seen an excellent buck feeding under the cover of darkness? Does this lead you to believe that the buck in question is nocturnal? If you have come to this conclusion, FORGET ABOUT IT, NOW! I have never observed or even heard of a buck staying bedded in the same spot all day long without moving at least a short distance. Even during heavy hunting pressure deer will get up and move during the daylight hours. The problem for hunters arises when the deer movement is confined to the most dense cover in the neighborhood, the bottomlands. When the big deer do move into the open, it is usually under the cover of darkness.

In areas of high hunter density the biggest deer will most often spend their entire day in these dense thickets and swamps, only venturing out at night. In areas of heavy hunting pressure the average age of a harvested buck is usually 1 1/2 years old. These "average" deer are the ones most likely to visit the big hardwoods and the open crop fields during legal shooting times. If you are looking for something above average, don't just rely on the rut and breeding scents to put a trophy buck in your sights. Find yourself a piece of dense bottomland. Chances are good there will be a trophy hiding in there somewhere.

Whitetail deer obviously have keen senses and can figure out what's going on without much help. When an area that's been free of human scent most of the year is suddenly visited by every sportsman in the area, the older mature animals will go to an area where there isn't much human harassment. Usually the best place for that is the bottomlands.

Your first step to bagging those deer is to get a topographical map of the area and look for

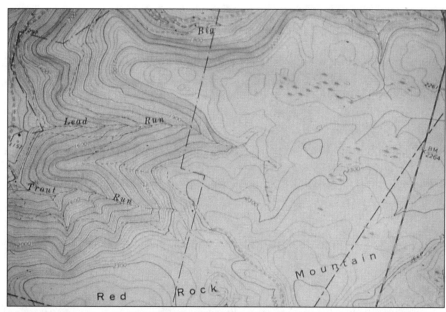

Finding obscure bottomland pockets is the first step to finding that buck of a lifetime. To start your scouting, get the best maps you can find and look for what you would consider the most inaccessible areas. Then try to figure a way in. Photo by C.D. Denmon

the local creek bottoms and swamps. If possible I like to find a swamp that has a stream running through it. These areas are usually very dense and offer deer the safety of cover, plenty of food and water and an easy escape route. A hunter simply walking through such an area will often do little more than spook the deer out along that favorite escape route. If the hunter is lucky enough to see the deer, it will probably be only a fleeting glance.

I will never enter an area I believe holds a trophy deer without a plan. The plan will include waiting for the correct weather, time of day, and a favorable wind. It is best to scout these areas late in the morning and during a moderate rain. The rain will help cover any noise you may make and will aid in washing away the scent you leave on the ground. As always, it is best to scout the area into the wind as much as possible. A crosswind blowing from the bedding area is also acceptable for scouting.

Scatter your scouting trips over the entire year, but limit your trips into the "hot spot" to as few as possible. You don't want to make the deer uncomfortable, but you also must not sacrifice knowledge of the area. In areas of mature hardwoods it is possible to see several hundred yards in any direction and be able to watch a deer's movements and travel patterns. Not so in the bottomlands. To be successful there you've also got to fight the dense

Using streams such as this as travel corridors for scouting and movement to and from your stand can greatly assist you in bagging your deer. Streams running through bottomlands provide easy access and often dictate deer movement. Pay attention to what you see there and jot important findings in your notebook. Photo by C.D. Denmon

vegetation. You might be able to see only 50 yards. You've got to pay attention to what you see.

Many times you'll find that these dense tangles are the deer's bedding areas, but often such cover may only be a travel corridor between their feeding and bedding areas. Some hunters will still insist that you stay away from a deer's bedding area. But the bedding areas can provide all-day, nonstop action. It is in their bedding area that deer will feel the safest. In my home state of Pennsylvania, where hunter density is over 23 hunters per square mile at the height of rifle season, I have observed groups of deer milling around bedding areas without a care in the world.

Keep in mind that what is a bedding area during the spring and summer months may not be a bedding area during fall and winter. A deer's bedding area will often change with the weather, temperature, insect density, or availability of local food sources. Knowing where a

trophy buck is bedding and feeding in August may leave you wondering where he went in October when food sources change. This is one of the most important reasons to scout throughout the year.

I prefer to hunt the dense travel corridors because you can catch deer moving earlier in the evening and later in the morning with less of a chance of disturbing a bedded buck. For some of the older and wiser bucks it may take only one unfortunate encounter to cause him to elude you all season.

One way to find good routes between feeding and bedding areas is to back-track well-used trails in the winter and follow them to where they originate. Most textbooks say these trails lead right into a bedding area, but this is not always true. In some cases you will find that between the bedding and feeding areas there is another area that I term a staging area. If the terrain leading to a crop field is relatively open, many times you will find

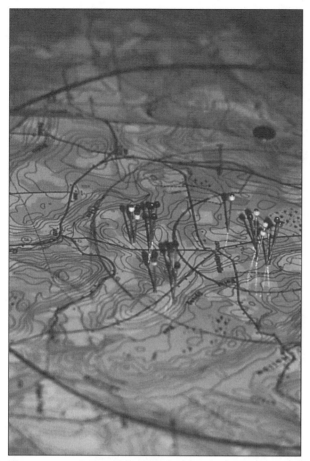

Plotting every piece of information you have on a topographical map will give you the big picture and a good visual reference to the things you've jotted down in your notebook. These detailed notes will aid you in pinpointing ideal stand locations. Photo by C.D. Denmon

deer meandering around these denser areas after leaving their "bedroom." They are apparently waiting for the cover of darkness to move out and feed. It may take hours of observation and days of scouting to determine whether or not the area in question is actually a bedding area or a staging area. At the same time, it is important to remember to pay special attention to the less-used trails nearby. Many times a mature buck won't follow a predominant trail, taking instead his own alternate route. This trail will most often keep the buck hidden in thick vegetation for much of the time. The deer you want is the deer that's old enough and smart enough to know it's best to stay hidden most of the time.

Your equipment for these scouting trips should include full camouflage clothing, including gloves, rubber boots(waders if necessary), cover scent, binoculars, compass, hand pruners, your topo map, a note pad, and a set of colored pencils or china markers. Plot as much

information as possible on the topo map with the colored pencils. This will make your scouting easier and a lot more detailed. Designating certain deer sign to a particular colored pencil will help you put together all the newly found signs when your're back at camp. You should consider having your map laminated to keep the rain from destroying it while on your scouting trips. If you choose to laminate your maps, use a china marker or grease pencil to mark on it. The colored pencils won't work.

If you've chosen a piece of bottomland with a creek the plan is simple: concentrate your search by walking the creek and looking for trails that cross it. Keep in mind that a large deer, particularly a buck, will often slide his feet on the banks of the creek. A smaller deer will step right onto the top of the bank if possible. It is alongside these creek beds that you will also usually find rub and scrape lines, just as you may find these lines of sign along a ridge or down a draw of a mountain. It is the topography of the land that draws bucks to a certain area and it is there he'll leave his mark.

As I begin my walk down the creek I will scan both sides and make note of all scrapes, rubs, deer beds, trails crossing the creek, and deer tracks that I may find. In addition to these recordings I will also add what direction the deer may have been traveling when he made the sign. Keeping very detailed notes will aid you in putting all the pieces of the puzzle together and hopefully pinpoint possible stand locations.

Once I have all this information logged and plotted on my topo map I'll then stray from the creek bed and plot the courses of every trail, detailing every bit of information I find, including surrounding vegetation. By plotting everything you find on the map you will begin to see the "big picture." You will soon begin to understand not only where deer move at certain times of day but you will also begin to understand why. When you start understanding all of that information you will be able to pinpoint ideal stand locations. One key to success in these dense regions is to not get discouraged. It may take several years to find the best possible stand locations within these areas, but once these areas are pinpointed the rewards can be unbelievable.

It's best to have all your scouting done and stands set at least two weeks before the hunting season. If you have made all the advance preparations and can set up quickly and qui-

Heavily used deer trails show up very well in the winter snows. By following these winter deer trails you can easily find bedding areas and escape trails. This is another reason it pays to scout year-round. If you know where the deer are hanging out in the winter, you can usually expect to find them there again in the spring and the fall. Photo by C.D. Denmon

On occasion it may be necessary to set up a ground blind because of a lack of sizable trees for a tree stand. When using a ground blind it is critical to be especially watchful of personal scent control and wind direction. One thing to remember is that ANY area can be hunted, but that area has to be hunted under the right conditions and with the right plan or time on that stand will be useless.

Proper camouflage is another important factor to consider in the bottomlands. Hunting in a tree stand in a mature hardwood forest calls for a light-colored camouflage. Hunting in a swamp that contains mostly pine and hemlocks means a darker tree bark pattern is needed. In my experience it is not the pattern of the camouflage but the color tones that really matter. Camouflage clothing that is made of a soft, quiet fabric such as saddle cloth or fleece is important when working the dense brush. Your approach will be much less noisy and the soft cloth will hide any movement noise created when you are on the stand.

Now that you have set your stands, donned the proper camouflage, have washed yourself and all your clothes in a hunters' clothes wash or baking soda and your equipment is checked for any squeaks, it is time to put into practice all the information you have gathered and go after that bottomland buck.

Let's go hunting. The first thing to remember is to use some kind of trail markers to lead you to your stand. Even if you think you know the area, you can easily become disoriented in the dark. In the swamps and dense thickets there is very little room for error when it comes to stumbling around while looking for your stand.

And don't wear all your hunting clothes while moving to your stand. Once you begin sweating all your scent preparation prior to your hunt will be for nothing. After you arriv

etly you can set up when you arrive at the site. But be very quiet if you're thinking of a same-day setup. In this thick terrain a deer may be closer than you think.

While many hunters like to obtain heights of 30 feet or more, I don't concern myself with minimum heights. It is more important to hunt at a height that offers you best vantage point possible. This may be as little as 6 feet or perhaps as high as 30 feet. Or maybe you may need to utilize a ground blind.

at your stand location and you are in position, put on the rest of your hunting attire and apply cover scent. One thing to remember when using cover scents is to use one that will blend in with the surroundings. When hunting in a cedar swamp use cedar, when hunting in a mixed hardwood and coniferous area go for a hemlock or pine scent. Personally I don't like to use any animal urine for a cover scent while hunting deer, especially skunk scent. I prefer to use non-animal scents such as hemlock, pine, cedar, oak, and natural earth because the shelf life of most animal urine is somewhat short. When an animal scent turns rancid it casts a vinegar-like odor. I prefer to avoid the risk of ruining my hunt with a bad scent. The use of deer urine as an attractant scent is fine as long as it is placed at the proper locations in relation to your stand (never on your stand) and is used at the proper time of the year in relation to the rut. The use of attractant scents is a whole other story that I won't get into now.

The timing of your arrival and departure is also very important. When hunting a morning stand I like to be at the stand and in position about an hour and a half before daylight. This will give any deer that may have heard me ample time to settle down. It also allows time for some of the scent you left on the ground while walking in to dissipate. If I am arriving at a stand for an afternoon hunt I usually like to arrive at my stand two to three hours prior to the time I expect to see deer. If I can, I prefer to stay on the stand all day when hunting the bottom lands. Deer may pass by at any time of day.

If I have not seen any deer while in my evening stand, I will often lower my bow and remain silent until well after dark. Many times I will hear deer moving past after shooting hours. If there is a lot of deer movement from one direction, it tells me to move toward where the deer are coming from. That way I can try to catch the deer during legal shooting hours.

Another important thing to remember is to be prepared for very close encounters with some exceptional whitetails. In this dense cover a buck can be almost ghostly and appear out of thin air. Before you know it you may be faced with a 5-yard shot. You might have to hold at full draw for quite a while. Other times only a quick snap shot through a narrow shooting lane will be offered. It is best to be prepared to make a good shot for a clean, quick kill during either of these scenarios.

As you hunt the bottomlands you may experience the thrill of a lifetime. Or you may just end up scratched, cut and tired from a long walk in tough cover. But remember, just because you have not seen a good buck doesn't mean one doesn't exist in the area. Just follow the biggest tracks you find into the toughest cover around. You might get the chance at one of the greatest prizes a bowhunter can claim: a bottomland buck.

CHAPTER 5

Recovering Bowshot Deer

By Norman E. Johnson

The subject of recovering bowshot deer is often shrouded in mystery. But before we can figure a solution to the problem, we must develop a better understanding of what takes place at the time of the shot and what we can do to recover more wounded deer.

It doesn't get any better than this. The author's son downed Wisconsin's largest 8-point Pope & Young buck in the past 20 years. In late afternoon the buck was hit in the liver and just walked away with snow beginning to fall. After waiting but 15 minutes to take up the trail, a fairly long, difficult search followed. The buck scored 166 7/8.

Despite our best efforts there will be some poor hits. A major magazine survey once reported 67 archery shot deer were wounded per 100 deer harvested. As responsible bowhunters we should be aware of our own personal statistics and learn ways to vastly improve these odds.

A few years ago a bowhunter called me, all excited about a large buck he had hit while on a morning hunt. He had followed the deer immediately after the shot and, after several hundred yards, lost the disappearing trail. Analysis of the place the deer was standing when shot showed some white belly hair. We eventually found the arrow, which indicated a paunch hit. We retraced the trail to where he had lost it and through diligent effort found his buck after five more hours of searching. It had indeed been hit in the paunch, with the arrow just nicking the liver. Had the hunter remained quiet after the shot and left the deer to bed down and die, the trailing job would have been much easier and shorter. He could very well have lost this deer to add to the unnecessary wounding statistics.

There really are no mysterious secrets about finding wounded deer. By applying some tried and tested common-sense trailing and recovery techniques, most anyone will experience a pleasant improvement in trailing skills. Some of those who trail wounded animals seem to possess a natural instinct to do so. But as you watch these individuals unravel the trails leading to even those most difficult recoveries, you will see the logical approach being used. The seemingly mysterious ways of finding wounded deer involve the sound thinking nearly any alert bowhunter can apply.

Making Better Hits on Deer

As bowhunters, don't we all recall those shots we wished we had never made? Making a poor hit on a game animal by attempting a shot beyond one's capabilities accounts for many of the wounded animals each season. Once we release the string we can do no more to improve the way in which the arrow will do its job. But a great number of things can be done before the shot is made to prevent unnecessary wounding leading to difficult recovery or a lost animal. Learning to shoot more accurately and developing a better understanding of arrow placement is the best place to start.

It is amazing how many bowhunters, particularly beginners, seem to think that deer or other animals die very near the area they were standing when hit. They are often misled by reading or hearing how deer die within sight of the bowhunter. While this may be true in some cases, it is far from the rule, and the average hunter should plan on becoming a good trailer. Without good tracking skills surely some animals will be lost. Even deer shot through a vital area can run surprisingly long distances leaving but a few drops of blood, if any, to follow. Though a lung-shot deer should never be lost, even some of these are not recovered by those who think the deer wasn't even hit or had sustained but a superficial wound.

There is a message for all bowhunters and this involves learning more about the kill-zone anatomy and better shot placement on deer. Knowing where these vital areas are relative to the position of the animal is the real answer to short trailing. The kill-zone of a

Clean kills and shorter trailing begins with improved archery. Practice using broadheads is highly recommended.

hooting deer from steep hooting angles makes shot lacement to the vital kill area ore difficult, and should also e practiced along with a udy of deer anatomy from is position.

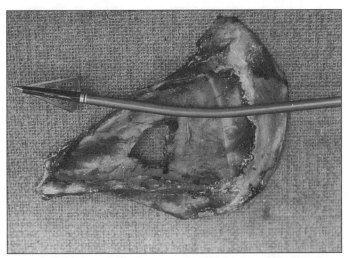

This sharp broadhead from a 60 lb. bow penetrated the shoulder-blade and one lung of a large, whitetail doe. Recovery was made after following a poor blood trail for nearly 350 yards.

broad-side, mature white-tailed deer is less than the size of the page you are reading, and quickly gets smaller as the animal assumes various positions. The vital areas include the lungs and heart and direct hits to the liver or spine and some arteries which are deceptively small but lethal. Detailed charts of deer anatomy are available and can benefit even the experienced hunters when they are reviewed from time to time.

Increasing our knowledge of arterial and venous anatomy too, can really pay off in the trailing of a wounded animal. Learn to distinguish the difference between arterial and venous blood. You can tell the difference between the two by color, texture, and often by its location on the trail or surrounding vegetation. I like to describe arterial blood as being more pink-like in color and thinner in viscosity when compared with the thicker, more purple, venous blood. The oxygen content in the arterial blood creates the difference. Arterial blood is under much greater pressure than venous blood, thus it will not clot as readily as blood flowing from veins. This high pressure often causes spurting which sends blood farther from the trail, assuring the hunter of a wound that will likely continue bleeding. The important lesson learned from all this is that animals hit by a broadhead all hemorrhage to some degree, and it's where they are hit that largely determines our degree of success or failure as we take up the trail.

We must use razor-sharp broadheads. Even the shock produced by the most powerful bows

contributes little to the overall hemorrhaging effect so necessary for quick, humane kills. I see broadheads carelessly dulled by mishandling, including hunters taking them in and out of the quiver or actually practicing with the broadheads they plan to hunt with. While penetration may be improved by faster arrows, sharp broadheads contribute more to the actual kill.

The difference between the hemorrhaging effect comparing sharp and dull broadheads is like night to day. In any wound involving bleeding, blood platelets break apart as they are pushed over the roughened surface in the blood vessel lining. At this time there is a

The Author points out correct shot placement on the broadside of a whitetail. Note where this buck was hit. The resulting liver/paunch shot allowed this deer, shot during the late afternoon, to live all night. It was found the next morning.

Shown here, on a model, is the ideal shot placement on a quartering away deer from an elevated tree stand. The shoulder is out of the way of the vital lung area.

release of a substance which causes the formation of clots. The clean, slashing cut produced by a razor-sharp broadhead blade greatly reduces or eliminates blood platelet formation and prevents blood clotting, whereas a dull, more ragged wound permits clotting to occur. A sharp broadhead can clearly make the difference between a clean kill and a wounded or lost animal.

But even the sharpest broadhead, poorly placed, will not produce a good kill. There must be some restraint by the shooter, and shots should be taken within reasonable range, at the vital area of our quarry.

Deer Reaction to an Arrow Hit

So you've made a hit—or did you? This will be your first reaction on releasing an arrow. Clues to where the animal is hit immediately follow the shot, but they are often uncertain at best. In many cases you can actually see exactly where the arrow enters the animal. Arrow exit can, however, be an entirely different matter as the deer turns, even as the arrow is moving.

Deer reaction can sometimes provide a major clue to where the animal is hit, but an arrow may hit several anatomical zones, causing a bizarre mixed reaction that can confuse you. For example, a gut (or paunch) shot deer will usually leave at a slower pace, sometimes as if not hit at all, or with head low or humped back; whereas, the mortally hit lung- or heart-shot animal will typically thunder off in a sort of death run, leaving less question as to the type of hit. The liver shot deer will usually leave in a hurry, too, but not always—some may remain after the shot as if they weren't hit at all.

Though the liver shot is regarded as a vital shot and such hits will invariably kill the animal, recovery can be most difficult with marginal liver hits. We must keep in mind

Careful examination of the hit site and arrow analysis should be done immediately after getting down from your tree stand. This may include searching for deer hair, blood, tracks and, of course, the arrow.

that deer reaction to an arrow hit can be misleading and should only be regarded as a starting point in the recovery process. You are likely to learn very much more as you follow the trail.

As we assume the roll of detective, major clues leading to deer recovery are nearly always found at or very near the location the animal was standing at when hit. Careful analysis of any clues here can greatly assist the hunter, not only in animal recovery but just when and how to go about it. In that short period of time immediately following the shot, much information can be gathered, and that which you observe and the things you do at this time can determine your success or failure.

As we have discussed, observing deer reaction to your shot is first followed by visually

marking exactly where the animal was standing at that moment. Sometimes a tree or stone or your arrow serves as a good marker. Then your undivided attention should be focused on the direction the animal departed, both visually and by sound. Frantically running animals will sometimes disturb other wildlife like squirrels, grouse, jays, etc. and provide directional feedback to you. Listen also for sounds like unusual brush cracking or the stumbling thuds of a dying animal.

Then We Wait

The actual amount of time you wait on the stand after the hit is perhaps less important than is your ability to move undetected by the animal you have hit. Assured of a perfect lung or heart shot, your waiting period may be less but don't assume anything. Deer frequently

After finding the arrow, look for dense cover. Deer will often head to the deepest cover around.

run but a short distance when hit only to stand or lie down within hearing range or in sight of the hunter. Disturbing these animals can lead to very difficult recovery or even loss. Wait at least 10 or 20 minutes. It may seem an eternity but this is a very important first step in tracking a deer shot with an arrow. Don't get too impatient because all you can accomplish when you get down is the initial examination of the area near where the animal was hit. Excitement and anticipation sometimes cause hunters to leave the stand too early and further frighten a deer.

Satisfied of a hit and that the departed animal can't hear or see you, sneak down from your stand, and get on with the analysis. I always go directly to the place the animal stood when shot at and look for deep hoof marks, blood, body contents, hair and the all-important arrow.

Examination of Hit-Site and Arrow

If you can find the arrow, careful inspection may confirm where the deer was hit and the degree of trauma caused by the broadhead. At this point your knowledge of blood will be very helpful. An arrow covered with thin, light pinkish blood often suggests a lung or heart shot. Conversely, an arrow smeared with paunch or bowel contents or dark, thick, purplish blood paints a bleak picture. Actual smelling of the arrow can tell you much. While blood has some odor, paunch, bowel and other bodily fluids will have a scent all their own.

Arrow analysis can sometimes be misleading because of the wiping or smearing effect as the arrow exits, sometimes at a bizarre angle from the body. In the fraction of a second it takes an arrow to reach a deer, the animal can react to your movement or unusual noise from a bow. Jumping the string is a primary cause of wounding where otherwise good shots would have hit the vital area.

Finding lots of blood on an arrow is a good sign but don't get your hopes too high for a short trailing job; you may be disappointed. Marginal liver hits can result in a very bloody arrow and hours of tricky trailing. On the other hand, finding half a bloody, broken arrow not far from the hit site is good news. As the arrow penetrates immediately behind the front leg, the deer bolts ahead, snapping the arrow off. If such an arrow wasn't broken by a stick or sapling, with few exceptions, you'll immediately find your deer close by.

Pink or bright red blood are the colors you most want to see on an arrow. They are often good signs an artery has been severed.

A hunter once called me from 150 miles away to assist in trailing. He reported a heavily blood-covered arrow and, being color blind, he decided to await my three-hour drive before searching for the deer. We found a fair blood trail but the odor on the arrow indicated an abdominal shot. Ample time had elapsed so we took up the trail. As the sun set, we failed to recover his buck, and resumed trailing the next day. It took another two hours of careful trailing before he was rewarded with a 10-point whitetail. The deer had covered more than half a mile, far more distance than the clue from the blood-covered arrow might have indicated.

Marking the trail with small pieces of tissue paper provides important directional information as well as a reference point to return to if the trail is lost.

Deer hair—and the less you find the better—can also relate to where the animal is hit. White belly hair is often a bad sign. Small amounts of dark, multi-colored hair indicative of a chest hit are far more encouraging.

Hair from different body areas varies in length, color, stiffness and texture, and this information can be vital to the bowhunter. Most hair left behind is cut as the broadhead enters the body, that's when the blades are sharpest and moving the fastest. Exit hair is less abundant.

After a quick and thorough site analysis, which may include sneaking some distance up the deer's trail, you can finally decide to pursue the deer or wait. At this point sufficient time has usually elapsed, and I find it difficult to resist following the trail far enough to determine how good a blood trail I have.

Not infrequently, high hits—even through both lungs—leave little, if any, blood trail with the deer falling dead less than 100 yards away. Then too, heavy bleeding from a muscular-type hit can quickly dwindle to nothing, making recovery next to impossible. Little is certain as you begin trailing what you've hit.

If the weather is threatening and rain or snow is likely to wash away any sign, it's often wise to begin trailing soon after the hit, even though immediate trailing would otherwise not be recommended.

Where a paunch shot is suspected, it's best not to follow too soon. If you take a shot near sundown, wait until the next morning to begin trailing. We have found many gut-shot deer still alive after more than 14 hours. Night trailing such animals can be a disaster.

Most wounded animals will bed down quite soon after being hit, leaving you only a short trailing job, if you stay off the deer's tail. Pushing wounded deer may cause them to run great distances, never to be seen again.

Stay With The Sign

The best advice in finding bowshot deer is to stay with any available sign you can—stay with anything you can find. The worst scenario a bowhunter can experience is to lose all sign of a deer you know you've hit and to be forced to begin a visual search for the deer.

Two hunters make a good trailing combination, with one doggedly following the blood trail or other signs and the other as backup, marking evidence of the deer's passage with a more wide-angle search. Of course, both hunters should get into the finer trailing as needed when sign begins to diminish or disappear. Marking blood or other signs with white toilet tissue shows the deer's last position, and by looking back over this marked trail it is often easy to predict where the animal will go.

Wounded deer will often travel the easiest route, such as trails heading for dense cover. Once a deer is on the trail, walk to the side of the trail so you don't disturb the blood sign or actual tracks. These tracks, as well as disturbed vegetation, ground or other signs will be important clues in trailing. If the bleeding deer brushed against small trees or brush, carefully note the height and position of blood or hair. Much can be learned about the type of wound and its location from this. If blood sign is on one particular side, look for more blood on that side of the brush or trees the deer may have passed. Once a deer wipes its side clear of blood on brush, further blood drops or smears may be much farther apart.

As a wound clots or plugs off, as is typical with paunch or gut shots, blood and other signs may become very scarce. But always try to stay with any sign you can possibly pick up before beginning the visual search for the animal. Paunch and gut-shot deer present the greatest challenge for most bowhunters. If you can acquire the skills to find these animals you'll likely be able to locate others with relative ease. My records show better than an 85 percent recovery on gut/paunch shot deer, so one must not become discouraged too quickly.

Always anticipate the unusual as you follow any bowshot deer, particularly older bucks and does. A very high percentage of these animals will make a circle and, without hesitation, or sign of doing so, make an abrupt or gradual turn. While making this turn, deer will frequently leave a well-traveled trail, even walking where it is more difficult. And, contrary to what is often written, badly wounded deer will sometimes run uphill. Always expect the unexpected. The deer is often found within a short distance of the telltale circle or directional change.

Most wounded deer will bed down. Look for them to bed down in heavy cover. If undisturbed, and a deer leaves its bed with relatively little blood sign, the animal may not be badly wounded. The sooner the deer beds after being hit, the more severe the wound. Gut-shot deer will usually bed and move several times before dying, even if undisturbed. These animals will sometimes head for water as they apparently experience a strong sensation of dehydration.

If an animal leaves little or no blood or other identifiable signs to follow, it can be very dis-

As described in text, the use of a properly trained dog can be a great asset to the hunter in search of hard-to-find, wounded deer. One must check with existing game laws before considering this approach.

couraging, but search carefully. A few times when others gave up the search, I have returned to find sign that eventually led to the recovery of the animal.

When you've exhausted all your leads and are forced to conduct a visual search for the downed animal, it is best to regroup your thinking and use a logical approach. Wounded deer like to head for good cover. Try to expand and extend your thinking over a broader area, as deer will sometimes bail out and head for a different area. But once this type of search begins you will need to use all the skills you possess. Get help if you need it.

Other Tactics and Strategies

Much time and thinking has gone into the subject of locating bowshot deer and other animals. Conventional wisdom would strongly suggest using the best methods available to us.

But gadgets can't make up for skill. First, learn to trail a wounded deer by reading the blood trail and the signs in the forest. Then think about investing in some of the gadgetry currently available.

Some hunters use and lay great claims to the use of a tracking string. Personally, I have never used one. I have seen evidence where such a device can alter arrow flight and actually lead to wounding. Yet a friend of mine credits the tracking string for finding his record-book buck during the 1998 season; others concur with him.

Some seek help with blood identification through chemical formulas using hydrogen peroxide. On contact, even dried blood turns grayish-white. The chemical is not intended to be sprayed around hopefully showing a trail anyone could follow. Perhaps those who are color blind may benefit by it.

Infrared heat detectors have gotten a lot of press recently. Again, I can't relate to experience in using these devices. Advertising claims of one unit tell of finding dead deer or bear 24 hours after the animal was shot. Perhaps I am missing something here, but considering the heavy cover and rolling terrain where I find most deer, the instrument would have a big job to do. Notwithstanding, any device that can successfully help us find any wounded animals should be considered.

Some use tracking dogs to find dead and wounded deer. Where legal, or with special permission, this can be a great help in deer recovery. With the keen nose of even your fireside pooch, most are adaptable to finding deer with even limited training. These dogs must be leash-trained and all you'll need is some paunch/blood juices (available as you field dress an animal) to lay a trail for training. Most dogs can easily follow-up the skimpiest trail, even after 24 hours. The smaller the dog the better. A prominent New York search team uses the little German wire-haired dachshunds in finding many hundreds of downed or dead deer.

Regardless of the methods we use, as bowhunters we owe it to the animals we hunt to make every effort to find them once we've made the shot.

CHAPTER 6

Do-it-Yourself Guide to Scoring Whitetails

By Bob Humphrey

The definition of a trophy buck can vary immensely from place to place and person to person. In some regions body weight is the most important consideration, while in others it's the number of points. For some hunters it is an individual assessment of the circumstances or difficulty of the hunt. But the most common and universally accepted objective measure of a trophy white-tailed deer is antler score.

In 1949, Grancel Fitz devised a scoring system for the Boone & Crockett Club's Official Record Book of North American Big Game. At the time his system was (and still is) considered the most equitable, and has since become recognized and used internationally as the standard method for ranking big-game trophies of North America. Virtually all other tro-

phy recognition organizations have adopted or adapted this system.

Nowadays, the pages of outdoor magazines and books are filled with descriptive terms like "book buck" or "150-class." Many magazines devote pages to reader-submitted photos, the captions of which invariably include the buck's score. And most readers are at least moderately familiar with what a record-class buck looks like. But how many of you know just how that score was derived? Furthermore, how many of you have a set of antlers on the wall and have always wondered how they would score? The answer is not that difficult to obtain.

The easy way to get your antlers scored is to consult an official scorer. Most states have their own trophy buck clubs and virtually every state has a few official scorers from one or more of the

The author admires a nice 10-pointer. But what does i score? See the text for basic instructions on judg ing the score of your buck

ational organizations like Boone & Crockett, ope & Young, Safari Club International, and uckmasters. However, these folks are volunteers. They devote their precious time and effort ecause they are dedicated whitetail fanatics ke you and me. But their time is limited and hey shouldn't be expected to go trekking round the countryside on a lark.

Whether you think you have a contender for he record books, or you simply want to satisfy our own curiosity, scoring a typical whitetail ack is something you can easily do yourself. In ct, with practice anyone can become proficient enough to make a reasonable "guesstiate" by eye. This ability can also come in andy when trying to judge trophies on the oof. If your score comes close to a state or ational minimum qualifying score, then conult an official scorer. It should be noted that coring non-typical racks can sometimes be a rmidable, and contentious proposition, and is est left for more experienced scorers.

To score a rack, all you need are a pencil, aper, tape measure, and, of course, a set of ntlers. Official scorers use a 1/4-inch flexible teel tape, but a cloth sewing tape will work. ou can also use a piece of string and a rigid uler. Care should be taken to avoid stretching he string. A better alternative is a length of teel cable of the type used for bicycle brakes. or a score sheet, set up a page as shown in the ccompanying illustration, or simply make a hotocopy of it.

The first three measurements are actually upplementary, and not included in the official core. However, they are the most commonly sed reference terms.

Number of Points: Count the number of oints on each antler and enter in the espective columns for each. In order to be ounted, a point must project at least one nch from the nearest edge of the main eam, and its length must exceed its width t one inch or more of length. The eyeuards or brow tines, and the tips of each nain beam are also counted as points.

Tip to Tip Spread: This is one of three neasures of space rather than antler. Simply neasure the distance between the tips of the nain beams (Figure 1). This measurement hould be perpendicular to the long axis of the kull. If the shortest tip to tip line is not perendicular, you will have to measure from an naginary point.

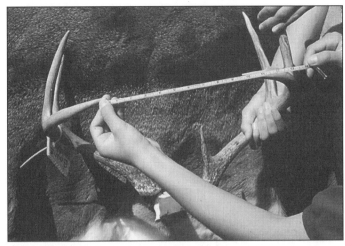
Fig. 1 Measuring the tip-to-tip spread.

Fig. 2 Measuring the greatest spread.

Fig. 3 Measuring the inside spread.

Greatest Spread: Also called outside spread, this measurement is also taken between perpendiculars at right angles to the centerline of the skull. Measure the widest part, whether across the main beams or points (Figure 2).

Official Scoring Sheet for White-tailed Deer - Typical

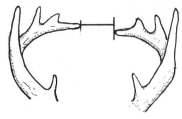

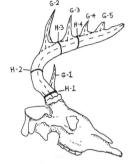

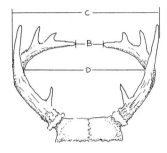

Detail of Point Measure

		Supplementary Data		Column 1	Column 2	Column 3	Column 4
		Right	Left	Spread Credit	Right Antler	Left Antler	Difference
A.	Number of Points on Each Antler						
B	Tip to Tip Spread						
C.	Greatest Spread						
D.	Inside Spread of Main Beams Spread credit may equal but not exceed lenght of longer antler						
	If Inside Spread of Main Beams exceed longer antler length, enter difference						
E.	Total of Lengths of all Abnormal Points						
F.	Length of Main Beam						
G-1.	Length of First Point, if present						
G-2.	Length of Second Point						
G-3.	Length of Third Point						
G-4.	Length of Fourth Point						
G-5.	Length of Fifth Point						
G-6.	Length of Sixth Point						
G-7.	Length of Seventh Point						
H-1.	Circumference at Smallest place Between Burr and First Point						
H-2.	Circumference at Smallest place Between First and Second Points						
H-3.	Circumference at Smallest place Between Second and Third Points						
H-4.	Circumference at Smallest place Between Third and Fourth Points or halfway between Third Point and Beam Tip if Fourth Point is Missing						
	TOTALS						

Column 1		Town/County where killed
Column 2		Date killed By Whom
Column 3		Present Owner
Total		Address
SUBTRACT Column 4		
FINAL SCORE		Remarks

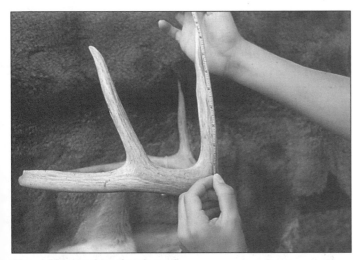

Fig. 4 Measuring tine length.

Fig. 4a Showing the point of measurement for the tine length.

g. 5 Locating the tine base.

Inside Spread: The greatest inside spread is measured at the widest point on the inside of the main beams, again perpendicular to the centerline of the skull (Figure 3). Enter this number in Column 1 of the score sheet. If this measurement exceeds the length of the longest antler beam, the latter measurement is used instead and the difference is entered in Column 4.

Total Lengths of Abnormal Points: A typical whitetail rack will consist of two symmetrical unbranched main beams with (usually) three to seven unbranched points at spaced intervals. Typical racks sometimes contain points that are not consistent with the symmetry and shape of the rack. These include sticker points, burr points, drop tines, or any (unpaired) point that does not have a matching point on the opposite beam. All such points are measured and the total is entered in Column 4.

This is your first measurement of an antler point and the same procedures will be used again to measure all other points. The easiest way is to lay your tape (or cable) along the outside of the main beam (or tine if the point protrudes off another point), at the base of the point (Figure 4). With your pencil, lightly draw a line across the base of the point in line with the top of the beam (see detail of point measurement). Next, hold the tab of your ruler at the place where the centerline of the antler point and your pencil line intersect. Holding the ruler firmly against the point, run it up the centerline and over the tip (Figure 4a). Read the length where the ruler curves over the tip of the point. If using a cable, you can mark this point with an alligator clip, then lay the cable against a flat ruler and measure.

A cable or steel tape are also helpful if you are having difficulty determining where the base of the tine is. Position the tape parallel to the main beam. Loop it around the tine, as shown in Figure 5. Slide it back and forth in a sawing motion several times until it settles into place. Have someone mark the main beam where the centerline of the tine intersects with the bottom of the tape.

Length of Main Beam: Measure the length of each beam from the lowest outside edge of the burr, along the outside curve of the beam, to its tip (Figure 6). Again, your measurement is taken where the tape bends at the tip. Measurements for this, and all successive points,

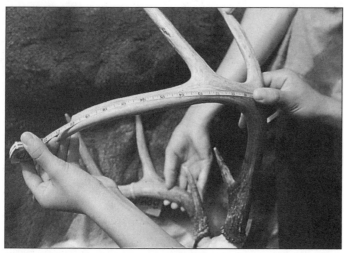
Fig. 6 Measuring the beam length.

Fig. 7 Measuring circumference at point H3.

In the case of webbed or palmate antlers, if both are webbed, the tine length is measured from the top edge of the palmation. If, however, only one antler is webbed, the individual point base line must be drawn along the main beam where it would be if the antler were not palmate. Tine lengths are then measured from this line.

Common base points are points that merge together above the main beam, and share common point material. Like the webbed tines, if the common base points are unique to one antler, tine length is measured from the tip to the main beam. If, however, both antlers display paired common base points, length is measured from the tip to the lowest part of a gap between the common base points. The definition of a point must also be considered here.

Circumferences: This measurement is taken at the narrowest place between points. The first measure, H-1, is taken between the burr and G-1. H-2 is measured between the first and second points, H-3 between the second and third, and H-4 between the third and fourth. If there is no fourth point (e.g., an eight-point buck), measure the circumference at a place halfway between the third point and the beam tip. There are no circumferences measured after H-4 regardless of the number of points.

To measure circumference, wrap your tape around the main beam. Then, holding the ends tightly, slide the tape up and down the beam. The tape will constrict as the beam narrows and will stop at the narrowest point (Figure 7). Enter these measurements in Columns 2 and 3, for right and left antlers, respectively.

You now have the numbers you need to calculate your score. First, total each column. Combining the totals of Columns 1, 2, and 3 will give your gross score. In Column 4, put the absolute difference between columns 2 and 3 for measurements A through F. The total of Column 4 is your deductions. Subtract this from your gross score to get your net or final score.

The minimum entry scores for the Pope and Young Club, which acknowledges deer taken by archers, are 125 for typical deer and 155 for non-typical deer. Typical whitetails scoring 170 or more are eligible for entry into B&C's official records. Non-typical deer, with antlers containing asymmetrical abnormalities, must measure 195 or more for B&C.

are entered for the right antler in Column 2 and the left antler in Column 3.

A cable may be better than a tape for this measurement as the measurement must be along the centerline of the beam. Following the curve of the beam can be a little tricky with a rigid tape. When you reach a point where the tape does not follow the centerline of the beam, pinch it firmly against the beam with your thumb; then pivot it on that point to realign the tape.

Length of Normal Points: The first point above the burr, often called a brow tine or eyeguard, is referred to as the G-1 point. Successive points along the beam, moving toward the tip, are referred to as G2, G3, G4, and so on. Measure these the same way as abnormal points described above and enter in their respective columns for right and left antlers.

Some questions may arise when measuring webbed antlers or points with a common base.

Don't be discouraged if your rack doesn't meet the minimum qualifications for the Boone & Crockett or Pope & Young Clubs. Try a local club. Minimum qualifications for states' trophy recognition programs are usually lower. Regardless of whether it makes anyone's minimum qualifying score, any deer taken by fair chase that elicits fond memories of an enjoyable hunt is a true trophy.

This text is designed to help you in scoring most typical whitetail racks. You may encounter abnormal points or other conditions not described herein. In those cases, or for scoring non-typical racks, you should consult an official scorer. An instruction manual entitled "Measuring and Scoring North American Big Game Trophies" is available from The Boone and Crockett Club, 250 Station Drive, Missoula, MT 59801, (800) 840-HUNT.

Scoring Sheds

Shed hunting is a great way to do a little off-season scouting and take stock of the local trophy potential, and an alternate way of getting into the record books. If you've ever picked up an enormous shed and wondered what that buck would have scored, you now have the knowledge to find out, at least with a reasonable margin of error. Individual antlers are measured the same way as described above. Assuming the deer was perfectly symmetrical (which it probably wasn't), double this number. Adding a spread credit of 18 inches (above average) will give you a hypothetical score. Some state and local trophy clubs have separate categories for scoring shed antlers or pick-ups. In the case of a matched pair of sheds, they may assign a hypothetical spread to derive a total score for the rack.

The Gear

CHAPTER 7

To Find the Perfect Bow: Look, Learn, Ask

By Terry Koper

A quest for speed has launched modern archery hunters into an era of complexity beyond the imagination of the founders of this popular pastime.

Speed is the most potent ingredient in what hunters hope will be a prescription to cure all their problems—from fatigue to taking the risk out of estimating ranges. The other ingredients of this prescription are reducing the weight of bows and increasing the amount of letoff.

Greg Kazmierski, owner of Buck Rub Archery, Waukesha, Wis., with a white-tailed deer he shot in his home state during the 1998 season. He used a Forge Flite AeroForce bow. Kazmierski said he prefers it for its accuracy and smoothness.

Some bow manufacturers have managed a pretty good mix of all these elements. They have produced superb products. Others' efforts have produced unwieldy concoctions too rich in either speed, lightness, letoff, or all of the ingredients. These products have missed the mark. And hunters using them will have a hard time staying on target.

So, rather than relying on a quick cure, it is up to the hunter to take the long course in finding the right bow. It is up to the hunter to find a way through the complex maze of cables, cams, pulleys, solid or split limbs, buttons, bushings, idler wheels, nock points, axle-to-axle ratios, brace heights, and a forest of other obstacles. The reward is that those who take the time end up with an efficient, user-friendly shooting tool. Though it may not be the fastest or lightest bow on the market it will be about as close to custom-made as many of us will ever get. Finding the right bow for you means getting an education.

"Even the slowest bow today is faster than the fastest bow available 10 years ago," said Greg "Kaz" Kazmierski, owner of Buck Rub Archery in Waukesha, Wis.

Kazmierski's hunting skills, bow tuning talents and general archery knowledge are respected widely beyond the borders of Wisconsin, a premier archery hunting state. Kazmierski, 43, has hunted for 31 years. He has 20 years experience in a busy shop cluttered with the tools and neatly stocked with the skilled help it takes to set up compound bows and keep them shooting at the maximum level of performance allowed by the bow.

Certainly, there are performance advantages in shooting properly tuned super-speed bows. They are lighter, shorter and more maneuverable. Higher speeds propel arrows along a flatter trajectory, reducing the risk inherent in judging distances.

But what makes a good bow the right one for you? There is no easy answer, because the deci-

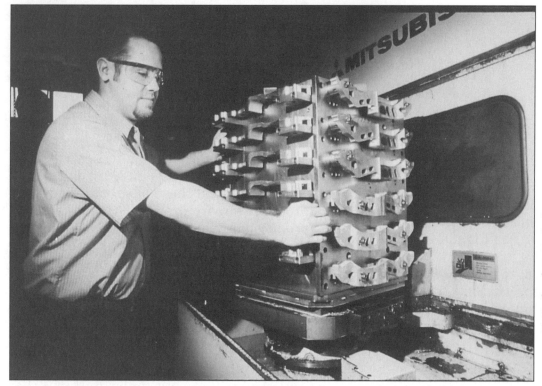

John Albanese moves a carrier of risers from a machining device at Forge Flite in New Berlin, Wis. The manufacture of modern bows has gone completely high-tech. The results are impressive.

sion is very personal. There are some things you should know that can help you make a decision.

If your objective is to have the fastest bow, ones with the most radical cams or single-cam bows send arrows on their way with blazing speed. Forge Flite's Fire Storm two-cam bow fires arrows at more than 300 feet-per-second. Bows from PSE, Oneida, Browning, Golen Eagle, Jennings, Bear, Darton and other well known brands routinely deliver speeds well over 200 feet-per-second.

For a bow that will take all the abuse of the most adventurous, aggressive hunters, a single-cam bow with solid limbs may be best. A single-cam bow is less likely than a two-cam bow to work its way out of tune. Avoiding split limbs averts the chance of having one twist to pieces while hunting in a camp far from civilization.

If accuracy is an archer's primary target, wheel bows still may set the standard. Generally, they are more for-

giving than cam bows, which reduces the degree of error caused by the many little mistakes a hunter can make during each shot.

These are just some of the considerations you'll be faced with. The best way to answer your questions is to introduce yourself to a respected archery pro and ask questions. Look around his shop. Tell him what you want to

The 296 (that's feet per second) speed was for one of Pagel's newer bows. He was testing the bow before shipping it out to a store.

int and how you want to
int and listen to his advice.
As in most other aspects of
fe, however, every advan-
age comes at a cost. In
rchery hunting, prices have
sen. It is easy to spend
400 for a good bow, and up
$700 for a product adver-
sed as an even better bow.
he trouble is, within a year
ose bows may be pushed
side by bows enhanced with
ven more technological
dvancements.

"Some manufacturers just
n't live in the real world,"
id Erv Wagner, owner of
rchery, Field and Sports, in
es Moines, Iowa.

"They want people to
ange every year, and want
em to believe the manufac-
rers made big changes.
ost people don't want that.
ost hunters who come in
ere still want to spend their
oney on something that
ill last, and is accurate and
rgiving. In addition to that,
ost of the people who come
here and are new to the
ort haven't yet developed
e shooting techniques to
andle some of these super-
arged bows," Wagner said.

So the increase in what a
unter pays will reach far

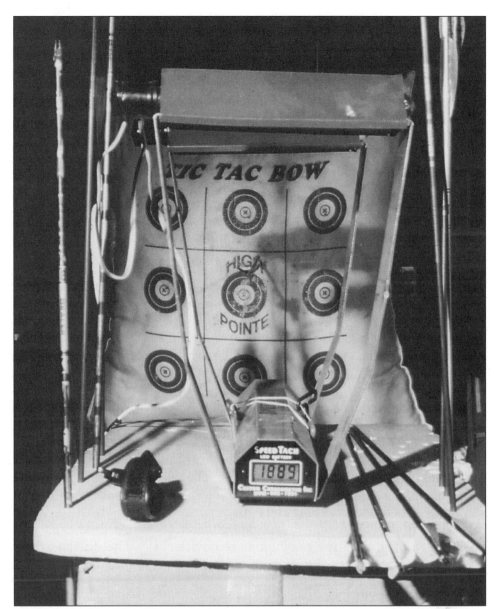

Steven Pagel's chronograph provides an accurate measure of arrow speed. For many modern archers higher speed is the single most important aspect of a bow. Still, there's more to a good bow than just how fast it fires an arrow.

eyond his pocketbook, digging deeply into a
unter's time and mental attention. Today's
rray of archery equipment demands hunters
e far more educated about equipment than
eir ancestors were about stick bows and
dar-shaft arrows.

Today's hunters seem to spend more time
udying the characteristics of a compound bow
an they do studying the characteristics of
er, elk, moose or bear. Modern hunters seem
spend much more time tuning equipment
an tuning hunting tactics.

This shift in the use of limited recreational
me isn't all the doing of hunters. Not directly,
nyway. Yet their need for speed has created an
a of zippy bows. These bows demand a lot of

a hunter's attention even before the purchase.
It takes some studying to determine which bow
will suit a hunter's needs. This is essential,
because some hunters won't ever be able to
shoot well enough, and some hunters who
could won't practice enough, to be able to take
advantage of all the benefits of shooting a
demanding, high-tech bow. Those hunters
probably would be happier with a bow that is
less challenging and less expensive. Of those
who can handle these more demanding bows,
some just don't want to deal with the changes
super-speed bows might impose on their hunting style.

After purchasing a bow, it takes a team of
experts to set up and tune it so that the bow is

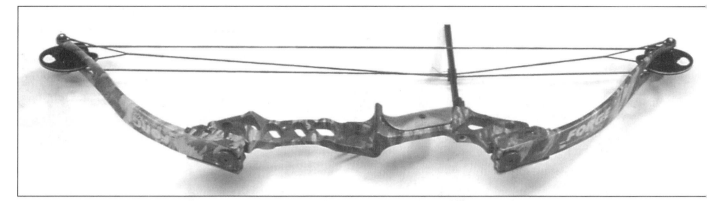

The Forge Flite Lightning Strike is one of a new class of bows designed for women and children. There is a growing market in archery that caters to this growing group of shooters.

able to perform up to claims in advertising. This isn't all bad, because it takes us to the days again when knowledgeable salesmen were the norm behind counters in stores that sold sporting goods. The complexity in modern archery equipment requires knowledgeable people to sell it and to help hunters make the best use of these products. The average hunter trying to tune a bubble-wrapped bow bought in a discount store will walk into a mire of frustration on his first step out of the door. Sadly, however, manufacturers would not market products in this manner if there was not a demand from consumers.

There are times when hunters force conflicting demands on the archery industry. It is not possible to produce high performance bows which weigh less than a quiver of old arrows and still sell them at bargain-basement prices, and still expect that they can be set up, tuned for an arrow and maintained by the customer. Especially those customers with a bargain-basement mentality.

Such goals are as unrealistic as imposing similar expectations on manufacturers and dealers of high performance sports cars. The fastest ones aren't for every driver, and it takes a specialist to sell such cars and keep them in tune. Even after that, an owner needs to know about a product's inherent quirks. An unsteady driver will spin a touchy, high-powered sports car right off track if he makes even a minor mistake in steering. Hunters who can't remain rock steady while shooting a high-speed, high-shock, lightweight bow will find arrows all over a target. Worse yet, they might not find any arrows in an animal after working for a once-in-a-lifetime shot.

These developments haven't happened overnight. When the last edition of this book was written by Chuck Adams, the famed bowhunter included note after note on the myriad of details required to take trophy animals with compound bows. The difference a decade later may be that hunters have to pay even more attention to equipment, without slacking off on any other aspect of hunting.

For history's sake, it probably should be noted that the man most recognized for success in bowhunting for big game animals was closing out the 20th Century writing columns about moderation in the archery industry. Adams was writing about hunters learning to match their own strengths and weaknesses with the proper bow for their applications. And Adams warned that we would walk with the entire archery hunting industry through a period of extreme expectations before stepping again into a time of moderation. The firearms industry struggled through similar changes decades ago. Everyone wanted a six-pound rifle with 20-inch barrel that would propel a bullet at blazing speed, flattening trajectory. After years of painful development, however, hunters found out that these little rifles were much more accurate at killing sound shooting habits than they were at killing big game animals. The curtain has closed on that act. The venerable .30-06 and .270 rifles, among others, were brought back on stage for a standing ovation. The crowd lost its interest in flea-weight rifles in calibers that would punish hunters and burn barrels out while adding little, if any, advantage to killing big game animals.

Hunters who look for bows with moderate characteristics probably will find them more enjoyable and productive hunting tools. Beyond extreme cams and short lengths, hunters should study the riser, Wagner said, cause it will show whether a bow will be forgiving or hard to handle.

Deflex risers place the handle on line with or forward of the limb buts. In reflex risers the handle is behind the limb butts, a configuration which generates more speed than does that of a deflex riser. While not as fast, bows with deflex risers are more accurate and forgiving, Wagner said. When combined with other advancements in the archery industry, modern bows with deflex risers still generate enough speed to get plenty of power for killing big game animals.

"If you just want to drag race through the chronograph and impress your buddies with how fast your bow is, buy one with a reflex riser," Wagner said. "If you want to hunt, buy a bow with a deflex riser.

"The old-timers seemed to have a lot more insight on this," Wagner said.

"The total faster-flatter attitude focuses most on distance, yet the biggest part of bow hunting has always been using hunting skills to get close to an animal. Archery always has been a close-range sport, requiring the hunter to use all his skills to penetrate the danger zone of an animal," Wagner said.

While visiting archery stores, hunters who can't tell the sometimes subtle differences in risers, or in the shape or positioning of other parts of a bow, should ask questions of those working in a pro shop. The skilled help in an archery shop is a buffer between marketing managers and design engineers who may necessarily spend more time in the office than they spend at a range or using a product under real hunting conditions.

Among the first thing a hunter must do in selecting a bow is to answer some questions about hunting conditions. What will be the distance for an average shot? How about the longest shot? Will a bow be used for just deer, or will it be expected to take an elk or moose as well? Will shots be from an elevated tree stand? Will they be made while sitting, standing, kneeling or any of these positions? Considering the kind of animal an archer will pursue, how fast does an arrow really need to travel to insure an accurate hit which results in an exit hole at the distances a hunter expects to shoot? How many pounds of pull can a hunter really handle? Macho image aside, truth is especially important here, considering that some advanced cam bows seem to require more muscle than their less-radical predecessors.

Does a hunter venture out only during the mild weather of early fall, or will trips include time on an icy stand in sub-zero weather? Does a hunter prefer carrying extra arrows on a bow-mounted quiver or one worn on the hip or back? Does a hunter prefer shooting with a tab, leather fingers, a glove or a mechanical release? On many modern bows this may not be much of a question, since they are too touchy for anything but a mechanical release. Some bows work well with some releases and not others, just as hunters find they may have preferences in mechanical releases.

Apply the answers to some of these considerations to a hypothetical situation, exaggerated a bit here to illustrate a point. The example will be made of a Midwestern white-tailed deer hunter who may venture west after elk—someday. Well, maybe someday, but better be safe now and buy the bow powered up for a long-range shot at a heavy elk. Since this possibility means the hunter may have to hike the mountains for elk and shoot from a kneeling position, he really doesn't want a bow that heavy or long. So he wants a lot of power and distance in a light little package, and still wants to shoot it with fingers rather than a release.

This hunter in need of guidance buys a bow from a catalog or discount house where questions about preference aren't given much consideration. The hunter selects a single-cam bow with 70-pound pull which manufacturers claim can launch an arrow at over 300 feet-per-second. It has a radical cam which provides an incredible let-off after breaking the hump to reach full draw. It has an axle-to-axle length so short it makes it look like a kid's bow, not one which would handle the archer's 30-inch draw and the leather fingers he planned to use. Only nobody said anything about that.

The hunter doesn't get to go elk hunting, but on a dreary, bone-chilling day in November he sees a big buck whitetail feeding peacefully toward his tree stand in the northern timber. His heart pounds faster and it is hard to control his breathing the way he does while practicing on targets in the backyard. The deer keeps coming, but by the time the hunter has realized it is well within range, he doesn't dare stand to shoot, and can't pull the bow from a sitting position. Especially with the new release he just bought only a few days earlier because his fingers were being crunched in the draw. Now the draw length doesn't even feel right.

The moment of truth has arrived. In another few seconds the deer will be dead, out of range, or its body blocked by the brush or a tree, with no opportunity for a shot.

"About this time the guy is wondering whether he really is going to need an arrow traveling at 300 feet-per-second to kill a buck at 15-yards," Kazmierski said.

"Really, just how much speed does it take to make two holes at 15 or 25 yards? How much deader would the deer be if the holes were made at 300 feet-per-second than if they were made at 250 feet-per-second? Except it doesn't make any difference because he can't handle this setup well enough to get a shot off," Kazmierski said.

Right. No matter now. It's too late. The buck bolted into the brush because the hunter was too noisy struggling for a shooting position. Answering questions, before buying a bow, about the hunter's strengths, weaknesses and hunting style, would have helped him get a shot. The style of risers, limbs, cams, cables, strings and the add-on parts are as personal to a hunter as his sleeve length, inseam, waist, neck, shoe and hat size. Trying to buy a bow package with a one-size-fits-all mentality won't work any more than it would work for clothes. You'd end up with a cap that came down over your ears, a collar too tight, sleeves too long, and trousers too short. Oh! The waist would fit, because somewhere along the way a salesman decided that was the only important measurement. Some deal!

Hunters aren't the only ones who can benefit from the day-to-day experience of pro shops. Manufacturers are learning to listen to the demands of hunters as they are filtered through these places. Steven Pagel, vice presi-

Steven Pagel, vice president of sales and marketing for Forge Flite, assembles bows in his New Berlin, Wis. factory. Much of the work that goes into creating a bow is still done by hand.

dent of sales and marketing for Forge Flite, a bow manufacturer in New Berlin, Wis., added a cushion to the wooden handles on his bows after comments from customers, most of which came through archery shops. Pagel substituted steel cables for part of the fiber string system in some of his company's single cam bows. The use of single cams became popular because it eliminated the need for timing two cams while increasing speed and letoff. However, technicians in archery shops kept pointing out that the system used was wearing through the integrated string-cable system at a rate which hunters did not like. Forge Flite changed. Other manufacturers were reluctant to listen to mounting complaints passed along from dealers in pro shops.

At this writing, Pagel at times was an army of one on a field of competition seemingly commanded by companies with legions of employees. Pagel, a design engineer who once worked for massive corporations, on some days at Forge Flite performed every task from assembling bows to tackling ways to incorporate consumer complaints or suggestions into the workings of his bows. Pagel also is able to combine his hunting experience with engineering knowledge to produce light, maneuverable, high-speed bows which are still accurate and forgiving. Among other bows, I shot one of Pagel's bows, a Flare, for hunting and daily practice through a long archery season. The single-cam bow was fast, blazing arrows out at 270 fps with only 65-pounds of pull. It was accurate, despite being only 38-3/8 inches long. I could cluster arrows so tightly I could not shoot too many at the same bull's-eye for fear of wrecking expensive carbon arrows. This happened anyway when on only the second day of practice with the bow I drove one arrow down the center of another. Tuning, courtesy of Ron Miller at Buck Rub Archery, and his suggestion to switch releases, had a heck of a lot to do with those tight groups. Those groups are the kind which create the confidence a hunter needs to know that a deer or an elk is going to drop after the shot. At this point, his actions are as instinctive as an archer with a recurve or long bow, and the archer's only thought is picking a place on the animal for the arrow to land.

Some other very good things have come from the archery world quest for speedy, lightweight bows with tremendous letoff. When these elements are added in sensible proportions they can combine to make excellent bows for women and children. Pagel is paying particular attention to these products in his line. His smaller bows aren't toys. They aren't even scaled down versions of standard models. They are individually designed to be comfortable for women and children, allowing them to spend plenty of time shooting at targets, while still packing the punch to kill big game animals, Pagel said.

"If we as manufacturers can't make performance bows that still are fun to shoot for everybody, women and children, too," Pagel said, "then we are going in the wrong direction to make bowhunting a more appealing sport."

CHAPTER 8

Modern Arrow Shafts: Better Than Ever

Today's bowhunter has more choices in top-quality arrow shafts than at any time in history. Here's a look at what's available.

By Bob Robb

If bowhunters can be defined, the definition would include a notation that they are people who love their "stuff." Bowhunters appear to be on a seemingly endless search for new products to improve their bow-and-arrow set-ups.

But lest we forget, the object of the game is to place a broadhead-tipped arrow into the vitals of our quarry. Essential to that task is a perfectly-straight, correctly-spined arrow that will fly with dart-like precision from your bow despite the attempts of a broadhead to steer it off course. In this search, today's archers are in luck. They have more top-quality arrow shafts and shaft components from which to choose than at any time in history.

Doug Easton: Arrow Shaft Pioneer

Talk about arrows today and most people automatically think of aluminum shafts. That's thanks to the hard work of one man and the company he built. Back in 1922, Doug

These two arrow groups were shot using the same bow, and same sight pin, at 30 yards. The lighter "SuperLigh[t]" aluminum shafts impacted well above the heavier, standard aluminum shafts, illustrating the flatter trajectory th[at] can be achieved from the same bow when choosing a lighter-weight arrow shaft of similar spine.

aston was a resident of the San Francisco ay area, an avid archer and bowhunter. He rst built his own hunting bows and arrows hile still in his teens. He experimented xtensively with wooden shafts, and many top ompetitive archers set records using his edar arrows.

In 1932 he moved his business to Los Ange- s, where he grew frustrated with the lack of onsistency and uniformity of the wood. After xtensive testing and research, the first Easton luminum shafts were produced in 1939.

Following World War II, Easton developed a rocess of drawing one-inch aluminum tubing own to the desired shaft size and continued nproving shaft quality using thermal and ork-hardening processes. These production echniques, innovative for their time, led to ne first trademarked aluminum arrow, the

24SRT-X. By 1948 Easton was producing 16 stock sizes of aluminum arrows.

In the early 1950s Easton developed the now-standard system of labeling arrow shaft sizes, where the first two numbers represent the shaft diameter in sixty-fourths of an inch and the second two numbers indicate the shaft wall thickness in thousandths of an inch. In 1958, Easton developed the XX75 shaft, avail- able in 22 different sizes. The company moved to a new plant in Van Nuys, California in the late 1960s.

In the early 1980s Easton introduced the then-radical concept of wrapping a thin-walled aluminum core with layers of lightweight, high-strength carbon fiber. The result was an extremely strong, stiff, lightweight and durable arrow shaft. In the mid-1980s Easton expanded its operation to include a modern manufacturing facility in Salt Lake City, Utah. By 1984 the first of its kind aluminum/carbon composite arrow was used by Olympic archers to capture Gold and Silver medals. This con- cept lives on today in the form of the A/C/C and A/C/E shafts, as well as the X10 and Hyper- Speed shafts. The X10 accounted for all but two of the medals awarded at the 1996 Olym- pic Games.

And in 1991, the XX78 Super Slam alumi- num arrow shaft system was introduced. It fea- tured new camouflage patterns and processes, a new adjustable nock system and new meth- ods of drawing aluminum tubing to thinner wall thickness with extreme consistency. Today Easton's aluminum arrow shafts dominate the market in terms of overall sales.

"From a cost/value standpoint, aluminum is hard to beat," said Easton president Peter Weaver. "For a very low cost you can get an arrow shaft that's very consistent in weight, in spine, is easy to build into an arrow shaft, easy to tune into a bow, and durable enough that they can be straightened. Aluminum arrows are a proven product, and they have darn good utility."

Carbon Shafts Coming On

A decade ago aluminum was without question the king of arrow shaft materials. Few bowhunt- ers gave much thought that new shaft materials on the horizon might challenge aluminum's dominance. And while aluminum arrows con- tinue to be the market leader in terms of overall

ston houses one of the country's largest aluminum odizing facilities. This raw aluminum tubing is on the y to becoming a finished batch of arrow shafts.

sales, carbon (graphite) shafts have come on like gangbusters the past few years.

While Easton stopped marketing their P/C pure-carbon shaft when they acquired carbon-arrow maker Beman in 1995, they continue to develop and aggressively promote both the Beman line of carbon shafts and their aluminum/carbon composite shaft line, the A/C/C.

"With the A/C/C, we're refining what we think is a superior use of materials, optimizing what you can get out of both aluminum and carbon," said Weaver. "When you take the hoop strength of an aluminum core, which gives a precise foundation for component fit and sizing, and reinforce it with carbon fiber, you're now utilizing the carbon fiber in the best way possible. A great example is the new Hyper-Speed shaft, which is the lightest weight shaft out there for a given spine. That would have been difficult to achieve with 100 percent carbon. We believe in this technology, and have invested a lot in it because we believe we can continue to refine it."

Carbon shaft sales are growing annually simply because they provide several performance advantages over aluminum shafts. One is raw arrow speed, achieved because carbon shafts of the same length and spine as a comparable aluminum shaft weigh much less. Another is durability. Carbon shafts are just plain tough. They are able to withstand much more abuse than aluminum and aluminum/carbon composite arrows. With carbon, the shaft is either as straight as it came from the factory, or it's broken—they can't be bent—and it takes quite a wallop to break them. When aluminum is involved, the shafts can bend, often imperceptibly, and these slight bends can destroy accuracy.

Carbon shafts also provide deeper penetration than any other shaft on the market. While there is no empirical, scientifically-valid research to back up this claim, after shooting a lot of aluminum, aluminum/carbon composite, and pure carbon shafts into all sorts of targets, including big-game animals ranging from deer to hogs to elk to bears to musk ox, in weather ranging from searing heat to 50 degrees below zero, there's no question in my mind that carbon shafts provide deeper penetration than aluminum or composites.

Another advantage to carbon shafts is the fact their spine covers a much wider range of bow draw weight/draw length combinations than aluminum arrows. "Spine" refers to the stiffness of the shaft, and how much it initially flexes or bends when the string is released. A shaft that over- or under-flexes is impossible to precisely tune.

Because of their wide range of spine options, carbon shafts give the archer a lot more flexibility and margin for error when selecting the right shaft. For example, Gold Tip sells only three arrow sizes — 35/55, 55/75 and 75/95, which covers all shaft lengths shot from bow draw weights ranging from 35 pounds to 95 pounds. It would take over a dozen shaft sizes to cover the same range with aluminum arrows.

Still, some dealers have been slow to stock or aggressively promote carbon shafts, which means that many bowhunters have not been exposed to them. In most cases, those dealers that do sell a lot of carbon arrows are carbon shooters themselves who understand both how to build quality carbon shafts, and how to tune bows to shoot these small-diameter arrows.

"Using carbon shafts is different than using an aluminum arrow," said Lenny Rezmer, Vice President of Game Tracker, which distributes the AFC carbon shaft line. "For example, I've found that when tuning carbons, a 'perfect' paper tear isn't always the best in terms of the groups you'll shoot. Instead, a tear that's slightly high and maybe 1/8- to 1/4-inch left is best for right-handed shooters. Also, arrow rests that work well with aluminum arrows often don't work well at all with carbon shafts. You have to get into a 'carbon mind-set' to get these arrows to work for you."

Today there are several manufacturers offering pure carbon shafts for bowhunters, including Beman (owned by Easton), Game Tracker/AFC, Gold Tip, Carbon Impact, Carbon Tech, and CAE (Custom Archery Equipment.)

Carbon Shaft Styles, Components

Early generation carbon shafts were so small in diameter that archers were required to use an "outsert" to affix screw-on broadheads, field points, and nocks to them. Outserts are carbon components that glue on over the shafts. This creates a slightly larger diameter part than the rest of the shaft. Outserts remain the common component attachment system today, but two companies, Gold Tip and Beman, began using internal components in their pure carbon shafts in 1997. This eliminated the need for outserts. Soon other companies, notably Game Tracker/AFC, followed suit. These finished shafts are a bit larger in diameter than other carbon arrows to allow for the inserts, but work very well.

"I began shooting the AFC graphite shafts with internal components when they first came out in 1997, and I really like the way they perform," said Tim Hooie, a highly-experienced bowhunter and host of the North American Fish and Game cable television show. "They fly like darts, are consistent, and the larger diameter makes it easier to keep fletch contact off the prongs of my shoot-through arrow rest than with other, smaller-diameter carbon arrows."

As is the case with aluminum shafts, archers can use an adjustable nock system with all carbon shafts on today's market. This allows for a precise nock alignment regardless of the type of arrow rest you choose, and makes it quick and easy to reset the nock position should you desire to change arrow rests.

In the Future...

One trend evident with today's bowhunter is that more of them are shooting the more expensive shafts. Modern bowhunters apparently want the best shafts they can shoot, and are willing to pay for them.

"One of the things we see in archery is an aging demographic. People in the sport are a bit older, and have a little more money to spend on equipment," said Weaver. "They're definitely starting to move up the ladder in terms of arrow shafts. The guy who shot GameGetters 10 years ago is shooting XX75s and XX78s today, and, in some cases, A/C/C shafts. 3-D archery has really helped promote these more expensive arrows."

Going hand-in-hand with that trend is a shift to bowhunters using shafts with tunable components, especially tunable nocks. Tunable nocks allow the archer to minutely adjust the position of the nock, which determines the position of the arrow fletching in relation to both the arrow rest and the bow's riser. This enables him to achieve perfect fletch clearance, which is critical to achieving

Modern archers can choose from several different sizes, weights, and styles of arrow shafts that are all designed properly for their bow. Each of these five different shafts will shoot perfectly from the same bow.

Old-style arrow nocks were glued in place, making them impossible to adjust during the bow tuning process. While this nock style is still available, smart archers avoid it in favor of a tunable nock system.

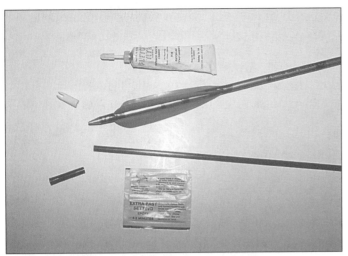

In addition to glue-on nocks, carbon arrow users were forced to use "outserts" to attach both nocks and arrow points. "Hip" modern bowhunters choose shafts featuring tunable nock systems and, if they select carbon shafts, choose those using internal components, which eliminate the need for the bulky outserts.

years, while the GameGetter class has fallen off about 30 percent during that same time. During the same period, A/C/C shaft sales have grown steadily, and now is about 1/3 of the total numbers of XX78 sales.

"That's a pretty remarkable number when you consider the price differential, with A/C/C's costing roughly twice the amount of XX78s at retail," he said.

So, what else is on the arrow shaft horizon? Only time will tell. But one thing's certain, today's manufacturers are not standing still when it comes to shaft development.

"We continue to work on improving our aluminum shafts, but we're continually looking at anything and everything out there, stuff like boron, kevlar, and so on," Weaver said.

dart-like arrow flight. Before the advent of tunable nock systems, archers determined the nock position of their shafts by trial and error, then glued their nocks in place. It was a slow, tedious process. And if you ever wanted to rotate the nock for any reason — like using a new arrow rest — you had to laboriously heat the nocks until the glue melted. It was not fun.

Weaver's data shows similar changes in what bowhunters want.

"I think we are getting a more knowledgeable group of archers out there," he said. "Maybe that's because we don't have as much influx of new archers as we did years ago, which may be a problem for archery in general but it is creating a more knowledgeable shooter as a percentage of the marketplace. These people appreciate the features of adjustable nocks, easily-replaced components, a choice of different arrow shaft sizes, etc.

"The other thing we've seen is the matter of just plain 'feel,'" Weaver said. "They ask, 'What do I like best as a shooter?' There's quite a few people who have tried a different shaft, say carbon or the A/C/C, and have decided that, 'I really like aluminum shafts best, they're the best arrow for my hunting, and that's what I'm going to shoot.'

"Still, it's nice to have so many good options out there." According to Weaver, the sales of the XX78 class of aluminum arrow shaft has increased about 2 1/2 times in the past five

Bob Robb took this nice 1998 whitetail buck from a tree stand using carbon arrow shafts. More and more tree stand whitetail hunters are using carbon arrows each fall.

Kevlar, for example, doesn't have any value by itself. It adds lots of strength and weight, but it doesn't have any stiffness. But that's the process. We look at all materials out there, all the resin systems, all the composites, thermo-plastics, and so on. Nothing is sitting on the horizon right now that we're aware of that will appear tomorrow as the all-new, breakthrough new material. Aluminum, aluminum/carbon composites, and pure carbon are really the only choices today that offer reasonable performance values to the consumer. But if we can find something that will work better, you can be sure we'll use it."

Arrow Shaft Manufacturers

Carbon Impact
2628 Garfield Rd. N.
Suite 38
Traverse City, MI 49686
616-929-8152

Carbon Tech
9050 Ranchview Ct.
Elk Grove, CA 95624
916/755-3622

Custom Archery Equipment
21529 Menlo Ave.
Torrance, CA 90502
310/212-5500

Gold Tip Corporation
140 S. Main St.
Pleasant Grove, UT 84062
800/551-0541

Easton
5040 W. Harold Gatty Dr.
Salt Lake City, UT 84116
801/539-1400

Game Tracker/AFC
3476 Eastman Dr.
Flushing, MI 48433
810/733-6360

True-Flight Arrow Co.
P.O. Box 746
Monticello, IN 47960
219/583-5131

CHAPTER 9

High On Hang-On Stands

By Mark Hicks

Before first light, Tom Lott slips his arms through the shoulder straps of his tree stand. With bow in hand, he makes his way across a cut cornfield to a wood lot that borders the southern fence line. Through previous scouting efforts, Lott suspects a trophy whitetail buck skirts the edge of the woods to scent-check the area before bedding down next to a small pond adjacent to the field.

Most bowhunting these days is done from tree stands. Of the many types hang-on stands are quieter to set up and more versatile than ladders or climbing stands and are much more portable than free-standing platforms. They also get you higher and work in multi-trunked trees.

Because the prevailing wind in the farm country of eastern Ohio where Lott hunts is from the southwest, it is impossible to penetrate a buck's bedding location without being detected. The buck can wind trouble approaching from the south and the pond prevents intruders from sneaking in from the north. For the deer, it's a sweet setup—one that could allow a buck to live long enough to grow heavy antlers.

Lott believes the buck circles around and approaches the bedding area from the west by traveling just inside the wooded edge of the fence line. Months before, he had picked out a tree that would intercept any deer that tried such a ploy. He had not been back since.

It is roughly 90 minutes until first light and Lott wants to be perched in his tree stand at least an hour before the horizon begins to brighten. Experience has taught him big bucks return to their beds soon after daylight even now, during the early phase of the rut. That leaves him only 30 minutes to find the tree, erect the stand and ready his bow.

Lott, an experienced hunter who has taken several Pope & Young whitetails, moves with steady purpose. Upon reaching the tree, he silently fastens screw-in metal steps, working up the trunk to a height of nearly 25 feet. He then screws-in the T-pin that supports his hang-on style tree stand. He silently places the stand in position and secures the stand's strap around the tree. Less than two hours later, a dandy eight-pointer passes only 6 yards from Lott's tree and he collects yet another trophy whitetail.

Hang-on Stands

No doubt Lott's scouting efforts and his uncanny ability to determine the movements of trophy bucks are two of the keys to his success. But he's convinced he wouldn't do nearly as well were it not for the hang-on tree stand system he has developed through trial and error over years of hunting. Lott is just one of several

Ohio hunters, all of them friends from Columbus, who dote on hang-on stands and tree steps. Each has collected several trophy whitetail bucks.

Hang-on stands may be rigged in practically any type of tree. They are quieter to set up than climbing stands and less cumbersome than ladder stands. These advantages are crucial to Lott and his friends because they constantly move their tree stand locations.

"I'm convinced," says Lott, "that your best chance to tag a big buck is the first or second time you hunt any given tree stand. If you keep returning to the same location, the deer soon figure you out and your odds for success plummet."

Lott and his friends are fanatical regarding the types of stands and tree steps they employ. He and hunting buddy Miles Clary prefer a steel Amacker stand with a woven mesh platform. At 12 pounds, this stand is heavier than many aluminum models on the market, but Lott and Clary feel the stand's advantages far offset its additional weight.

"I've tried a lot of aluminum stands made with tubular platforms," says Lott. "Some of the ones that are welded and not riveted do a fair job. But even the best of them are noisy compared to a steel mesh stand. That's doubly true when the weather's extremely cold. A big buck just won't tolerate a creaky tree stand. I've learned that the hard way."

The T-pin feature is another reason Lott and Clary favor the Amacker. You first screw the pin into the tree and then hang the stand on it. The pin helps stabilize the stand and leaves both hands free to fasten the chain, strap or rope that wraps around the tree's trunk. It's a much quieter and safer process than trying to hold the stand against the tree while fastening it. Lott and Clary weld an extended handle to the T-pin. This provides needed leverage for screwing it in, since you are limited to the use of one hand at this point in the stand-hanging operation.

Steve Pinkston, another of Lott's friends, favors the Lone Wolf stand which features a patented molded aluminum platform. There are no welds, rivets or hollow tubes to creak or emit other unwanted noises. Folding the seat to the down position moves the stand away from the tree, which tightens the anchor rope or chain, creating a strong, stable connection.

If you plan to leave a stand in a tree for an extended period, a chain-on system is best,

Trees with protruding limbs are no problem for hang-on stands. This tree would have been and impossible site for a climbing tree stand.

since it may be secured with a padlock to help prevent theft. A quieter strap or rope system is preferred by Lott and his friends who remove their stands after almost every hunt. They strive to get up a tree as quietly as possible to avoid alerting deer. Chains can clink or inadvertently bang against the stand during setup. This noise only serves as a warning to any nearby deer.

Adam Hays, another member of this close-knit circle of hunters, opts for a different system. He modified a Lone Wolf tree stand by bolting two down-turned metal hooks to the stand's stem. The hooks slip behind a heavy metal cable that is first fastened to the tree. Large rubber grommets on the cable leave room for the hooks to slip into place. This system may be used in areas where screw-in tree steps and T-pins are not allowed, such as on public lands. The cable affords the same advantage as a T-pin, since you can first hang the stand on the cable and then secure the strap or chain.

Some hunters will weld a tree step to the T-pins of their hang-on stands to provide needed leverage for inserting the T-pin, which stabilizes the stand, into the tree.

Steppin' Up

Metal tree steps, where legal, are the choice of these successful Ohio buck hunters. They especially like Loc-On and Cranford EZY Climb steps, because these models start fast and screw in easily. Some tree steps can work you to death before they take hold. A dozen tree steps will do the job in most cases, but it's wise to carry a few extra steps just in case you need to gain additional height.

When hunting where screw-in steps are not permitted, strap-on tree steps offer a viable option. Mike Rex, who regularly takes trophy bucks from the Appalachian region of southeast Ohio, prefers the Deer Me brand tree step, which he has used for many years. It features a quick-cinch rope system that he claims is faster than installing screw-in steps.

"The only problem," says Rex, "is keeping the ropes from tangling. I've had my best luck draping a half dozen steps over the back of my neck and pulling them off one at a time as I climb the tree."

Strap-on climbing sticks offer another option. Though not as light as screw-in and strap-on steps, climbing sticks attach quickly and afford one of the fastest means for getting up a tree. They are especially applicable when you don't need to get much higher than 15 feet or so.

Tree Stand Safety

All these hunters wisely wear a safety belt when hunting from a tree stand. When they step up onto the platform, they secure the belt before doing anything else. Where they leave themselves vulnerable, however, is when

Some brands of tree steps screw in with much less effort than others. Screw-in tree steps let you quickly and quietly climb any tree that will support a hang-on stand.

climbing the tree and fixing the stand in place. Anytime you are attaching steps, only one hand is free to hold onto the tree's trunk. And when securing a stand's chain or strap, you sometimes find yourself grappling to complete the task without any handhold on the tree. It's an invitation to disaster.

I've taken to wearing a safety belt while climbing and placing hang-on stands, which is something too few hunters do. The climbing belt I use, the Treehopper, features a cinch-rope that adjusts to the diameter of the trunk which usually narrows as you ascend the tree. A similar belt is made by Southland.

Wearing a climbing belt not only prevents falls, it takes much of the work out of hanging a stand. You can lean back into the belt and have both hands free for placing steps and securing stands. Once the stand is fixed in position, I unhook a latch on the belt so I can climb up onto the platform. Then I immediately refasten the latch and use the climbing belt as a safety belt while hunting from the stand.

Best Trees

If you can find one where it's needed, an ideal tree for a stand is a thick, multi-limbed specimen, such as a spreading oak. When you climb above the lower limbs, deer are less likely to see you.

A thick pine tree does an especially nice job of breaking up your outline and hiding your movements. Instead of trimming the boughs, tie them back with monofilament fishing line. When you leave, untie the line and the boughs bounce right back. Other hunters will never suspect you've been there.

Such trees help you go undetected while hunting only 12 to 15 feet above the ground. Hang-on stands excel in these situations.

Tree Stand Height

When hunting weary bucks that regularly elude hunters, as is the case with this Ohio bunch, 18 feet is about the minimum height for a tree stand. This is particularly true when hunting from a straight-trunked tree. Most of these hunters routinely climb higher than 20 feet. In order to take a buck that was passing through a funnel of woods with a group of does, Rex once erected a stand at the nose-bleed height of 40 feet to avoid being detected.

Only hang-on stands let you easily attain such high perches without sawing off limbs. Ladder stands are too short and there are few trees that have trunks bare enough to let you get much higher than 15 feet with a climbing stand.

In addition to getting you above a deer's line of vision, a high stand sets your scent aloft where air currents, with luck, whisk it away. This helps you avoid being winded. One down side to a high stand is that it presents bowhunters with a steeper, more difficult shot angle when deer pass close by the tree.

After picking the brains of these Ohio hunters, I've incorporated much of what I've learned in my own hunting. I started by investing in a hang-on stand, a welded aluminum model with a tubular platform. The stand's light weight, about 7 pounds, convinced me to try it. It proved to be stable and easy to erect, but, true to the advice of my Ohio peers, it was noisier than their stands.

The author finds that a climbing safety belt, such as this model from Treehopper, makes hanging stands safer and easier. For safety's sake, never scale a tree without some type of safety equipment.

I glued outdoor carpeting to the stand's platform to help silence it, which worked reasonably well when temperatures were above freezing. The carpeting proved to be a catastrophe, however, in subfreezing weather. Any mud or snow caked on my boots would freeze to the carpeting and crunch whenever I moved my feet. In order to stay silent, I had to leave my boots, literally, frozen to the carpet.

I did pay closer attention, however, regarding the amount of time I spent at each tree stand site. I hunted most stands no more than two times and was within bow range of more whitetails than ever before. Because you are allowed only one buck per season in Ohio, I passed on dozens of does and small bucks. A few stand sites looked so promising I hunted them four or five times, but to no avail. If I didn't see deer the first or second time I hunted a stand, additional visits to that location usually proved futile. Just as the other hunters predicted.

By mid-November I was beginning to wonder if I'd ever see a buck worth shooting. On a day when the temperature never rose above the freezing mark, I hiked about half a mile into a wooded public hunting area for an afternoon hunt. I had selected the tree weeks before and was at the base, ready to climb at about 4 p.m. Minutes later, I strapped my hang-on stand to the tree's trunk more than 20 feet above the ground. I had taken great pains to keep noise to a minimum during this process.

About 5:30 I heard a deer coming down off the ridge. Its hooves crunched the crisp leaves as though they were crushing potato chips. Then I saw the deer 70 yards off, a big-bodied seven-point buck with a wide spread. He wouldn't make the Pope & Young record book, but I deemed him good enough.

Two short grunts on my grunt call pulled the buck to my stand. When he offered a quartering away shot at eight paces, my longbow drove an arrow down through one lung and into the heart. I watched him drop seconds later. A first-time hunt from a hang-on stand had produced a nice buck. It surely wouldn't be the last.

CHAPTER 10

Getting Organized Can Make Your Hunt Even Better

By John Kasun

In many ways bowhunting is like a giant jigsaw puzzle. Both are made up of many small pieces but the picture won't be complete until all are in place. Most hunters focus on the bigger pieces of the bowhunting puzzle such as properly tuned equipment, shooting skills, preseason scouting, etc. While these major components are obviously important, the one thing I have learned in more than 40 years of bowhunting is that attention to detail is the glue that binds the pieces together. Attention to detail is one of the things that spells the difference between success and failure. One of these important details is organization.

Bowhunting is a sport that requires hours, days and even weeks of extreme patience. This time is periodically interrupted by a few seconds of intense activity requiring split-second decisions and automatic responses. Because we never know when those few seconds will occur and that big buck will appear out of nowhere, it is important to be ready at all times. This means spending your time hunting, not hunting for things. It means having what you need at your fingertips when you need it, knowing it will be there and being able to find it in the

eeping equipment organized makes hunting easier and reduces the frustration associated with misplaced or maged equipment.

This tree stand/backpack combination makes a convenient way to transport your hunting necessities. Photo by John Eicher.

While top-loading packs are common, front-opening packs allow for complete access to the pack's contents without "digging" through everything in the pack. By design, the pack should be broken down into several subcompartments. This simply means several outside pockets and possibly an inside divider that make the organization of the pack much easier.

Gear

When organizing your gear it helps to break it into two categories. First are the items that you use often or may need access to quickly during a hunt. Second are the items that you may need only occasionally but should always carry with you. Separating these items into categories also tells us how they should be packed and where in our pack they should be located. Although the gear each of us carries will vary because of personal choice and changing conditions, let me use the following example of the contents of my backpack on a typical afternoon hunt in early November.

CONSTANT USE ITEMS	OCCASIONAL USE ITEMS
Outer Garments (Coat and Pants)	Spare Release
Extra Clothing as required	Spare Keys
Knit Camo Hat	Extra Flashlight
Gloves	Emergency Red Flashing Light
Facemask	Shoulder-Length Gutting Gloves
Release	Gutting Knife
Arm Guard	Paper Towels
Safety Belt	Plastic Electrical Zip Ties
Binoculars	Emergency Space Blanket
Upper Arm Bands	Hunting Tags and Pencil
Compass	Tracking Tape
Flashlight	Fluorescent Tracking Tacks
Camera	First Aid Kit
Water Bottle	Extra Film
Energy Bars	Extra Batteries
Deer Calls	
Deer Lure	
Scent Canisters	
Tree Steps	
Topo. Map	
Folding Saw	

And the Last Shall be First

One of the secrets to organizing your pack is to pack the items in the reverse order of use. In other words the last things you may use are the first things you pack. Let's look at how I would pack the above items and why.

dark. It means having every item you may need while hunting and not one item you will never use. It means being prepared, disciplined and well-organized.

This organization occurs on several important levels. Let's start with the gear required at our hunting site and work backwards. Although this may seem a bit strange at first, it really makes the most sense. We never should wind up with anything at our hunting site we don't need or want, so what better place to start than at the end.

Backpack

Any gear I require for a hunt is packed into my backpack for transportation to and from my hunting site. I prefer a camouflaged, waterproof, polar fleece pack with padded shoulder straps and a waist belt. The fleece material is quiet while the padded shoulder straps and waist belt makes carrying whatever load is required easy and comfortable.

A well-organized backpack is essential to the bowhunter. Photo by Sandy Kasun.

Side Pockets

From the "Occasional Use Items" list I would first select all the items that would be logically grouped together. The extra flashlight, emergency red flashing light, spare keys, spare release, extra film, emergency space blanket, extra batteries and first aid kit are all items that I could need and therefore should carry. As they are emergency items I could go all season without ever having to reach for these items. I place them in a resealable plastic bag and store them in the bottom of one of the side pockets.

The next logical breakdown of items from the list are the shoulder length gutting gloves, gutting knife, paper towels, plastic electrical zip ties, hunting tags and pencil, tracking tape and fluorescent tracking tacks. These will all be used if and when I get a hit. They are very important items and I need to carry them any time I am afield. However, I don't need to be handling them all the time and I

don't want them scattered all through my pack. Again, I place all of these items in a plastic bag and place them in the same side pack pocket with the items previously packed. I now know where all of my "special need or emergency items" are located. If I need them I don't have to go "hunting" for them and yet they are never in my way.

From the "Constant Use Items" list I would again follow the same logic but with a slightly different twist. The deer lure and scent canisters will be placed in a plastic bag and placed in the second side pocket. Filling out that pocket will be the compass, flashlight, camera, topo. map and folding saw. I will be using all of these items on a regular basis when hunting and, therefore, they are all logically grouped together in the same side pocket. The water bottle, energy bars and any additional food I may carry, fills out the last outside pocket. Now that the side pockets are packed, I focus my attention on the main compartment.

Main Compartment

When stand hunting, I do not attempt to hunt my way in or out; I go directly to the stand as quickly and quietly as possible. I dress lightly, packing any clothes needed for the actual hunt in my pack. This does several important things. It keeps me from getting overheated and sweating. In turn, this reduces the odor I generate and keeps my clothes dry and fresh for the hunt. When I arrive at my stand, I add any additional garments required capturing the built-up body heat. I am dry, warm and comfortable and will be able to stay in my stand for a long period. Again this logic must be reflected in the way in which I pack the main compartment.

The knit hat serves two purposes. First as an additional head covering if required and second as an expandable inner pack. I pack the following items inside the knit hat in the order listed: release, gloves, combination deer call, binoculars, arm guard and facemask. I place the upper arm bands around the knit hat to make a small package about 1/3 the size of a football. (Note: The upper arm bands are 1-inch wide elastic bands that I place over my jacket on my upper arm to keep the bulky material out of the way of the bowstring.) The knit hat and its contents are now placed in the bottom of the main compartment. Next comes the safety belt, which can also double as a deer drag (eliminating an extra item). Next, I place my outer garments, jacket first, then pants, in the main pack compartment on top of the safety belt and knit hat.

Installing a quiver mounting block on the side of the tree stand not only provides perfect storage for the quiver but gives the hunter quick and easy access to his arrows. Photo by John Eicher.

These are followed by any extra clothing, shirt, vest, etc., that may be required. If I am using tree steps they will be packed in a small canvas bag and packed on top of the clothing. If I am carrying rain gear, it is tied to the outside of the pack. All items are now separate but grouped according to use and packed in the order in which I will need them. When I arrive

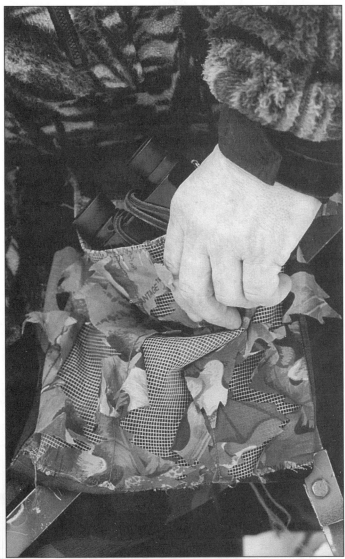

Pockets mounted on the side of the tree stand seat keep necessary items close at hand. Photo by John Eicher.

The small light is always attached to the zipper of my pack and is easy to find even in total darkness. The light it casts will let me get out my back-up light if required without any unnecessary fumbling. Other emergency items such as a compass, whistle or thermometer can also be used as pulls. The object is to make any item serve dual purpose if possible.

Using Your Tree Stand as a Backpack Frame

The best way to transport a tree stand is with the use of backpack straps. Many tree stands now come equipped with such straps or they are readily available as an accessory. The problem arises when you have a tree stand to transport as well as a backpack. A simple solution is to find some way of attaching the backpack to the tree stand. As tree stands vary in construction, this will vary from stand to stand. I found that the attachment of a simple metal hook to the stand, combined with the use of a bungee cord, permits an easy attachment of pack to stand. I have used this method to pack stand and gear long distances comfortably.

Customize Your Tree Stand

Getting organized means paying attention to the slightest detail and making the most of every move while eliminating any unnecessary moves. Adding a few modifications to your stand can help you do exactly that. When hunting from a stand I prefer to sit as much as possible, often shooting from the sitting position. Sitting is more comfortable over a long period and it helps minimize my movement. The more comfortable I am, the less I move; the longer I remain in the stand, the better my chances are of seeing game.

I get the best padded seat I can for my stand, then my wife adds some touches of her own—she covers the seat with polar fleece material. It is soft, quiet and dries quickly if wet. To each side and the front of the seat she adds a large pocket. When seated in the stand these pockets are easily accessible with a minimum of movement. Depending on the situation and the amount of time I intend to spend in the stand, these pockets serve a variety of uses. I can place sandwiches, snacks and a water bottle in one; my camera and binoculars in the second; and deer lure and calls in the

at my stand location and open my pack the first thing I find are my steps. Second is any extra clothing, depending upon the weather, then my outer pants, then my jacket, etc. Everything is packed in order of use. A simple way to think of this process is to first consider yourself fully dressed at your stand. If you were done hunting, the first item you remove goes into the bottom of the pack, the second next and so on and so on.

Zipper Pulls

I replaced one of the zipper pulls on my backpack with a micro AAA flashlight. Although I know exactly where my spare light is packed chances are I will only need it if my first light burns out and that only happens in the dark.

third. If I choose to stand for a period of time, I place the lower limb of my bow in one of the pockets. It removes the weight of the bow from my arm yet keeps the bow close at hand. The possibilities are endless. The pockets keep any items you need close at hand while keeping the movement needed to get them at a minimum.

Like most bowhunters I use a bow quiver but I prefer to remove it from the bow when I am actually in the stand. When I am moving the bow to get in position for a shot it is just one more thing to catch the deer's attention. But if you remove your quiver, where do you put it? I mounted an extra quiver mount on the right front corner of each of my tree stands. In just seconds I can remove the quiver from my bow and snap it into the mounting block on the tree stand. The block is positioned to place the arrows just to the right of the seat. If a second shot should present itself I can reach down and pop an arrow from the quiver without looking and with a minimum of movement. Another plus is that I never have to worry about bumping the quiver and having it tumble to the ground at the worst possible moment.

Drop cords attached to the stand are another useful addition. I have two drop cords tied on each of my tree stands. On the end of one cord is an electrical alligator clip. A second cord is fitted with a plastic snap clip. When I use a rope-on stand, I normally have to climb the tree with the stand on my back, a difficult and dangerous thing to do. Now, before climbing the tree I reach into my tree stand seat pocket and unroll my two drop cords. I clip the one with the plastic snap clip onto the cable of my bow and clip the alligator of the other onto my belt loop. Now my bow is attached to the tree stand with a length of cord and the stand is attached to my belt with another length. At this point I simply climb the tree using tree steps or a ladder if necessary. When I reach the desired height I grasp the cord attached to my belt loop and draw the stand up into the tree to me. As I raise the stand the second cord is playing out to the bow which is still lying on the ground. After the stand is in place and my safety belt is attached I simply grasp the second cord and draw the bow up. This procedure is reversed when breaking down the stand at the end of a hunt. The cords are always in place and the

Attaching a drop cord to the bow before ascending the tree helps this bowhunter to reduce his set up time. Photo by John Eicher.

clips are quick and convenient to use even in the dark.

Every bowhunter has found at some time or another, the need for a little more cover. I have attached four Limb Locks to each of my tree stands. These simple clamping devices not only allow me to quickly attach branches to the stand but they can be easily adjusted to any position required.

Your Hunting Vehicle: A Mobile Camp

By the middle of the hunting season most hunting vehicles look like a sporting goods store that got hit by a tornado. Not only are these conditions frustrating but they often lead to the damage or loss of some valuable equip-

This "custom bow rack", fabricated from scrap material, provides safe yet easily accessible storage for the bow. Photo by John Eicher.

ment. I selected and outfitted my latest hunting vehicle with organization foremost in my mind. Like many hunters, my basic hunting vehicle is a small four-wheel-drive pickup truck with a cap. I also wanted to have easy and total access without climbing into the back each time I needed something. While I intended to carry extra gear in the truck, I didn't want it banging around, getting broken or damaged.

The cap access problem was solved by the addition of side-opening windows that exposed all areas of the truck bed. I fabricated a bow holder from PVC pipe and mounted it to the inside of the truck bed under one side window. This not only provides safe storage for the bow but also allows me access to the bow using the side window. For the storage of miscellaneous items, towing straps, ropes, extra steps, tools etc. I purchased a plastic cargo box with a top-opening lid measuring approximately 32 inches long, 14 inches deep and 14 inches wide.

From a piece of scrap plywood I built a bracket to hold the cargo box. A bow holder mounted on the lid of the box allows for the storage of a second bow. Canvas pockets fastened to the side of the bracket allow for the storage of clippers, bottles of scent remover, extra tree steps and various other miscellaneous items. Also mounted on the outside of the bracket are a saw, folding shovel and a pair of gas tracking lanterns for nighttime tracking. The bow mounted on top of the box and the contents of the box are accessible through the side window while the items stored on the sides of the mounting bracket can be easily reached through the rear door of the cap. This setup allows me to carry all the gear I might need, keeping it both organized and accessible. It also keeps the bed of the truck free for a sleeping bag, storage of tree stands or the transportation of game.

The items carried will obviously vary from hunter to hunter and the methods of storage vary from vehicle to vehicle. The important part is to find the best way to carry your gear, keeping it organized, easily available and safe.

The benefits you get from being organized are directly proportional to the effort you put into it. Being organized won't guarantee you success but the lack of organization could easily cost you success. Put every piece of your bowhunting puzzle in place. Get organized.

CHAPTER 11

Single-Cam, Split-Limb Bows

While these futuristic tools certainly aren't Robin Hood-pure, they represent the cutting edge of compound bow technology. Are they destined to dominate the market, or become nothing more than a passing fancy?

By Bob Robb

While bows have undergone technological advances since the first prehistoric hunting implements, the introduction of the compound bow in the late 1960s sent the wheel of progress spinning at warp speed. Since that time, we've seen innovations that have made a huge and measurable impact both on how a bow works, and how quickly they sell on the marketplace. We've also seen more than one design change that has proved to be nothing more than a passing fancy.

The latest "hot" design changes have been the single-cam bow, followed closely by the use of a split-limb design. Together these design changes are the epitome of the state-of-the-art, high-tech compound bow designed to help you—the bowhunter—become a more efficient shooter. The question is, do they?

Single-Cam Bows

Traditional compound bows have a pair of wheels (or cams) of exactly the same shape, size, and design. These have generally been classified into three basic types—round (energy) wheel, soft cam, and hard cam. All other things being equal, the more radical the design of the cam, the more raw arrow speed produced by the bow. As the buying public began demanding more efficient bows that produced faster arrow speeds, manufacturers produced more hunting bows with hard cam designs. On the surface, this would seem like a good thing. But one must remember, as with all things in life, nothing is free. Shooters found that hard cam bows were, generally, much less forgiving to inconsistencies in shooter form, noisier, and more difficult to keep in perfect

tune than bows with softer cams. They are also more difficult to draw, making them better suited to advanced shooters than the average weekend bowhunter.

While bow makers have dabbled in the single-cam design for many years—the old Dynabow of the early 1970s is a prime example—they really didn't grab the market's attention until Matt McPherson, an engineer who had previously worked for McPherson Archery, introduced his single-cam design to the archery

Bob Robb poses with a Kentucky 10-point whitetail taken with a solid-limb, one-cam Browning bow.

Single-cam bows, like this model from Mathews, Inc., have taken the bowhunting world by storm in recent years, when their performance levels reached those of comparable two-cam bows.

world in spring, 1992. In just five years it took the industry by storm.

"For years, all savvy engineers working on compound bow design knew that a single-cam design would be better than a two-cam design, if they could make it work," McPherson said. "The old Dynabow had the problem of very poor nock travel, which really doomed it from the start.

"The problem we all faced was making a single-cam design that was simple, because there was lots to be done to control nock travel. When the answer finally hit me, I wasn't really trying to design a bow. It just sort of popped into my head, more of a gift than something I really worked for. I went and built a model, and, by golly, it worked. I then started Mathews Archery. It has been successful beyond my wildest dreams."

Basically, a single-cam bow features a nearly round "idler" wheel on the upper limb, and an oversized cam on the lower limb. The question

everyone asked at first was, simply, why should I make the switch?

From an engineering point of view, the advantages of the single-cam to the shooter are many.

"The primary benefits of the single-cam are centered around the issue of wheel timing," said Derek Phillips, field staff manager for Mathews Archery and himself a highly-accomplished bowhunter. "With two-cam bows, it's very difficult to synchronize the oblong-shaped cams to roll over at exactly the same time. When they do not, the result is inconsistency in performance. But since you only have one cam, not two, with a single-cam bow, the issue of wheel timing has been eliminated altogether."

There are other benefits as well.

"The key to the success of any new product, in any field, is whether or not it will perform better than the existing product," said McPher son. "Often, the new product will perform better, but it is also more complicated, and therefore more expensive. But with the single-cam bow, it not only performs better, but it is also simpler, which makes it competitively priced with two-cam bows.

"The key to the single-cam's success is certainly wheel timing, but it's more than that. They (the bows) are easier to tune, and to keep in tune. They are also much more consistent shot-to-shot and they have a much more solid wall at full draw than a two-cam bow. This means they are much easier to anchor and 'aim' exactly the same every time, which helps the shooter release the arrow exactly the same every time. And as we all know, it is this kind of consistency that breeds accurate shooting."

That these points are true is underscored by the fact that the vast majority of the nation's top 3-D tournament shooters—folks who make their living shooting a bow-and-arrow with surgical precision—are shooting single-cam bows today.

With all the hoopla over the single-cam bow, let's not forget the inevitable trade-offs. At first, single-cam bows were measurably slower than comparable two-cam models.

"It took lots of design work, but we've solved the speed issue with current models," said Jim Jordan, Vice President of Sales and Marketing for Precision Shooting Equipment (PSE), a man who is not only a serious bowhunter but one of the finest bow mechanics around. "Today's single-cam bows are very comparable, in terms of raw arrow speed, with two-cam bows while retaining all their other benefits."

McPherson sold his single-cam patent to Bear/Jennings while retaining some royalty rights, which means that all other manufacturers who use this new design must pay a royalty for the privilege. Still, that has not deterred other bow makers from jumping on the single-cam bandwagon.

"The single-cam trend is not coming, it's here," said Jordan. "It's just too good a design not to build and promote."

"As an engineer, I was trying to design out all the things that were problematic with two-cam bows when I designed the single-cam," said McPherson." As I see it, the handwriting's on the wall for the two-cam bow. I think in the very near future you'll only see two-cam models on lower-end bow models from manufacturers who don't want to pay the royalty. When

you have a bow that's quieter, more consistent, more accurate, produces less recoil, and gives you the same raw arrow speed as a two-cam bow, why wouldn't you want to shoot it?"

Split-Limb Designs

The "rage" design of the late 1990s is the space-age looking split-limb compound bow. While the split-limb design has been floating around the archery industry since the 1960s, it didn't achieve stardom until Hoyt hit the market with a split-limb bow design in 1996. Five bow makers jumped on the bandwagon in 1997 and in 1998 at least 13 major bow manufacturers are using a split-limb design in at least a portion of their new bow line-up, with both single- and dual-cam models available.

When you first look at a split-limb bow, you can't help but think, "Can this thing hold up?"

Two-cam bows have been the rage with bowhunters for years. Despite the emergence of one-cam bows, this proven design is still both popular and an effective bowhunting tool.

Split-limb bows have become more and more popular in recent years, although not all bow manufacturers believe that they will be a significant player in terms of numbers of units sold. They are lighter than comparable solid limb models, which many archers like.

What the heck is going on here?" Split limb bows use bow limbs that have eliminated the center portion of the limb, in effect creating a bow that uses four thin limbs instead of the more traditional two wider limbs. Removing this portion of the limb reduces weight, an advantage for shooters seeking a lighter bow they can hold at full draw longer without fatiguing their bow arm.

"Except for single-cams, the split limb design is the hottest thing out there right now," said Randy Walk, President of Hoyt and an experienced bowhunter. "I think the main reason is that, when you look back on the industry over the years, the things that have been successful have been a win-win deal for all involved. Right now, the number

one cost of warranty repair work for all bow manufacturers is limb fork cracks. With the split-limb design, this goes away because there is no limb fork. And from the consumer standpoint, split-limbs are a bit quieter than solid limb bows, and they're about one-third lighter in mass limb weight because you've eliminated the solid limb's center section. So the consumer gets a quieter, lighter, less-fatiguing bow, which he loves, and the dealer doesn't have as many warranty problems to deal with."

While a large segment of the bow manufacturing community has jumped on the split-limb design and are singing its praises, not all have completely embraced the concept. For example, Jim Taylor, President of McPherson Archery, said he was reluctant to jump on the split-limb bandwagon at first.

"Every time we introduce a new bow, we thoroughly test the product to see how it performs and how it will hold up," Taylor said. "We ventured into the split-limb market in a reluctant manner, mainly because I felt this was one of those items driven mostly by perception and visuals, while in reality these bows were not any faster, nor do they offer any other significant performance advantages over solid limb bows that I can see. They do tend to be a bit lighter, but not as much as one might at first think because of the special limb brackets that are both heavier and needed to hold the limbs securely on the bow.

"Right now, in the late 1990s, it's easier to sell and promote split-limb bows because there's a visual 'wow, this is different' thing, but we think it's a fad as much as anything else," Taylor said. "One thing I've always believed is that if there are true performance gains on various design changes in bows, they'll stay around over time. If not, they'll run their course. We're not sure on split-limbs at this time, because we just haven't seen the performance benefits they provide yet."

There are some performance concerns with the split-limb bows.

"In my testing, I've found split-limb bows to be somewhat unstable, with some independent movement of limbs which can translate into side-to-side cam movement," said McPherson. "This will hurt accuracy, and for this reason we've not made any split-limbs at Mathews

Two-cam, solid-limb bows are still the most common type seen in the deer woods each fall. And for good reason — they work!

hunting bears, caribou, and moose in Alaska to spot-and-stalk western hunts to conventional tree stand hunting for white-tailed deer. In 1998 I switched to a single-cam, solid-limb Mathews Z-Max. It was the easiest bow I've ever owned in terms of the amount of time and work it took to set up and tune. It also shoots a very quick arrow, and is extremely accurate. With it I've taken Alaskan grizzly and black bears, caribou, and one of the largest mountain goats ever bagged by a bowhunter. It, too, has worked well on white-tailed deer in the lower 48. It's a superb hunting bow.

The final judgments will be made by you. Each "advancement" in bow design will be judged by hunters in the field. Each hunter will have to answer the same questions we all do when trying out a new bow design. Right now,

Archery. Right now I think that, unless these kinds of problems can be fixed, split-limb bows will be a passing fancy."

What's Next?

A wise man once said, the only thing constant is change. In the world of high-tech bow design and manufacture, this is certainly the case. Today, the consensus among both manufacturers and top shooters is that the single-cam design is a winner that will, many industry members believe, dominate the market in the very near future. However, the jury is still out on the split-limb design.

In 1997, I shot two different Browning single-cam, split-limb bows exclusively. I found them to be smooth to draw, consistently accurate and able to provide good arrow speed. They worked well for me both on the range and under field conditions that varied from

One-cam bows are characterized by a smallish round "idler" wheel on the top limb, and the oversized cam on the bottom limb, which can be easily seen in this silhouette of a Mathews Z-Max bow.

the hottest things going are the one-cam and split-limb bows. Do these designs work for you? Do you like them better than conventional two-cam, solid-limb bows? Do they perform shot after shot under the kinds of hunting conditions you most often face? If you're like me, you'll find the single-cam design to be a real winner. Split limbs? The jury, as they say, is still out. Right now some people love 'em, and some people hate 'em. Visit your local pro shop, shoot one yourself, and see what you think.

And remember, there will be more changes in the future. That means more tests and more discussion on what's better and for whom.

CHAPTER 12

Choosing The Right Arrow Rest

Not all arrow rests are created equal. Here's a look at the evolution of this important accessory, and how to choose the right rest for your own bow-and-arrow set-up.

By Bob Robb

When you look back at the basic bow-and-arrow set-ups we were using to shoot at game and pop targets with just a decade or two ago, then compare them with the hot-rod set-ups so popular today, the differences are astounding. In just 30 years, we've evolved from a

recurve bow/wood or aluminum shaft/glue-on broadhead/finger tab or shooting glove crowd to a short-axle compound bow/advanced aluminum, carbon, or aluminum/carbon composite shaft/screw-in broadhead/release aid bunch. If you'd been asleep for 20 years and just woke up, you'd have a hard time recognizing one of today's most popular bow-and-arrow set-ups.

Few archery items have evolved over the years as dramatically as the arrow rest. And while often overlooked by new shooters more enamored with hype about raw arrow speed, using the wrong arrow rest is the best way to insure consistently mediocre shooting.

Old-Time Arrow Rests

In the beginning, archers with longbows did nothing more than rest the shaft across the fist of their bow hand, usually protecting against friction with a leather glove or, sometimes, nothing more than an adhesive bandage or

Modern all the way: Bob Robb used a one-cam Mathews Z-Max bow, Golden Key-Futura 3-D Rover ee-launcher-type arrow rest, carbon arrow shafts, and Pro Release Pro Roller release aid to harvest this nice point Kentucky whitetail in 1998.

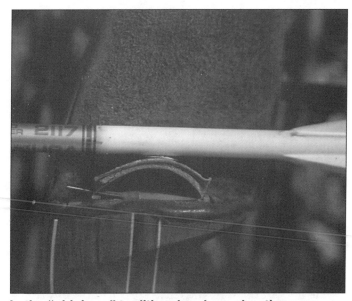

In the "old days," traditional archers shooting recurve bows and releasing their arrows with their fingers often shot their arrows "off the shelf." With no way to adjust the side pressure on the shaft, this makes it difficult to get perfect arrow flight.

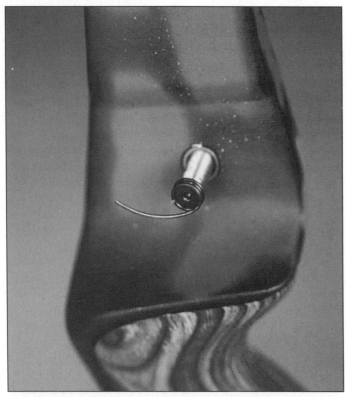

The springy rest had a short life. Some bowhunters still carry springy rests in their tackle boxes as an emergency spare rest. They can be used by both those who shoot with fingers and release aids.

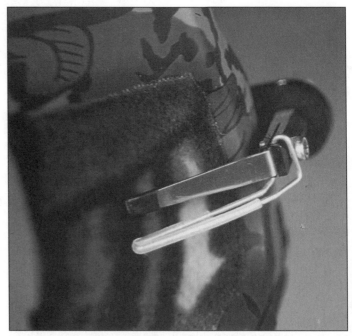

The Cavalier Super-Flyte rest is a version of the cushion/plunger design, which supports the shaft on both the bottom and side. While this rest type can be used by release aid shooters, it is more commonly used by those shooting with fingers.

strip of cloth tape. Then, in the 1950s, the then highly-evolved recurve bows were designed with an arrow shelf that was carved into the grip. Archers covered these shelves with an old piece of low-pile carpet, cloth, or leather, and found that shooting "off the shelf" was a big step up in consistent accuracy.

It was in the 1960s that archers began using the first removable arrow rests. These simply-designed rests were usually little more than a horizontal plastic (or, sometimes, hair or feather) shelf for the arrow to rest upon, and a plastic or nylon side plate for the shaft to rest against. Soon there were a few of these rests that permitted some horizontal side plate adjustments, which greatly aided in the bow tuning process and made accurate shooting at longer ranges a reality for skilled archers. Most of these rests attached to the bow with double-backed adhesive tape. These types of inexpensive arrow rests are still available today.

Arrow rests took a giant step in the evolution process in the mid-60s with the introduction of the Berger Button. Actually invented by tournament shooter Norman Pint, but named for well-known tournament shooter

Victor Berger, this button cushioned the shaft against side-to-side oscillation as it was released, which helped tighten arrow groups dramatically. When used in conjunction with the popular adhesive-backed Flipper or Flipper II arrow shelf, this combination became the standard against which all other rests of the late 1960s and early 1970s were judged. Today this type of arrow rest is generically called the "cushion plunger."

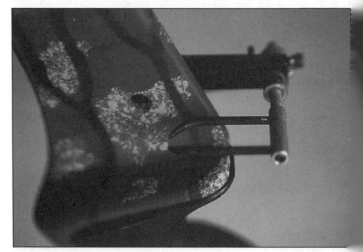

The Vee-launcher type rest, like the Golden Key-Futura TM-Hunter shown here, is the most common type of arrow rest sold today. That's because this design lends itself to use by release aid shooters, who make up the bulk of today's archers.

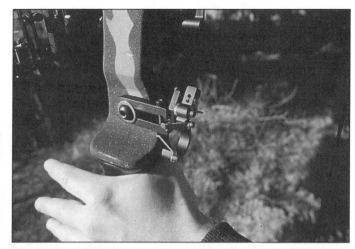

The Bodoodle is a type of modern-day cushion/plunger rest design that also incorporates some of the features of the Vee-launcher type rest. These types of rests, the Golden Key-Futura Star Hunter is another, are very rugged, making them good choices for bowhunters.

In the 1970s, a variation of the cushion plunger was the springy rest, which was nothing more than a threaded brass barrel connected to a coiled, one-piece spring wire plate-and-shelf unit. Springy rests were sold in a variety of spring gauges and tension weights to accommodate different bow weights and arrows of varying stiffness. These rests could be adjusted horizontally as well. These simple, rugged rests were popular with bowhunters of that era, but they're as rare as a four-leaf clover today.

In the 1980s we saw the rise in popularity of the launcher-type arrow rests. These rest types were actually invented in 1967 by southern Californian Fred Troncoso, a professional musician and serious tournament archer who founded Golden Key-Futura a year later. He wasn't making arrow rests in 1968, but the first rope release aids and a nock aligner device.

"I was shooting tournaments with a guy named Roy Hoff, and he got me started making rests back then," Troncoso said. "I first just whittled rests out of wood and plastic. The first prong-type rest came about after I acquired my first Sable center-shot bow in '67. It had a little wire rest, so I made a prong-style rest to fit this bow. This was before release aids were around, but it worked great anyway. But no one was really interested in them, they were too radical and complicated at that time."

Troncoso kept tinkering with his new arrow rest design, "just trying to improve my own shooting," he said. His first patented arrow rest was the Match One, patented in 1973-74, followed by the Pace Setter Vee-launcher type a year later.

"Even though my wife won three national field championships using this new rest, people still weren't that interested in this new design," Troncoso said. "After all, the arrow fell off if you turned the bow on it's side! Sometimes it just takes a while for a good idea to catch on."

Troncoso said it wasn't until 1982-83 that his Vee-launcher rest first became accepted by a significant number of archers. Back then, these rest types were commonly called "wrap-around" rests because the rest unit attached to the Berger Button hole tapped into the off-side of the bow's riser, then "wrapped around" the back side of the bow's handle. Initially there were two basic styles of this rest. The "Vee-launcher" type, like the old PSE Hunter Supreme and Martin Slide Rest, featured a

Archers using a mechanical release aid—the most common modern method—generally choose a Vee-launcher type rest.

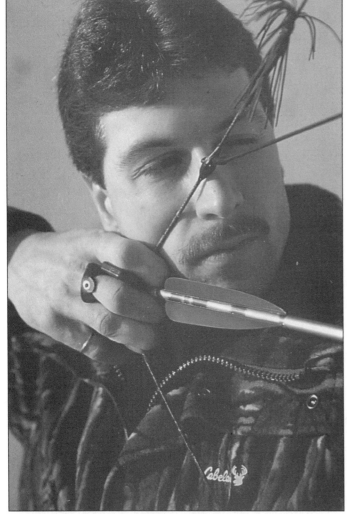

Fingers shooters usually choose a cushion/plunger type of arrow rest, although some buck tradition and use a Vee-launcher design.

solid metal post with a Vee-shaped cut-out in which the arrow was rested. The "Shoot-Through" rest featured a pair of up-thrust metal prongs, between which the shaft was rested. The Townsend Lodestar and PSE-CF-TM Hunter were two early examples.

Modern Arrow Rests

Today, arrow rests have evolved into a seemingly endless array of styles and designs. The questions asked by shooters are always the same. Why is rest category A better than category B? What features do I need on an arrow rest? Can I use the same rest for target shooting that I do for bowhunting?

"Our surveys indicate that somewhere between 80% and 90% of today's archers—and that includes both bowhunters and target shooters—use some type of release aid," said Bob Mizek of New Archery Products, an arrow rest

manufacturer. "That means that the basic shoot-through rest design is the basic type of arrow rest that most of them will be using. To that end, you're seeing a lot of the industry's research and development efforts in the arrow rest segment directed towards this type of rest."

"Bowhunting is where the money's at in the archery industry," Troncoso said. "While the target market is there, most arrow rest innovation is heading towards making people better bowhunters."

Desirable Design Features

A look at the many different arrow rests offered for sale today will turn up everything from simple to complex. Some rests have few adjustment features, while others — notably those designed with the serious target archer in mind — have more screws and adjustment knobs than a nuclear submarine.

In recent years, the industry trend has been to try to give all archers a rest that could be micro-adjusted. That is, a rest with vertical and horizontal adjustments that could be made in very small increments. The goal being to permit the very precise vertical and horizontal rest adjustments that need to be made as the archer attempts to perfectly tune his bow-and-arrow combination. However, many of these rests ultimately disappointed bowhunters, who found their complex adjustment systems difficult to work with, and that the many tiny adjustment screws and knobs often rattle loose or slip during hunting season, which of course changes the shaft's point of impact.

In the late 1990s, the pendulum began to swing away from complex to simpler arrow rests. Manufacturers have learned that bowhunters, their bread-and-butter customer base, want simpler designs that require less maintenance during the course of a hunting season.

"We feel that basic arrow rest design is returning to a more simplistic style," said Mizek. "Our conversations with our bowhunting customers show that they want, first and foremost, reliability in their arrow rests. Second, they need to be able to make both vertical and horizontal adjustments easily, but then once they have been made, not worry about it again. They want simplicity without giving up the features. We know we can make everything super adjustable, but the reality is that often you end up with a bow-and-arrow set-up that, once it's tuned and the arrow rest set, you never use the adjustment features of the rest again. We're trying to make rests simple to set up, quick to dial in, and built so they won't get beat up during tough field use and will hold up in extreme weather conditions."

"The number one factor in an arrow rest for bowhunting is reliability," said Troncoso. "Simplicity is also crucial for bowhunters. And yet, savvy bowhunters want the micro-adjustments that permit them to precisely tune their bow-and-arrow set-up. After all, all archers, whether they be target shooters or bowhunters, like to tinker with their equipment, and want to be able to tune their bows as precisely as possible. They're always looking for a little extra edge in their equipment, and this is one factor that gives it to them."

The Cushion Plunger: Obsolete?

With 80 percent to 90 percent of all bowhunters using a release aid and, therefore, some type of shoot-through arrow rest, is the cushion plunger style of rest now headed for the scrap heap?

Not necessarily.

"I find that, when it's all said and done, using a reliable cushion plunger rest, especially one that offers a bit of downward give, can be an excellent choice for bowhunting, even with a release aid," said Lon Lauber, a well-known bowhunting writer, member of the Mathews Archery Pro Staff, and winner of several state field and broadhead target shooting championships. "Especially on what I sometimes call a 'he-man' hunting trip, like backpacking for deer or elk, hunting in Alaska, and so on. The simplicity of these types of rests, the ease at which they can be adjusted in the field with a minimum number of tools, and their almost indestructible construction makes them a good choice."

"We've found that we can still sell a quality cushion plunger style of arrow rest," said Mizek. "The Centerrest, for example, with its downward give, sells about 60 percent to finers shooters, but about 40 percent to release shooters. That tells us that there are still many, many bowhunters out there who value the rugged simplicity of this type of rest enough to put them on their hunting bows, even if they're shooting a release aid. So really, cushion plungers aren't fading away at all."

"We don't find many release shooters asking for our cushion plunger type rests these days," said Troncoso. "By far the prong-type rests are what they're buying. The closest thing we have to a cushion plunger that's a large seller for us to the release crowd is one of my earliest designs, the Star Hunter, and the newer version, the Rising Star Hunter."

The Carbon Arrow Challenge

Although large-diameter aluminum arrow shafts continue to dominate the market, more and more archers are discovering the benefits of small-diameter carbon arrow shafts for both target shooting and bowhunting. They're also discovering the challenges posed by these small-diameter shafts in terms of choosing and using an arrow rest.

"Carbon arrows are selling more and more units every year," Troncoso said. "The challenge to making them fly straight and true is the same as it is for any shaft — fletch clearance. With the reduced space between the fletching on the shaft, it can be tough. One thing we've done is made some thinner prong arms, and designed different arm shapes to help accommodate these shafts."

Other changes are coming, too.

"One other thing we see that is starting to make a difference with fletch/arrow rest contact problems is that the smallest-diameter carbons are beginning to fade somewhat in popularity, with the larger-diameter shafts like the Easton A/C/C, Gold Tip, Game

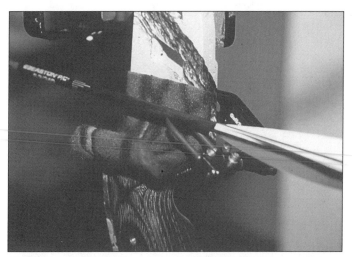

Carbon arrows pose unique problems for arrow rests, the most common being the inability to achieve 100 percent fletch clearance.

Tracker, and Beman ICS with internal components instead of overserts, coming on in popularity," said Mizek. "This slightly fatter shaft helps tremendously in eliminating fletch clearance troubles."

Often, new technology is needed before an idea can really take off.

"I experimented with Teflon launchers back in the late 1960's," said Troncoso, "but found the material too soft to really be of value. Today, though, the use of space-age plastics is helping solve the abrasion problem of carbon, and helping quiet the rest as the shaft is drawn and shot over it. We look for improvements in this regard in the coming years."

Arrow Rest Costs At Retail

"While there are several price categories of arrow rests, we believe that today's archer that's not a beginner won't get sticker shock if a quality arrow rest falls into that $25- $40 price range," said Mizek. "Beginners may buy something a bit cheaper, but much higher than that and you'll find some resistance."

Troncoso agrees.

"Top target shooters will pay anything for a rest, because they want the ultimate in performance," Troncoso said. "But with the mass market, and that includes bowhunters, rests selling in the $20-$40 range are the mainstay of the business."

Down The Road

What's down the road for arrow rests, in terms of design? Manufacturers tell us not to hold our breath waiting for a new "radical" design anytime soon.

"There is a tapering off point for everything, just like the efficiency of bows," said Troncoso. "Most all quality products are built on a variation of some tested theme. But creativity will tell. For example, we have some arrow rest designs that we're working on right now that, while we could bring them to market today, we don't want to saturate the market with too many new products at once. You also have to educate the public to the benefits of a new rest before it will sell well for you, which both takes time and some of the focus off your existing product line."

That doesn't mean manufacturers are holding back.

"We're always working to make our existing products better, and to design new products we know will both work and sell for us," said Mizek. "But right now there's nothing on the horizon I can see that will set the industry on its ear."

"I think two things are important in any archery product design and development, not just arrow rests," said Troncoso. "First, dealers need to be able to sell the product, customer awareness is critical. The best manufacturers support their product lines with advertising and promotions. And second, you have to be a shooter to design quality new products. Our family goes hunting primarily to think and brainstorm about how we might tweak this or that to make it better.

"So who knows? Maybe on our next trip to the woods, one of my boys will come up with some crazy idea that will work, like I did with the prong-type rest back in the 1960s," Troncoso said. "We'll all just have to wait and see."

CHAPTER 13

Return to Tradition

As modern bowhunters look for new challenges, many find retracing archery's roots the biggest challenge of all.

By Rob Reaser

Traditional bowhunting is one of the fastest growing segments in archery today—and little wonder. After enjoying years of hunting success, many modern-tackle bowhunters are looking for new challenges afield. Some want to remove all mechanical advantages and face their prey on even turf. Others succumb to the romantic lure of longbows and recurves and seek to relive the adventures painted by our archery forebears.

Regardless of the reasons for switching to "old-style" hunting weapons, returning to traditional archery is more than dusting off an old recurve and grabbing some cedar shafts. There is a science behind the "antiquity," and more equipment choices than you may imagine. Of

urnament archers and avid bowhunters "Cricket" Simmons (left) and Clark Freeman (right) show their winning ms. Traditional archers enjoy a special camaraderie on the 3-D range. Missed shots and broken shafts are taken stride, and celebrated with whoops, hollers and good-natured ribbing from fellow shooters. Photo by Rob aser.

course, learning to shoot a bow without mechanical let-off and sights offers its own challenges.

My goal is to introduce newcomers to the world of traditional archery. It's not for everyone, but if you're looking to step up to a new bowhunting challenge, you must first take a few steps back.

What is Traditional Archery?

"Traditional" is a relative term. Generally speaking it is archery involving all manner of longbow, flatbow, recurve, and composite designs—from high-speed recurves sporting carbon fiber laminations to reproduction Turkish war bows and anything in between. Practitioners mostly use wooden shafts shot off the shelf (no arrow rests), hand-sharpened broadheads, feathered fletching, Flemish-twist bowstrings, and such leather accouterments as armguards, shooting gloves and quivers.

Yet while equipment serves to define traditional archery, there's more to it than hardware. It's also a philosophy—a removal of physical and psychological barriers between the archer, the bow, and the target.

Modern vs. Traditional

There is more than gear to distinguish the traditional from the modern archer. The physical and mental adjustments needed to accurately and consistently perform with traditional equipment differ significantly from that required of modern-day tackle. Two dissimilarities jump immediately to the fore.

The first is drawing the bow. An archer anchoring a 65-pound compound may only hold around 20 pounds. An archer drawing a 65-pound recurve to anchor at, say, 28 inches, will be holding a full 65 pounds. That's because the recurve or longbow continues to build stored energy as it is drawn, with draw weight peaking at the archer's anchor. That's a difference which manifests itself through all facets of the draw, aim, and release.

Sighting, or aiming, provides another stark contrast. Launching an arrow with a contemporary setup is akin to shooting a rifle. At anchor, the arrow is aligned with the target via front and rear sighting devices, much like the sights of a gun. Traditional archers, who typically forsake sighting apparatus, learn to send their arrows to the mark with good ol' fashioned hand-eye coordination.

Shooting traditional equipment doesn't mean forsaking conveniences like bow quivers. Selway Archery's Stick Quiver can be used on a variety of longbow and recurve models. What's more, many traditionalists feel these quivers help stabilize their inherently light bows for improved accuracy. Photo by Rob Reaser.

But perhaps more than anything it is disciplining the mind, body, and bow to work in unison that separates the modern archer from the traditional. That is not to say mental and physical discipline is not required when using compound bows and sights. On the contrary, all the gadgets in the world will not make you an accomplished archer without the mental and physical control to use them effectively. Nevertheless, mechanical aids offer much in reducing the mental and physical discipline needed to accurately shoot the modern bow. The traditional archer, lacking these amenities, must forge mind, body, and bow into one.

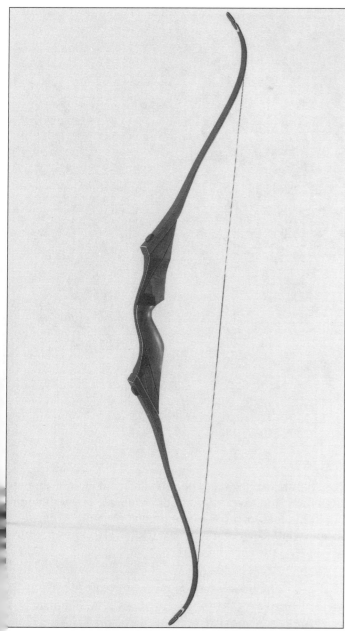

Even the big boys recognize the growing interest in traditional bowhunting. Industry giant Darton is just one of a handful of compound manufacturers now offering longbow and recurve models. Marketed under the Predator Traditional Bows trade name is Predator II take-down recurve. Photos courtesy of Predator Traditional Bows.

Of Mind...

All archers demand a high degree of mental discipline to effectively hit their mark. With mechanical let-off, sights and release mechanisms removed from the equation, mental control takes on even greater importance for the traditional archer.

The stick-and-string bowhunter learns to shoot instinctively. Instinctive shooting is like throwing a baseball. With practice you just sort of "know" how hard and high to throw it. Shooting a bow without sights is no different. Looking at your target with the arrow drawn to anchor, you "know" when to release in order to hit the mark. If you've ever used a slingshot, you already know how to shoot instinctively. It's exactly the same.

Understand, however, that learning to shoot traditional equipment effectively, consistently, and instinctively requires dedication, practice, and good mental control. It's not unrealistic for a first-timer properly outfitted with a compound bow, sites, and release, to be knocking on the bull's eye in a half-hour. Not so for the traditional archery newcomer.

...and Body

Like the mind, the body of the traditional archer must also be in tune with the shooting process. Drawing and holding to anchor requires greater strength and stamina than shooting modern tackle. More significantly, the body plays an integral part in the instinctive shooting process.

In many respects, the body is like a real-time computer. By assessing the weight of a drawn bow, for example, the practiced archer knows how high to aim the arrow in order to hit the target.

Fred Bear best illustrated the flexibility of instinctive shooting with traditional equipment when he downed his 41.5-inch curl ram on a British Columbia hunt in 1957. The ram, standing 35-40 yards over a ridge crest, faced Fred with only its head showing. A full-draw shot from his bow would offer only a head shot, so Fred took a short-draw shot, allowing the arrow to arc over the ridge and drop square into the brisket for a quick kill. Although such shots are not recommended, they illustrate the instinctive archer's capacity for allowing the mind and body to work together to achieve perfect shot placement.

Hunting With the Stick and String

It doesn't take a great mental leap to realize the limitations of bowhunting with traditional archery tackle. The simple longbow or recurve archer, shooting heavy wooden shafts without sights, understands the difficulty of making quick, clean kills with his gear.

First, instinctive archers tend to lose accuracy much more quickly than the practiced

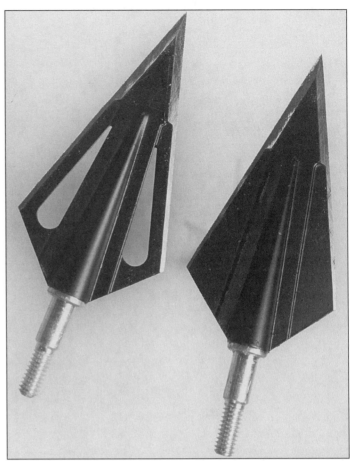

Most stick-and-string bowhunters favor hefty, fixed-blade broadheads for optimum penetration and maximum cutting surface. Modern archers may balk at the two-blade designs so often favored by traditionalists, but with accurate shot placement the two-blade is no less effective than the replaceable, multi-blade heads. Magnus Archery Company offers their popular Magnus heads for use with wooden (left [5A]) or aluminum (right [5B]) shafts. Photos courtesy of Magnus Archery Company.

compound shooter. Most traditional shooters, therefore, limit their hunting shots on big game to 20-25 yards. A 30-yard shot is usually considered "long-distance," and taken only by those archers who are confident in their equipment and ability to make a deadly hit.

Another cruel fact of shooting traditional gear is the absence of draw weight let-off. While the compound shooter can draw and wait for that buck to step out from behind a bush, the traditionalist, holding a 50- or 60-pound bow, cannot. Accuracy suffers exponentially the longer the bow is held at anchor.

These two factors alone may make one reconsider taking up traditional bowhunting. But for these perceived "detractions" there are a number of aspects to shooting longbows and recurves which make them the ideal weapons in big game hunting situations:

Lighter Equipment - A compound bow can weigh 6 to 8 pounds when rigged for hunting duty. A longbow or recurve sporting a quiver full of arrows can be as light as 2 to 3 pounds.

Quicker Shooting - The simplicity of traditional tackle lends itself, by necessity, to much faster shooting. While the modern archer may see the lack of mechanical let-off as a handicap, the stickbow shooter views it as a blessing, allowing him the flexibility of making split-second shots under the most adverse conditions.

Improved Mobility - The lighter, more streamlined gear of the traditional bowhunter offers improved mobility in heavy brush.

Reduced Parallax - Parallax is the difference between your line of aim and the arrow's line of travel. You may have a clear sight picture, but you may not see that twig right in the arrow's path. The instinctive archer practically eliminates this situation because the eye and arrow are much closer together.

It must also be pointed out that while distance diminishes accuracy for the traditional archer to a greater degree than the modern archer, the two become more evenly paired in hunting situations. Realistically, most killing bow shots are made in the 20-25 yard range—usually no more than 30 yards. So, in the field, the shortened effective range of traditional hunting gear is really no more of a handicap than that faced by the archer using all the gizmos and gadgets.

Never-the-less, traditional bowhunters strive for the closest shot possible simply to ensure lethal, humane hits. This, arguably, leads to perhaps the most important by-product of hunting with the stick-and-string—improved hunting skills. Let's face it. If you hunt on the ground (as most traditionalists do) and limit yourself to taking shots at 20 yards or less, you're either going to hone your skills to a razor's edge or spend many frustrated days watching game mingle out of bow range.

Equipment Selection

Once you've convinced yourself that traditional archery is the way to put the spark back into your bowhunting passion, the next step is to gear up. The beginner will have many questions as to what type of bow to start with, draw weight, arrow selection, shooting style, and accessories. The best teachers are self-exploration and other traditional bowhunters.

First, try out traditional gear before spending big bucks on an outfit. This is done by contacting a few traditionalists through your local archery shop or club, or by attending any of the growing number of traditional shoots held around the country each summer. Traditional bowhunters enjoy bringing newcomers into their sport. They are a proud lot, yet will put their prized bows and arrows in the hands of anyone willing to try them out.

Try a few different bows in the 45-55 pound range. Compound shooters who pick up a longbow or recurve for the first time can be easily dissuaded if the bow is too heavy. You should draw and shoot a few different models before deciding which type suits you best.

The Longbow

The term "longbow" is given to bows typically made of long, straight limbs, usually between 67 and 72 inches. Most have small, rounded handles, or slightly dished grips, with small arrow shelf and subtle sight window.

The generic classification of the longbow is somewhat inaccurate. Purists refer to true longbows as those of English descent. These are typically longer and narrower of limb than the modern longbow and are characterized by their deep core and round belly. The modern longbow, typified by wide, flat, and shorter limbs, are more accurately referred to as flatbows. These represent something of a hybrid design between the English longbow and the flatbows used by native North Americans. The most common of these in use today are the laminated flatbows, featuring wooden limb cores laminated with fiberglass. For the sake of this discussion, we'll simply call them longbows.

Longbows come in a variety of designs and materials. Some are straight limbed while others offer deflex/reflex or reflex limb profiles. In general, those longbows which incorporate a reflex in the limb (where the unstrung limbs angle away from the archer) tend to shoot faster than those which don't. The idea of reflex limbs is to build additional energy into the drawn bow for quicker arrow flight.

Although high in romantic appeal, the longbow is not for everyone and may present a steep learning curve for those just coming off of a compound. With its long limbs, slower cast, and lack of center shot window, the longbow can be a significant challenge to the newcomer. On the other hand, it is perhaps the most fun of the traditional bows to shoot and offers some definite advantages in the field. One is its forgiveness. The longer limbs help make the bow rather stable in hand, and it is less critical of poor shooting form than the shorter recurves.

Once you are comfortable shooting the laminated longbow, you might want to graduate to a selfbow. Selfbows are drawn from staves or billets of a particular wood—most often yew, osage orange or hickory. These are the simplest of all the longbows, but require extra care and maintenance when used in hunting applications. Most are backed with glued-on rawhide, snake or fish skin to prevent checking or breakage, and to provide the limbs with extra cast. Selfbows owe their performance to the single piece of wood from which they are made, and to the master craftsmen who created them.

The Recurve

Recurve bows offer newcomers the best entry into the world of traditional archery. Although

Phil Rathburn congratulates Kevin Butts on his traditional Michigan whitetail kill. If you're looking for a way to spice up your deer hunting, try your hand with the stick-and-string. Photo courtesy of Great Northern Bowhunting Company.

they draw like a longbow—without let-off—their grip design and large, near center-shot sight window make them familiar in the compound shooter's hand. They also tend to shoot faster than the longbow.

The magic of the recurve is in its limb design. In contrast to the straight limbs of a longbow, the recurve has wide limbs with an acute deflex/reflex profile. The idea is to develop more stored energy in the limbs during the early and middle stages of the draw, and transfer that energy to the arrow. It is this energy capacity during the latter part of an arrow launch which contributes to the recurve's speed.

Like all stick bows, the recurve is available in unlimited styles, sizes, and wood materials. Among the most popular recurve designs are the three-piece takedown models, which allow

separation of the upper and lower limbs from the riser.

Like any stick bow, you should try out a few different models before making your selection. One of the most important things to consider before purchase is bow length. For bowhunting most archers tend to lean towards short or medium-length bows, as they are less restrictive in the bush. The drawback is that stability and subsequently accuracy, tends to diminish with a reduction in bow length. Longer bows, thanks to increased mass and longer limbs, are inherently more stable and forgiving of shooting errors. Sample a variety of bow lengths and designs before finding your optimum recurve hunting bow.

A couple more words before we leave the topic. First, the incredible demand for top-quality longbows and recurves has sent price skyward in recent years. Good models, especially custom bows, can command prices exceeding top-of-the-line compounds. Buying a new stick bow should be considered a serious and long-term investment. After sampling a few models, the beginner would do well to purchase a good used bow to bang on for a season. There are plenty out there at bargain prices, and they will help you decide if you're into traditional for the long haul, or if it's just not right for you at this time.

Finally, make sure you purchase a bow that you can handle. You may have been shooting a 70-pound compound, and you may be able (with considerable effort) to draw a 70-pound stick bow to anchor, but the beginner WILL NOT be able to accurately and comfortably shoot a 70-pound longbow or recurve.

Selecting a stick bow weight is something of a compromise between your physical ability and, for the bowhunter, the need to shoot a bow that will deliver a hunting shaft with enough energy to quickly take down large game. Lighter bows in the 40-50 pound range are fairly easy for the beginner to master. At anchor you will not be shaking and straining to aim the bow as you would with a 65 or 70 pound bow. The absolute worst thing you can do is "overbow" yourself. Too strong a bow and you will shoot poorly, develop and reinforce bad form, and most likely become frustrated with the whole thing and go back to a compound.

In reality you do not need a monster bow to take down large game. A razor sharp broadhead and good shot placement with a 50-55 pound bow can put down an elk in short order. Sure, a heavier bow boasting 10 or 20 extra feet-per-second will send an arrow downrange packing more energy, but it's all for nothing if you can't accurately shoot it. Set aside pride when picking a bow's draw weight, and select one you can shoot comfortably, but will pack enough punch to put down a large animal. For the average stick bowman, that means longbows and recurves in the 55-60 pound range.

The Feathered Shaft

One of the greatest pleasures of shooting the stick bow comes with launching the wooden arrow. Yes, they are longer, heavier and slower than aluminum or carbon arrows, but are arguably more effective in delivering lethal energy than the modern arrow, and are without doubt

"sweeter" to shoot. A lot of traditional bowhunters stick with aluminum shafts after making the transition, and that's OK. Properly spined aluminum shafts are faster than wood and can accommodate the range of modern broadheads. But there are good reasons why most traditionalists cling to the trusty wooden missile both in the hunting fields and on the target range.

In comparison to aluminum or carbon, wooden arrows are downright weighty. In the hunting arena this added weight works to the archer's advantage. The heavy arrow takes on, or "absorbs," more of the bow's energy than a lighter arrow. It may fly slower and have less energy at launch than a lighter arrow shot from the same bow, yet the added weight leads to more impact momentum and better penetra-

If you think stone heads are going too far, think again. Archaeologist W. Hunter Lesser of Elkins, West Virginia has taken two whitetail deer using flint-knapped broadheads like this one. The hunting heads and hand-cut turkey feathers are secured to cedar shafts with sinew, and make for deadly missiles in the hands of practiced archers. Note the cut-in "self nock" behind the turkey feathers. Photo by Rob Reaser.

tion. That may be a hard nut to swallow for the compound shooter flinging ultra fast carbon arrows, but consider this: would you rather be hit with a 3/8-inch wooden dowel or a broom handle of similar length?

In addition to penetration, there are a few more good reasons traditional archers tend towards wooden arrows. The heavier weight absorbs more of the bow's energy, thus offering less hand shock than a lighter arrow. The added weight also makes the wooden arrow more stable since it takes more energy to knock a heavy arrow off course than a lighter arrow. Finally, wooden arrows are fun to build, and offer the amateur arrowsmith ample opportunities to exercise his or her creative inclinations.

Bowhunting with traditional gear is not as difficult as it may seem to the newcomer. The longbow and recurve, however, can be harsh taskmasters, and will definitely raise your shooting and hunting skills to new heights. If you're looking to put the fun and challenge back into bowhunting, you'll do no better than picking up the age-old stick-and-string.

CHAPTER 14

Making the Switch

By Bob Butz

Traditional archery gear draws more and more hunters each year. It could be the challenge or the romance of getting back to "sticks and strings" or it could be something more.

A little history...

Archeology shows that bows and arrows have been around for some 23,000 years. History tells that in that time they've been utilized the world over as everything from a recreational toy to a devastating weapon of war.

Though innovations in construction and materials used for bow making were drastically different between cultures, the configura-

tion of the bow remained relatively unchanged for most of this period. Even after the advent of fiberglass in the 1950s—which replaced sinew, rawhide, and horn as a backing material—the configuration of modern bows was basically the same.

Howard Hill, a hunter, bow maker, and celebrated trick shooter who appeared in seven Hollywood films in the 1950s and 60s, favored a longbow, a bow design used by the legendary English bowmen centuries ago. Fred Bear made the recurve bow popular. It is a design little improved upon since the days of the Turkish Empire.

In the late-1960s, bowhunting and the sport of archery was forever changed through the

n Linehan searches for black bears in northwest Montana during a spring hunt. Traditional archers usually say
ey enjoy the simplicity of their equipment and the challenge it provides.

Jim Welch, shown here, hunting in southeast Iowa during a November snowstorm, is a professional bowyer and owner of Toh-Kah Bows. He specializes in crafting traditional Osage self-bows. An increasing number of archery hunters are returning to traditional gear.

and recurves in favor of those strange new wheeled contraptions that, to many old-timers, didn't even look like bows.

These same curmudgeons said the compound was a fad, one that would never really catch on. Fred Bear boldly declared that his company, Bear Archery, would never manufacture such a bow. But of course they did, while everyone else who turned a blind eye to this booming new industry found themselves pushed out of the archery business in only a few years.

But, as is so often the case, the pendulum has swung back. Ironically, the technological advances that made compound bows all the rage with hunters 25 years ago now seem to be the very thing that is driving many to look for something else.

From this has come a renewed interest in so-called traditional equipment, that is longbows and recurves. It's a "back to the basics" movement, one whose participants are looking, at least in part, to rediscover the romance and sense of adventure—qualities seemingly lost in bowhunting today—by simplifying their equipment.

Aldo Leopold long ago talked of how gadgets invariably end up replacing woodsmanship. Bill McKibben wrote of how money has become a supplement for skill. Whereas the modern hunter, using a compound bow, tends to be equipment-oriented and bent on results, the traditional bowhunter prides himself on the process of going afield and taking game with the barest essentials.

Today...

Though there's no way to measure, maybe there is something to be gained when success in the field is had despite overwhelming personal limitations set by oneself. But these days you have to be careful about taking up one kind of hunting or fishing over another. If you're no

introduction of the compound bow. The new "wheel" bows were a marvel of modern ingenuity. Hunters who had never thought to try bowhunting before because of the difficulty involved in shooting a primitive-style bow, were now buying into the compound craze.

The compound bow delivered on the industry's promise of greater accuracy and ease of shooting. Before long, competitive archers and even old-school bowhunters from around the country soon put away their obsolete longbows

The author shows the results of hunting with traditional gear. This buck was taken in Iowa a couple of years ago. It was shot from the ground at 25 paces with a 56-pound longbow and Sitka spruce arrow.

careful, you end up sounding like a snooty elitist, which is unfortunately the case when somebody really gets going about things like fly fishing, wingshooting, and traditional bows.

Most of the hunters taking up traditional archery are former compound shooters. And whatever your reasons for wanting to learn about traditional bows, the time has never been better than now. For the past 25 years it seemed, you were hard pressed to walk into most pro shops in the country and find a bow on the racks that didn't have a set of wheels on it. Today, however, longbows and recurves are everywhere. Even most of the bigger compound bow manufacturers have recognized the trend and have responded by adding them to their lines.

Compound bow users making the switch typically find the recurve the most user-friendly of traditional bows. Recurve bows are center-shot—just like compounds—and the way you grip the bow is the same. They are inherently faster—flatter shooting than longbows. Some

friends, recent converts to traditional-style equipment, have also told me that a recurve seems more forgiving than a longbow in their novice hands.

Proponents of the longbow have gone so far as to say that shooting one effectively is a whole different kind of archery. The bow itself, with its gently curving limbs, straight, leather-wrapped grip, and a tiny arrow shelf covered with a bit of moleskin, is a model of utility and function. Whereas the standard recurve is 56 inches to 60 inches tip to tip, the typical longbow used for hunting is anywhere from 62 inches to 68 inches long.

This is another reason why the recurve is more popular with traditional shooters; recurves are more easily maneuvered both in tree stands and tight ground blinds. Also, if you're fresh off the compound bow wagon, even the fastest longbow will seem sluggish to you. Surely, you'll also hear tons of erroneous scuttlebutt regarding handshock, something synonymous with longbows. Excessive handshock

Jim Welch shot this bison from 20 yards with a homemade cedar arrow and unbacked Osage selfbow of 60 pounds.

is only an indication of inferior workmanship. It is not indicative of all longbows. The best ones are as smooth and pleasant to shoot as the finest recurve bow.

Whichever way you choose to go, the biggest mistake many people make when buying a traditional bow for the first time is in "over-bowing" themselves. That is, getting a bow that is too heavy for them to learn to shoot comfortably.

Because there's no let-off with primitive-style bows, one rated in the 50- to 55-pound class is a good place to start. Game as big as elk has been taken with bows of this draw weight. Longbows or recurves in this class are easy for your muscles to get used to (45-pounds is even better). This is important since shooting, in the beginning, is every bit a muscular exercise as a mental one.

Unlike compound bows that take a rocket scientist to tune, outside of setting your brace height and nocking point traditional bows require little in the way of tuning. In fact, any

problems with arrow flight can usually be traced back to the arrow.

There's a certain sense of romance and style that comes with a well-worn leather quiver filled with finely crafted wooden arrows; it's something you just don't get from arrows made of fiberglass, aluminum, or carbon. But wood arrows are something you either love or you hate.

Be they crafted of Port Orford cedar, Sitka spruce, Douglas fir, or any of the other 20 or so North American hardwoods used to make arrows today, wood arrows can be just as accurate and effective as any of the "modern" arrows...provided they are properly spined and weighted for your particular bow.

With wood arrows you get what you pay for. Arrow making is a dying art. And the truth is, a good set of them will probably cost you quite a bit more than would a dozen aluminum shafts. Best if you start out with aluminum shafts which are durable and more

Instinctive shooters should keep their muscles in shape through practice. Shooting at 3-D targets during the off-season is a great way to keep the keen mental edge needed to find the target with precision. The archer shown here, Mario Eusi, keeps his skills up year-round.

forgiving over a wider range of bow weights. For example, with a 26-inch draw I can shoot the same 2116 XX75 Easton shafts out of my 45# longbow as I do from my other longbow rated 58# at my draw. With wood shafts I need two separate arrows with spine weights of 45#-50# and 55#-60#, respectively, to achieve proper arrow flight.

Regardless of your choice in arrows, for longbows and recurves designed to be "shot off the shelf" (most are) there is no alternative to shooting feather-fletched arrows. Though the drawbacks of feathers are well-documented, plastic vanes simply don't allow for proper arrow flight.

If there is anything that defines a traditional bowhunter, it is this business of instinctive shooting. Even though you can mount a sight aid on any kind of bow, with a fine custom longbow or recurve the mere mention of it seems a sacrilege. Shooting instinctively has been touted as an art by some; by others, a mere physical act of hand-eye coordination.

Surely, the masters make it look easy, you could even say artful.

True instinctive shooting is not sighting down the arrow, or using the gap between the tip of the broadhead and the target as a reference. It is "pointing" rather than actually "aiming." If you're a shotgunner, the mechanics of it may be easier to understand since the basic tenets of the discipline are the same.

Fred Asbell, author of the two books on instinctive, claims that he can teach anyone to shoot a bow without the aid of any sighting mechanism. And he probably can. But it is this one facet of traditional bowhunting that most limits the bowhunter, and therefore defines him. It is why traditional bowhunting is simply not for everyone. Shooting instinctively takes plenty of practice and years to maste,. And some people, frankly, never quite get the hang of it. The method forces the hunter to get close to his quarry, closer than close. Fifteen to 20 paces is the self-imposed limit of most of the best who shoot using this method.

I read something wonderful not long ago, some profound observation about bows and arrows in a book entitled, The Bowyers Craft, by the late Jay Massey. Massey was another kind of bowhunter entirely. He was a staunch independent, a do-it-yourselfer, who crafted his own bows from Osage orange trees, his arrows from raw blanks of Sitka spruce, and knapped his broadheads from chunks of flint.

In an essay about why some people hunt with truly primitive-style equipment, Massey supposed that perhaps the bow and arrow has been part of our culture for so long that our affinity for it is ingrained in our collective psyche. By crafting his own archery equipment and taking game in the manner in which men have hunted for generations the world over, Massey felt as if he was getting to the core of what it meant to be a hunter. Ultimately, he believed that by learning about the bow and arrow, by stripping the exercise down to its bare essentials, we could learn something about our ancestors. And maybe more importantly, we would end up learning something about ourselves as well.

CHAPTER 15

Good Clothing Is Part Of A System

by Terry Koper

Bowhunters looking for an excuse for a missed opportunity can forget about blaming their clothing. After decades of development clothing manufacturers have covered every angle. From proper camouflage to comfort in extreme conditions, hunters should think of each piece of their clothing as part of a system.

The author heads to his deer stand in northern Wisconsin decked out in Sleeping Indian Design's Gray Ghost camo. It's hard to beat wool for cold-weather hunting and a camo pattern as open as the Gray Ghost design really helps to break up a hunter's outline.

That system must keep them hidden and help them regulate temperatures found in the field.

A seemingly infinite array of camouflage patterns allows hunters to blend into any type of foliage, in any season, in any corner of the world. Manufacturers have kept up with hunters' demands as seasons have expanded and spread across the world. There is a pattern for every destination, from sparse shrubs on the gray shale slope of a Montana mountainside, to a stand of oaks in Arkansas, to tall grasses on an African plain, to a white expanse of snow on an Arctic caribou hunt.

These same camouflage clothes assist hunters by being functional in other ways. They can keep hunters warm and still while waiting on the coldest stand during a late December bowhunt in Wisconsin's Lake Superior country. They can keep hunters cool in the desert-dry sun of a Wyoming antelope hunt and dry in an all-day rain in the Pacific Northwest. The same clothes also are quiet, allowing a draw so silent that not even the most wary white-tailed deer will know an arrow is almost on its way. Modern fabrics no longer sound a krinkly alarm as a hunter shifts position or begins the critical, heart-thumping draw of an arrow.

The most recent development in hunters' clothing even eliminates the oldest excuse of all: a hunter's cover being blown by an errant breeze casting an alarming human scent toward an animal. What experienced hunter hasn't heard a deer or elk snort in fear before crashing off through the timber?

Manufacturers have found ways to use charcoal liners to absorb scent. They've found ways to lock human scent within clothing to keep it from reaching the sensitive noses of animals that rely on keen senses of smell.

Hunters thumbing through catalogs or prowling the clothing sections of sporting goods stores will notice that the developments can come at a high cost. The prices on certain sets of clothing would cover the cost of an expedition to some prime hunting locations. Fortunately, however, hunters also will notice that the tried-and-true wool, cotton and canvas clothes they've been buying for years still hang on racks at reasonable prices. And, under the right circumstances, an inexpensive cotton or wool shirt in a muted plaid pattern is silent, and still almost impossible for animals to see.

If there is one thing that manufacturers hope isn't hidden in their camouflage clothing it is this: Among the ranks of their workers is a growing number of bowhunters whose experience and ideas have resulted in superior products for consumers.

"I can't count the number of hours we've spent out on tree stands that have gone into the development of our MT050 cloth," Steve Culhane said of his work with Ev Terrell, a fellow clothing designer at Cabela's.

What started as a small business in 1961 has grown and expanded in popularity to such a degree that Cabela's sprawling store near Sydney, Neb. is a landmark to hunters driving along Interstate 80. No one can miss the bronze, battling bull elk, standing twice as large as life in front of the 75,000-square-foot retail showplace. No wonder the store has become Nebraska's number one tourist destination.

Long before Cabela's retail stores attracted attention, hunters learned of its products through catalogs. More than 60 million catalogs are mailed annually. A recent Cabela's archery catalog offered hunters more than 20 pages of clothing, including Cabela's Whitetail Extreme System, featuring its propriety cloth, MT050. Hunters wearing this clothing also are protected from the elements by Gore-Tex and Thinsulate Lite Loft. ScentLok, activated charcoal in a unique fabric lining, contains human odor and yet is supple enough so it does not interfere with a hunter's freedom of movement.

From experience, I can say that the parka and bib overalls in this system had to have been developed by a bowhunter who in the past had

struggled for freedom of movement, or to stay warm and dry, or simply to find an accessible pocket in which to stash a deer call. My son, Pat, and I wore all or parts of the Whitetail Extreme System through a long archery season and a rifle season as well, with no complaints.

Even when a hunter chooses not to take a shot, the right camouflage clothing can unlock the marvels of the outdoors. Deep in the Wisconsin wilderness just south of Lake Superior Pat watched while a young buck with forked antlers sniffed and pawed at the bed of an

A hunter who intends to spend long hours in a tree stand needs t dress for the occasion. A good clothing system will keep you dry and that's the foundation of warmth. Pat Koper was able to spend hours in a cold northern Wisconsin stand thanks to good clothing

older buck. Pat sat on a mossy old log downed decades ago along the banks of a noisy river in an ancient mountain range.

The buck spent several minutes within 20 yards of Pat, pausing many times to gaze right through him. As mentioned earlier, often it is easier to remain unseen and unheard than it is to prevent being winded by an animal as cautious as a deer. Hunting along slopes or cool streambeds can compound the problem. This deer never got wind of Pat, despite tricky breezes and cross currents. After it lost interest in the larger buck's bed it wandered off, leaving Pat undetected to wait for a chance at a trophy we'd stumbled across a few days earlier.

The taking of a trophy animal with a bow and arrow, however, is a journey which winds through many months, sometimes years, of careful planning, including deciding what to wear. Slapping a cover coat of camouflage over an unprimed body probably will be about as unsuccessful as painting a house without scraping and priming first. Dressing properly may mean scraping the body down with special soaps to eliminate human odors. After working to prevent detection by odor, the next step is choosing the right underwear. Not even Cabela's extreme wear can keep a hunter warm if sweat has soaked through a set of cotton long underwear. Cotton is appropriate for warm weather hunting but is dangerous in cold weather. It takes underwear of natural wool or the new synthetic blends to keep hunters warm and dry in the varied demands of cold-weather hunting.

Dressing from the inside out is so important that Ted Ranck will pass on an important sale of his pricey Sleeping Indian Designs woolen wear if a hunter wants to start with buying a coat.

"Even our best parka won't work the way a hunter thinks it will if he hasn't dressed from the inside out," said Ranck, whose business is based in Jackson, Wyo.

"I want him to have the right kind of underwear first and then we fit him for a shirt, pants, a hat, gaiters, and then an anorak or a parka," Ranck said.

Veteran hunters, especially those from cold climates, instinctively seem to know about layering with the proper materials. Not until I worked as a wrangler in a remote Wyoming elk camp and was exposed to hunters from across the country did I understand how mysterious this concept can be to some of them. It can be very hard for some hunters from warmer climates, or for infrequent hunters who don't spend much time outdoors, to comprehend what winter can do in the northern mountains, the tall timber country or plains. If nature

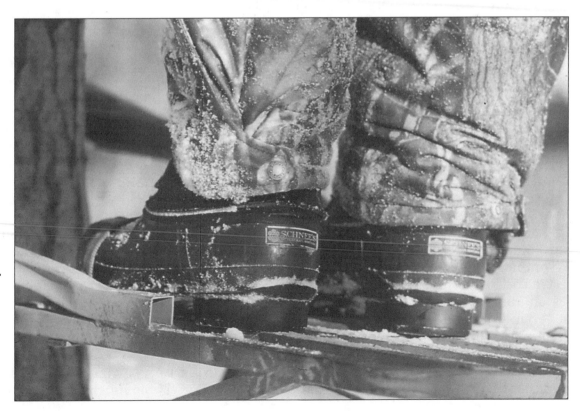

Good Footwear is a blessing in the cold. Don't skimp on boots, you'll ruin your hunt.

Dudley Hole shows off the results of staying hidden in plain sight. His King of the Mountain camo, kept him warm enough to wait out this Alberta whitetail.

sinks into a bad mood the question of proper dress rapidly escalates beyond keeping warm enough to avoid fidgeting and not be detected by an animal. It becomes a matter of survival.

Almost any time after the opening of archery elk season in Wyoming wind, and snow can clog mountain passes until it takes scoop shovels to clear a trail for pack strings and mounted hunters. A combination of woolen and synthetic clothes kept me warm and dry upon riding into camp in Wyoming's Thorofare Country at the end of a 14-hour struggle through the snow. More than five of those hours were spent scooping head-high drifts off the steep, perilous Deer Creek Pass as a blizzard officially had closed the rest of the state of Wyoming.

Wearing combinations of wool and synthetics on another wilderness elk hunt in Idaho saved my son and I from freezing during a terrible, wet storm, the end of which was made more serious by a drastic drop to sub-zero temperatures. We were wet (I was soaked) and just about ready to tuck up into the shel-

tered bottom of a deep, timbered canyon to build a fire for the night when my son found our one way up and out of the canyon. Continuing would not have been an option had we not been dressed properly. We would have been forced to spend the night around a drying fire because we would not have made it out without freezing.

Clothing manufacturers, outfitters, guides and wranglers never seem short on stories of similar outdoor adventures with the weather. Unfortunately, they also have an abundance of stories of hunters well off enough to pay for a costly hunting trip to Alaska, Alberta or Montana, but who balk at buying the right clothing that could save their lives in perilous situations.

For safety's sake, don't cut corners on buying long underwear, the first layer of clothing a hunter should consider in putting together an outfit. Underwear must wick moisture away from the body to an outer layer where it can collect and evaporate at a reasonable rate. If there is too much moisture wicking away too quickly, heat will escape with it and a hunter will become cold.

Quality long underwear at reasonable prices is readily available in stores and catalogs. Read labels and descriptions. Be sure the underwear is the proper weight and of the right material for the kind of country and weather in which you will be hunting.

I have found Patagonia's Capilene underwear in various weights to suit almost every situation I've encountered. Patagonia seems to take more time in tailoring products so they fit comfortably, which is important on an all-day ride to camp or an extended hunt. A heavyweight, Patagonia pullover of stretchy fleece fabric was a very good grab off a sale rack at a mountaineering shop not far from my former home in Butte, Mont. Over the years it has taken some serious beatings, and still shows almost no sign of wear. I bought it on impulse during an unexpected stop in that shop while on my way to the grocery store, not knowing quite how it would fit into my wardrobe. Since then it has ended up being packed for almost every back-country trip, being worn in more conditions than I ever imagined.

Before moving out to the next level, hunters need to know that under some stressful conditions even the most appropriate long underwear won't keep them from becoming damp and overheated. It is essential to know when to peel off a layer, or just avoid putting one on for a while. Several hunting companions and I once stuffed our warm outer clothes in frame packs and made a long, fast hike in the cold pre-dawn. We were in a hurry to butcher and bring back an elk, which was shot just before dark the day before. We raced up the mountain in long underwear, donned warm clothes to bone and pack the meat, and stripped to long underwear again for the exerting work of backpacking the meat back to camp. Any other way we would have overheated on the hike, and frozen while working at a slower pace to carve up the animal.

In addition to avoid overheating, stripping layers averts another problem. Being overdressed while hiking in deep snow, in steep country or at high elevations will drain a hunter's limited reserve of energy. It is much easier to remove a piece of clothing and carry it in a pack.

After hunters have selected long underwear, it is time for the next layer. In warm weather this can be cotton. Long underwear in very warm weather can be cotton, because it will hold moisture against the body, keeping it cool. Never have hunters had a wider selection of cotton clothing for mild weather hunting. Since life-threatening weather is not generally a consideration in mild weather, hunters need to place more emphasis on selecting the appropriate camouflage pattern of cotton or another material that is not too noisy for a close-range shot.

Again, catalogs and magazines are packed with pages of varied patterns of camouflage, almost all of which can also be found in abundance in retail stores. Picking a pattern is not nearly as complicated as the wide variety of choices would indicate. Be sure the pattern blends well with the country in which you will hunt and be sure the pattern is not one which will turn to a dark blob at any distance.

As the weather slips from cool to cold it is time to switch to wool. Despite the popularity of synthetic fabrics, woolen hunting clothes still may be the most useful, durable and versatile clothing hunters can buy. Old reliable products from companies such as Filson, Woolrich, Pendleton and others still are readily available. Inexpensive army surplus woolen trousers are warm and durable, though they may not be the most fashionable items.

There are alternatives for hunters who want more sophisticated wear. Because of the evangelistic dedication of two competing clothing manufacturers, hunters now are offered systems of wool clothes, the quality of which surpasses anything ever on the market.

Few manufacturers even come close to the attention to detail given to clothing from Sleeping Indian Designs, and King of the Mountain, of Loveland, Col. The utmost attention is paid to tailoring, placement of pockets and in providing useful accessories, such as caps, vests, gaiters, gloves, mittens and packs. Furthermore, quality in these products begins with buying the best wool and being sure it is pure so that its longer fibers can be woven into a fabric which is durable, yet soft and comfortable.

Ranck's interest in outdoor clothing began while hunting in wool with his father and grandfather. It became a more intense passion over the years when his father was in the Air Force and family fun centered on outdoor survival drills. To learn about wool, Ranck studied

Clothing technology is changing as fast as any other segment of the bowhunting industry. Manufacturers continue to produce innovative products to keep hunters, warm, quiet and scent-free. Mossy Oak has recently introduced it's QT (Quiet Technology) line of camo. The fleece garments are designed to be not only warm, but silent as well.

sheep and the quality of wool they could produce. He went to mills and learned tailoring the hard way. He spent four months sleeping on the cutting table of a demanding Korean tailor who allowed Ranck to learn by watching his work during the day. Ranck and King Cavalier II, Chief Executive Officer of King of the Mountain, worked together at King of the Mountain until Ranck struck out on his own.

While the prices for their clothes may seem high, the cost of quality clothes of synthetic fabrics has risen to the range of these woolen products. Those who favor wool will argue that the clothes will last longer and will not be

bumped off the rack by yet another wonder product claiming to answer all a hunter's needs. They are probably right, considering that hunters have been wearing wool since settlement times, hundreds of years ago.

"That's one of the big reasons people get started wearing wool," Ranck said. "Their grandfathers and fathers wore wool and told them to wear wool. They just didn't tell them why, because they didn't know all the real reasons wool can keep you warm."

Wool has the ability to radiate heat from the sun, said Cavalier.

"When the sun comes out on a cold day and starts to radiate through your wool it makes you feel good, like you were up against a wood stove," Cavalier said. "It is really comforting."

And yes, wool will keep a person warm even when wet and has a good ability to repel water. Wool will not prevent a soaking in a downpour, but hunters in any clothing should be headed out of the weather in such conditions. What wool offers that many synthetic combinations don't, is a reasonable rate of wicking away human moisture while retaining much of that warmth. The inner core of a fiber of wool is absorbent, covered by an outer layer which is not absorbent. The two layers act somewhat as a thermostat, controlling temperatures depending on a variety of demands from the weather and a hunter's level of exertion.

Body moisture transformed to vapor contains a significant amount of latent heat, which wool can absorb. Wool puts this heat to use before allowing moisture to pass along. Some synthetic products either hold too much moisture, resulting in a clammy feeling, or release too much moisture, and heat, causing a hunter to feel cold. Wool is a living fabric and breathes in a naturally regulated manner. This is one reason a hunter wearing wool won't need to alternately peel and put back on layers of clothing through the various demands of a hunting day as frequently as will a hunter wearing mostly synthetic clothes.

These varied conditions are not so critical while walking only a short distance to sit on a tree stand. They are very noticeable, however, when exertion levels vary widely, and when the weather in one day can vary more than some people see in one season. With wool, a hunter can dress with less bulk and weight and be comfortable through a day of strenuous climbing at high elevations, through the inactivity sitting on a mountainside as the brittle chill of evening begins to displace the fading sun.

Wool has two other important qualities not matched by synthetic products. It is silent and its camouflage patterns just fade into the surroundings. After testing a number of quality clothes of synthetic fabrics and a variety of wool products, it became apparent that animals at times still can detect the draw of an arrow while wearing synthetics. Even the best of these fabrics is not silent as a hunter shifts position. Wool is absolutely silent, a quality which when combined with warmth can mean the difference between getting a shot at a prized animal or not.

Veteran hunters know how difficult it can be to get a chance at a real trophy, and just how many obstacles they face along the way. Cavalier cited an instance when wearing wool would have allowed a hunter shots at very large white-tailed bucks in Canada.

"Twice he couldn't draw his bow back because he was too cold," Cavalier said.

Sixteen hunters had spent over a week archery hunting for trophy white-tailed deer. These were the only opportunities offered any of the hunters, Cavalier said, and they fell to a hunter who could not take advantage of them because he was dressed improperly.

In addition to being warm and silent, the texture of wool is fuzzy, and camouflage patterns woven into clothes are far less distinct than those printed on synthetic fabrics, or even on wool. Weaving a multi-colored pattern into a wool fabric, however, is labor intensive, and therefore one of the details which drives up the cost of these quality wool products. Also, there still are those who believe that no new camouflage patterns are any more deceptive than those provided by muted plaid patterns in wool or cotton.

Through fall and winter I wore wool from both of Sleeping Indian and King of the Mountain and can attest to their products' superior warmth, silence and deception. One still November day in Wisconsin's North Woods I sat in a ground blind and watched a six-point buck for more than 20 minutes while wearing King of the Mountain's Standmaster jacket and bibs in their blowdown camouflage pattern. The deer was never more than 25 yards from my stand. At its closest point of about 15 yards it stopped and stared right through me while munching a mouthful of buds stripped

from a dogwood bush. Several times while it had its head to the ground to bite at grass or drink, I slithered into a shooting position, without detection, finally letting the buck slip over a timbered ridge.

King of the Mountain's Standmaster Jacket is a versatile five-in-one layer system, including a shell with a hood and built-in, wind-blocking cotton liner, and a fleece liner, the sleeves of which may be removed to create a vest. The jacket is tailored with gusseted, raglan sleeves, an important tailoring design allowing the ultimate in freedom of movement for hunters. On raising the arms, the sleeves do not raise the rest of the jacket or bind under the armholes, restricting the movements of a bowhunter at a critical time. The bibs are lined to block the wind and have pockets conveniently placed on top of the thighs for easy access for seated stand hunters wearing gloves. When worn with the right long underwear and one of King of the Mountain's wool shirts or sweaters, a hunter can last for hours on a tree stand in late-season weather which causes deer to move for feed. I stayed on stand for hours at a time in temperatures that dipped to 25 below zero. The wind chill factor, a serious consideration in an exposed tree stand, was 50 below zero that day. I remained warm enough so that at periodic intervals I could still draw a 65-pound pull, solo-cam bow.

The Standmaster system is as carefully-crafted as comparable clothing from its competitor, Sleeping Indian Designs. One late December sub-zero morning while wearing Sleeping Indian clothes, a chickadee buzzed onto my shoulder as I sat high on a tree stand. I remained motionless while it pecked at my sleeve for quite some time. Eventually, finding no food in the look-alike bark, it flitted off to a real tree. I was wearing Sleeping Indian Designs' clothing in its silver camouflage pattern—patches of dark gray and black on a dusky silver-gray background. This pattern seems to take on ghost-like qualities when worn in the gray, brushy vegetation growing along the edge of aspen and evergreen stands, where deer and elk can be found.

"These camouflage patterns work so well because they look like nothing," Ranck said. "Too many other patterns try to look like something. They only work when you wear them in exactly the same kind of cover. They don't work when your hunting takes you through several kinds of cover during a day. Ours do."

Sleeping Indian offers a useful variety of lined and unlined wool jackets, parkas and an anorak for wear over layers of long underwear and its shirts, trousers and bibs. At the insistence of hunters, it added a fleece lining to its Archer's Anorak, a pullover parka. For hunters in arctic conditions, Sleeping Indian's Extreme Parka includes a liner of Polarguard under a wool shell.

Hunters spending any time in the quality clothes of these two manufacturers generally conclude that their wool clothing offers more warmth, maneuverability and durability with less weight and bulk than any other product on the market—whether it is of other wool or a high-tech fabric. While the costs of these products, including those of high-tech synthetic materials, may seem high, you won't be thinking about the money when your clothing makes the difference in being able to take a shot while on an expensive trip, or just staying alive in the conditions which can develop on true wilderness hunts.

CHAPTER 16

The Return of Traditional Archery

By Tony Kinton

The hog, a big ugly brute of some 300 pounds or so, broke from a thick tangle of Mississippi cutover. He had seen me or heard me or detected my presence by some other manner and determined then that all was not well. He was moving off to the side to better apprize the situation. In so doing, he slid across a logging road that offered an open shot.

The bow was a recurve, a Cherokee Hunter built by my friend Gary White, himself a solid bowhunter turned bowyer. The draw weight was an even 60 pounds at my length, and the arrows were cedar, tipped with Zwickey Black Diamonds. This unit swung into position as second nature, and the arrow zipped through its target. I don't really recall the draw nor the release, but I do recall that feeling of "just right." Such sensations are common to traditional shooters.

The boar made his way into the tightest cluster of vines and briars he could find. It was there he stopped, some 30 yards from the shot. He swayed briefly, then dropped to the ground and rolled over. It was the end of a spectacular hunt. It was also the time for some reflective moments.

First of these was the shaking and the adrenaline rush centered around the predicament I could have found myself facing. Hogs can exhibit nasty behavior, and with no backup it was of paramount importance that I do my

Traditional archery is facing a new dawn in the bowhunting community. More and more archers are trading in the gadgetry of high-tech hunting for the simplicity of traditional gear.

One secret to success in traditional shooting is regular practice. The hunter would do well to shoot under hunting conditions, such as at the 3-D range.

deed with great certainty. That done, the second reflection was that of the grand endeavor of traditional archery. Nothing in hunting can match it.

Archery—traditional archery if you will—has its roots in antiquity. It dates back to the early developments of mankind, and reached a point of high proficiency, at least in military terms, with such historically colorful gatherings as the English longbowmen. These were formidable enemies to all who found themselves on the opposing side of the battlefield. The bow was proven; its usefulness went unquestioned.

But for a more pertinent survey of the pursuit from the hunter's perspective, traditional archery is best viewed in the experiences of individuals such as Saxton Pope and Art Young. What they did is no secret. The contributions they made to what we now enjoy can not be overlooked.

Following the lead of these two were many others, now legends: Howard Hill, Fred Bear,

Glen St. Charles. The list goes on, and there are new names being added annually that time will likely reveal as giants in the field. They, all of them, have learned what their predecessors knew: Traditional archery gear is effective, challenging and pure magic. This latter superlative is probably the driving force behind the near incredible growth the sport has enjoyed over the past decade or so. It is indeed magic.

Once was the time when traditional gear was all that was available. Longbows and recurves were the tools of the trade, and bowhunting took these and moved into a viable position during the 1950s and '60s. Hunters previously skeptical of the rigs began to take notice. With the exploits of some of the men named above presented on video to mass audiences, the idea that the bow and arrow were suitable for taking large game took hold. Bowhunting was entrenched.

In all fairness, it must be noted that while bowhunting was recognized and somewhat respected, it took the development of the com pound bow to move it to where it now resides. These modern marvels, along with the various gadgetry that made shooting a bow a skill practically anyone could master, brought bowhunting to the attention of thousands who had not tried it. This simple addition of numbers was a plus, for numbers mean strength and political persuasion. Both were and are vital to continued growth of the sport.

As time moved on and archery continued to grow, prodigious numbers of hunters found themselves in the field with no knowledge of the more traditional approach. Indeed, most had never even handled a traditional bow. They grew up and entered the ranks of bowhunters under the shadow and mystique of the compound. Only a few old hands remained married to the simpler ways. The art of bow building and shooting appeared doomed, something akin to the dinosaur. But a few resisted the lure of the compound bow. It was these archers who kept the tradition alive, and it is these archers who have provided the impetus for others to try this, the grandest of all shooting.

My own hunting experience is not unlike that just outlined. I began as a child enamored of the bow. I fashioned crude rigs from branches, saplings, vines, and just about anything else that would bend under string tension then spring back into position. These units were far from sophisticated, but they were easily made and more than entertaining.

In the 1960s, as a hungry college student, I somehow managed to acquire a recurve, and I entered the hunting woods with a broader view of the possibilities. Few deer were taken, but this in no way diminished my enthusiasm; it simply grew with time. Then the compound bow came to my hometown.

The first one I saw showed little resemblance to the super-charged bows of today. It was heavy, cluttered with pulleys and cables, and generally an unattractive monster that we all predicted to be little more than a misplaced

Hunters have discovered that traditional archery tackle is more than adequate for taking big game. As a result they are turning to this gear in record numbers. Like this hunter, many combine the traditional bow and cedar arrows with modern tree stands and tactics.

and misshapen fad. It would never catch on. We were wrong! I bought one myself.

My first compound was a good performer. Its pins allowed a bit more accuracy than I had grown accustomed to, and its let-off permitted a draw and hold not possible with a recurve or longbow. I took several whitetails and my first mule deer with it. Its connection to my life lasted several years, and spawned the purchase of two or three later and improved versions. Still, there was a deep nagging within me that would provide no rest. I recalled with joy and perhaps a touch of nostalgia those more basic bows of days past. I wished to revive the thrill, and a reentry to traditional archery seemed the proper route.

The first "new" bows I tried were not new at all; rather, they were leftovers from my first years at the game, and most were in an ill state of repair. But, they provided the miracle of rediscovery. I was off and running. A custom-built recurve followed. This is the bow with which I took the hog, as well as a number of whitetails and assorted small game.

That bow is still with me, but there are others that complement it. The latest endeavor has been an attempt to build my own laminated longbows, and this effort now occupies my shooting and hunting time. The magic is stronger than ever!

Some might ask, with ample justification, why anyone would take an apparent step backward in any hunting ploy. Modern rigs and their accessories are truly amazing when performance is the bottom line, and there are so many varieties on the market that it seems futile to use anything else. That is the thinking of a solid majority, but there exists a clear and impressive increase in the traditional field despite such propensities.

I can speak only for myself, but there are easily some elements present in the traditional approach that are not present in the world of technology. Traditional gear puts a romance and human factor into the sport that is difficult to realize with more advanced tools. The aiming is a function of instinct, and the simple act of stroking a traditional bow brings to mind days past, as well as grandeur and self sufficiency. This interpretation is in no way slanted to take away from the advancements; it is simply a truth that can not be denied by those who have ventured into this somewhat unknown realm of shooting.

Many who know only modern gear find a burning within to experience what the earlier generations of bowhunters did. They may begin with the idea of adding little more than some novelty to their shooting. They likely emerge as traditional hunters if they persist in the pursuit to the point of becoming handy with the old ways. Remember, there is magic, and that magic has a way of inching itself directly into the very being of the participant.

The tremendous growth of traditional archery is evidenced in the number of new and established bowyers across the country today who have more work than they can get to. Also, scan the catalogs of reputable manufacturers, and you will likely find a line of fine traditional

Without question, the white-tailed deer is the No. 1 big game target of bowhunters. One collected with traditional gear is an animal in which a great deal of pride can be taken.

gear added to what was, only a few years back, a long list of compounds. There can be no denying that these may be the glory days of the traditional hunter. A check with some of the bowyers verifies this thinking.

"Traditional archery is most definitely seeing a huge growth," says Mark Horne of Horne's Hardwoods and Laminations in Boyd, Texas. Mark, along with wife Sandy, owns and operates a hardwood lamination business that supplies laminates for the purpose of bow building. He is also a skilled bowyer. The two of them hunt and compete regularly with traditional equipment.

"Our feel on this is partly that people are enjoying the simplicity that traditional has to offer," Mark said. "They enjoy being able to watch an arrow fly to its mark. They have realized that traditional bows are more than adequate in a hunting environment. Most of the folks that go to the shoots are just there to have fun, which makes it a great family outing.

"We have noticed in the last few years more and more guys are wanting to build their own bows. A lot of them just want to shoot with equipment they built, but there are also quite a few that want to become full-time bowyers. As a result of this influx we are seeing more and more choices offered in custom bows.

"We started the hardwood business in May of '95, and in that time we have gone from just offering the hardwoods to where we are today. We now stock over 20 species of hardwoods, glass, Smooth-On Epoxy, Fuller Plast, and the bolting kits. We will also be adding new woods in the next few months. We have always tried to keep our time of delivery to no longer than two weeks from time of order, but this past year it was almost impossible for us to do that. In December 1998 we brought Jeff Schultz in as a full-time employee to help keep up with the demands.

Although deer are the most popular game sought by traditional archers, small game can play a vital role in honing shooting and hunting skills. Rabbits and squirrels are nearly perfect for some fast-paced action with traditional gear.

"We have also started with a full line of custom bows under the name Horne's Archery. We offer our Ridge Runner, a large-handle three-piece take down recurve; the Mountain Bow, a small-handle '50s-style model recurve in a one-piece or take down; the Combo Hunter, a traditional longbow handle with bolt-on recurve or longbow limbs; and the Brush Bow, a 60-inch or 62-inch longbow. We have been looking at a six- to nine-week wait on our finished bows."

Most traditional bowhunters prefer a basic broadhead of cut-on-impact design. These projectiles, cast from a good longbow or recurve, will penetrate like no other heads.

Horne says his business showed a 40 percent increase in sales during 1998.

Mark says he feels that simplicity is one reason for the tremendous growth of traditional archery. And he says you can't overlook the fact that a custom bow is an entity unto itself. It possesses its own unique beauty, and each rig is quickly an extension of its owner.

The simplicity theory is shared by Bob Lee of Bob Lee Archery in Jacksonville, Texas. This long-time bowyer feels that archers want to get back to a simpler system of shooting and hunting. "They have burned out on all the gadgets," he says. "They want to get back to having a good time. I'm happy to see it coming."

He also feels that the complicated systems of compound bows are part of the reason that shooters are opting for traditional gear. "Shooters are tired of having to work on bows all the time. And they are tired of the weight. They want something uncomplicated."

Traditional gear certainly fits this latter requirement. Lee notes that 60- to 70-percent of his business is from compound shooters switching over.

He says traditional archery will continue to grow. There are now more bowyers in the business to provide gear, and he notes that the pastime has been around forever.

"I have some bows in stock for sale," he says. "Some orders take three months to fill. We average two to three weeks now.

"We just started making two one-piece bows; we are beginning to get more and more requests for one-piece bows. But by far the best seller is the takedown recurve. I still think this is the best system offering all the advantages."

For anyone remotely interested in traditional archery the name Bighorn has a familiar sound. The company, King of the Mountain in Loveland, Colo., has been around for many years and produces a line of fine traditional bows that have an enviable reputation. Bowyer Ron Buchholz has a feel for the pastime of traditional shooting and shares his views regarding the rise in its popularity.

"It is my opinion that the increased interest in traditional archery stems from several factors," he says. "The nostalgia and challenge of traditional archery seem to be the overriding factor that draws people to it.

"Most all baby boomers started shooting traditional tackle of some sort, and now seem to be revisiting the fun they had with that type of equipment. The phenomenon could possibly be likened to the person who has been hunting with a modern rifle with a high-powered scope and decides he wants to experience the challenge of shooting an open-sighted muzzleloader.

"Most of our customers tell us that the simplicity, quietness, and light physical weight of traditional tackle is what has led them to put down their compound bows. It seems that many archers have grown tired of the gadgetry associated with compound bows, such as sights, arrow rests, stabilizers, releases, and the like. Traditional tackle will almost always be lighter and quieter shooting than compound tackle.

"Finally, the beauty and physical appearance is what attracts many people to traditional bows. Most bowyers offer a wide range of gorgeous woods for bow construction. The advent of clear fiberglass has allowed them to make beautiful limb cores from most any type of wood.

"As for sales figures, it appears that we will have about a 12-percent increase in sales this year [1998]. This is an unaudited number as we haven't closed out 1998 yet, but it is probably a pretty good estimate. Some of this increase is probably due to the introduction of our new take-down limb design. It has proven to be quite successful. All in all, we have experienced a steady increase in sales, but we may not be on pace with industry averages as there has been a great proliferation of traditional bowyers over the past years."

There is no question that traditional archery is on the rise, and it is on the rise in a significant fashion. Annually, more shooters are added to its ranks, and there seems no end in sight. Is it for you? That is a question only you can answer. It is, however, wholly satisfying, challenging, and sure to generate a spark not found outside its mysterious reaches. It is, after all, magic.

Chapter 17

Get It On Paper

By Terry Koper

To be an effective hunter, the selection of a bow is critical. But choosing your weapon is just the beginning of the process of creating a high-performance shooting tool.

If all the right accessories aren't added, and if they aren't adjusted in the proper manner, the puzzle that is archery will not end up as the satisfying picture of a system that will drive arrows into the center of a target. If the puzzle is going together poorly, the hunter should look for a remedy long before heading out into the field. Adjustments will have to be made, or frustration will be a constant companion at the target range, and later in the field.

Though the continuing development of high-tech bows continues to push custom tuning to higher levels, the required set-up and tuning of bows dates back to prehistoric times. As simple as those stick bows may have seemed, individual archers still found ways to set them up and tune them for personal preference and higher performance. They shaved slivers of wood off bow limbs or applied thicker rawhide to them, or twisted strings until a bow was tuned to its peak level of performance.

The concept of paper tuning appears, from the outside, to be very simple. An arrow is launched through a piece of paper which is set up in front of a traditional target. After the shot, the size

Ron Miller, a technician at Buck Rub Archery, Waukesha, Wis., paper tests a bow after setting it up for a customer. Paper tuning is a great way to judge an arrow's flight and improve accuracy.

Greg Kazmierski, owner of Buck Rub Archery, Waukesha, Wis., works on a bow that's secured in a bow press. The right tools are one of the keys to properly tuning a bow.

and shape of the tear in the paper is studied and modifications are made to the bow, its accessories or the arrows to improve the flight path of the projectile. The goal is to launch arrows that regularly punch "pencil" holes in the tuning paper. Nice, evenly round holes mean the arrow is flying straight and true. If the arrow is "fishtailing" it will show up on the paper.

While we use paper today to tune an arrow to a bow, one of the most noted archers of nearly a century ago used a different target to test obsidian and steel broadheads. Archery pioneer Saxton Pope, who introduced us to Ishi, the Yana Indian hunter, once used a target box filled with bovine liver and covered with a fresh deer hide. It is doubtful that any archery shop today will use that method to determine which broadhead would be best for a bow and would work best on an animal. The degree to which early archers were willing to go to perfect their pastime, however, is a reminder of what archers must expect of themselves today.

Really, technology isn't offering any shortcuts to a perfect shot. This requires time to select the proper bow, and more time to decide which accessories will turn your bow into a complete shooting system. It takes still more time to adjust these accessories and then to find an arrow that will fly straight towards a target, without wobbling along the way. Most archers also need to find a professional to set up and tune a bow, because they do not own all the tools necessary for such work, and rarely have the experience or talent to do the job.

Once an archer has purchased a bow, accessories must be added to make it useful. On a recurve bow a hunter may wish only to have a nock point for consistency in the correct placement of an arrow on a string, and then buy a glove or tab for shooting.

A few more items will be needed to get the most out of a modern compound bow. A nock point will be necessary, as will an arrow rest, a sight and a stabilizer. The stabilizer is necessary to dampen the shock generated from today's high-powered bows. Most of today's bows also will require a hunter to use a mechanical release. Each of these items must be selected to accommodate the bow and the personal preferences of the archer.

Before these items are attached to a bow, it must be brought into proper adjustment so that everything will work correctly once the package is put together. Once archery advanced to wheeled bows, the requirement of adjusting them became much more complicated than with recurve and long bows. This complication may have peaked with two cam bows, since synchronizing the cams is essential to getting the bow to shoot properly. From manufacturers' recommendations and from the experience of archery shop technicians, there are various written and unwritten guidelines to balance these sometimes-touchy bows. Generally speaking, however, it is the accumulated knowledge of a team of archery technicians that will get the most out of a bow.

It is doubtful anyone will find it written anywhere that a hacksaw is needed to deepen the groove in the metal cable holder on the older Darton two-cam bow I had shot for years. Truly, every individual bow has its own personality. Skilled archery technicians get to know the bows, the way old aircraft mechanics got to know the quirks of the propeller-driven airplanes they managed to send out and bring back to the deck of an aircraft carrier.

"It's just experience," said Greg "Kaz" Kazmierski, owner of Buck Rub Archery in Waukesha, Wis.

Kazmierski had been back and forth, from the target to the bow press, with an old Darton 60MCX. Though it was old, heavy and slow compared with other newer bows out on the line, when tuned properly it could drive tacks with the best of bows. After more than a decade of being bounced about in trucks, boats and on horses, this bow was in need of an adjustment or two. And it was not responding to adjustments normally prescribed for the type of tears it was making in the paper target. After some quiet cursing, mumbling and talking it over with other technicians in his shop, Kazmierski cranked the bow back into a press and reached for a hack saw blade. Once the cables were slack he used the blade to deepen a cable keeper at one end of the bow. After a few more minor adjustments with a wrench and shooting an assortment of arrows, I was able to punch a

pencil hole through the paper, a sign that the bow was in tune.

"Just experience," Kazmierski said.

"We look at a lot of bows coming through here every day. Some of the set-up goes by the guidelines, but a lot of it does not. You can't always follow the charts. That is why a guy will get frustrated when he is trying to paper tune a bow and things aren't working out the way they show in some guidelines or books," Kazmierski said.

A guideline may suggest a nock point be moved or a cam adjusted to compensate for a paper tear in a certain direction. Paper tuning, however, is an art which combines information from a multitude of guidelines and experience. Strictly speaking, Kazmierski said, paper tuning is the art of matching an arrow to a bow. All it requires is a piece of paper on a target. An

The right arrow might be the most important factor in tuning a bow. Greg Kazmierski, owner of Buck Rub Archery, Waukesha, Wis., has hundreds of arrows in the shop for use while tuning bows, one of its most sought after services from customers.

The results of paper tuning. One obvious tear indicates the bow is way out of tune. The hole at the other end of the line is just a pencil point with little slices for fletching. This indicated perfect tuning.

arrow is shot through the paper, leaving a tear, which offers clues as to how to adjust the bow.

The trouble is, deciphering the tears can be a mystical process. And paper tuning also requires a wider selection of arrows than are available during a home-tuning process.

"We've got 500 arrows," Kazmierski said.

"That's the key to paper tuning," Kazmierski said. "You need every arrow on the chart in every length any archer might shoot. We know from experience which range to start in after we get someone set up."

Setup is separate from tuning, although some minor adjustments may overlap. More frequently, however, when a bow is set up properly, tuning is merely a matter of adjusting an arrow to the bow.

"An inch in length may mean the difference of several inches on a target when you are trying to get a good group," Kazmierski said.

So before tuning, attention must be focused on set up. A nock point must be crimped on the string, usually at an angle almost square to the bow. Sometimes this may vary a fraction of an inch, depending on the equipment and the archer. An arrow rest must be added. There are several schools of thought on which type will work the best. Kazmierski's is inexpensive and simple, an important consideration for field archers. Kazmierski favors a shoot-around rest rather than a shoot-through rest.

A shoot-around rest can cost about $12 while shoot-through rests generally cost many more times that amount. A shoot-around rest is simple, often just a spring or piece of plastic, requiring little adjustment. A shoot-through

rest has more moving parts and requires more adjustment and more maintenance.

The different ways each rest works are main considerations for their selection. When shot, an arrow has minimal contact with a bow using a shoot-around rest. An arrow maintains contact with the bow a lot longer using a shoot-through rest. This increased time of contact can cause an arrow to veer off target, Kazmierski said. The difference in characteristics of these two releases often is difficult for average hunters to understand, he said.

An arrow on a shoot-around rest is on a tiny wing attached to the bow's riser. When shot, the arrow bends back and forth several times under the tremendous pressure of the release. During this process the arrow bends around the bow for a minimum of contact. This is important, since the bow is in the hand of a human, and not braced in a machine. The more movement and contact, the more there is a chance for an error in a shot as that movement is transmitted into the arrow.

With a shoot-through release, the arrow is cradled on the bow, does not bend as much and remains in close contact with the bow as it is shot. This contact increases the chances for human error. In addition, some archers have problems dropping an arrow between the cradle and the bow handle, creating a launch sequence for a projectile that could end up anywhere but on target.

Once an arrow rest is secure and adjusted, an archer must install a stabilizer to the front of the bow. Stabilizers add a little forward weight for balance, but their most important

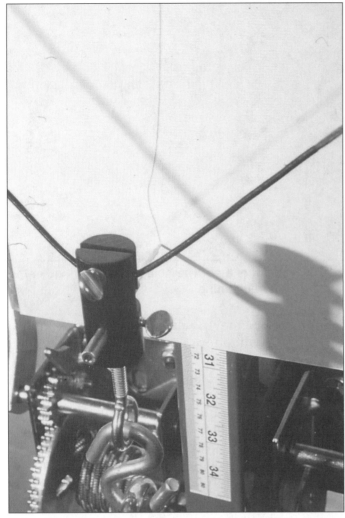

One of the machines maintained by better bow shops uses a stylus to track the travel of a bow's nock point. This photo shows a nock point traveling on a curved line indicating the bow is out of tune and will need work.

function is to reduce the shock inherent in modern super-speed bows. A sight must also be added. Certainly it is possible to shoot instinctively, without sights, but this does not take advantage of the accuracy these modern bows are able to deliver. Taking quicker shots while shooting instinctively also would not take advantage of the let-off in a compound bow, which allows an archer to hold longer on target. This can be essential while drawing on a wary white-tailed deer. Choosing a sight is a matter of personal preference. They can range from simple and inexpensive to very sophisticated and expensive. With most modern sights a peep sight must be woven into the bowstring. This is where an archer certainly will need the assistance of a shop pro, who will need to mark the location of the peep on the string while the archer is at full draw. At this time, the pro also

will use a blunt test arrow to determine an archer's draw length.

This will depend, in part, on the type of release an archer shoots, or if the archer still wishes, and is able to use leather finger guards or a tab. The differences in draw lengths can be considerable by changing the method of an archer's release. Changing bows may mean an archer has to trade off a favorite release because it does not work well with the particular bow he has just purchased. That same release may work well on that same bow in the hands of another shooter, but if it no longer works right for him, it is time to find one that will. The time to find this is before the bow is totally set up or tuned to the specific arrow it favors. Good archery shops generally have a selection of releases for archers to test.

Once a sight is installed an archery shop technician probably will have the archer shoot a few arrows at a large target at close range. This begins the process of allowing the parts to meld—to show if more major adjustments are needed and if the archer is adjusting properly to this whole process.

The draw weight, for example, must be set. On that matter, here is a tip from bowmaker, Steven Pagel, vice president of sales and marketing at Forge Flite, in New Berlin, Wis. Try to shoot the bow at the heavy end of its weight range, Pagel said. This takes some of the slop potential out of the bow, which is still an assembly of a number of moving parts. Shooting at the heavy end of a bow's power range reduces or avoids altogether any slop where the bow's limbs are attached to the riser. To be sure that he can do this, a hunter will have to pay attention to the weight range that is selected in a bow. Hunters should not select a 60-70 pound range if they only ever intend to or are able to pull 62 pounds. This hunter might find it more accurate to buy a bow in the 50-60 pound range and crank it up as high as it will go. Most likely, since power ranges still only are estimates, the lighter-powered bow will still reach 62 pounds.

I found great accuracy in Forge Flite's solocam Flare model in the 50-60 pound range. Tuned at Buck Rub Archery and cranked to the max, this one tested on two scales at 64-pounds and shoots more accurately there than it did at lesser weights. Once an archer has a bow set up so it will shoot clusters of arrows in the bull's eye, it is not advisable to mess with the myriad of movable parts on the bow. As in precision hand loading for firearms, making the most minor adjustment can throw everything out of balance, opening up groups on the target.

One day my Flare fell into the hands of a well-intended person who hoped to correct a perceived imbalance that he noticed. The gaps where the limbs bolt to the riser were uneven, suggesting to him that the bow might have been shot out of adjustment during a long archery season. He evened the gaps. Paper testing later that day showed that the bow now was way out of tune.

"That's because for you to shoot this bow and make a pencil-point hole in the paper, the gaps weren't supposed to be even," Kazmierski said. "The bow was tuned, individually, for you."

Evening the gaps moved the string. That put the nock point off, and changed the draw weight of the bow. That would have called for a different arrow altogether. Fussing with a bow requires a chronograph to check the speed of an arrow, a paper target to read the holes, other targets to adjust sights and see if arrows cluster in tight groups, a bow press and a wall of tools. Kazmierski now has added another tool to his collection. He has a device that traces the travel of the nock point on a string. This device delivers clues to adjustments needed to make sure the nock point is traveling along a straight line.

For those who have the tools and the desire, there are entire books dedicated to tuning bows. Two of them are by noted archer Larry Wise. They are "Tuning Your Compound Bow," and "Tuning & Silencing Your Bowhunting Shooting System." Both are third edition books and published by Target Communications, 7626 W. Donges Bay Road, Mequon, WI. 53097.

These books will tell most hunters all they need to know about tuning bows. For me, and probably most average hunters, the books told me to take my bow to a professional. I'll never have the tools, time or talent of a Larry Wise.

Tactics

CHAPTER 18

A Complete Scouting Package

By Greg Miller

The big buck was 30 yards out and walking straight towards me when I first spotted him. With no time to waste, I quickly grabbed my bow from its hanger and got ready. Within seconds the buck was walking by broadside at a mere 10 yards. I quickly and quietly came to full draw and put the top site pin on his vitals. It was now or never.

Even though the arrow was a blur, I still managed to see exactly where it struck the deer. In fact, I saw the arrow hit the ground on the other side of the 10-pointer before he even had time to react. The next thing I knew, however, the thick-necked buck was crashing away into a nearby stand of thick pines. I waited five minutes before taking up his trail. In all, I'd say the buck managed to run 75 yards before going down for good.

Several years later and 125 miles to the south I managed to harvest another big whitetail. The 18-point nontypical, which I arrowed during my home state's late archery season, was substantially larger than the northwoods buck I'd shot two years earlier. But these weren't the only things that made this hunt different. The 10-pointer's home turf consisted of miles and miles of heavily forested, roadless cover. The nontypical, on the other hand, had spent his entire lifetime running around on mile-square (and smaller) tracts of rather open farm land.

There was a significant difference in size between the aforementioned bucks. Also, the two deer lived in completely different environments. Regardless of the differences, however, the same basic scouting strategy proved effective on both deer. This strategy, which has proven deadly in dozens of other instances as well, is one that I developed and perfected some years back. But interestingly, even though the strategy is both very easy to describe and relatively easy to understand, a good many hunters seem to have a problem with the actual application. No doubt this is because my strategy requires expending more than just a little bit of energy.

What is a complete scouting package?

My strategy entails incorporating a complete scouting package into your hunting efforts.

The post-season is a great time to search for buck bedding areas. You can use this information to figure out how to best hunt the area in the future. It is this type of work in the field that creates a total scouting package and a more successful hunt.

Those hunters who prefer to limit their pursuits exclusively to mature bucks, should be especially interested in incorporating a complete scouting package into their hunting efforts.

And just what do I mean when I talk about a complete scouting package? In the simplest terms, it means spending time in the woods during all four of the major scouting periods. Namely, the post-season, spring, pre-season and in-season periods. It also means doing all you can do to learn more about your hunting areas at other times as well.

Those hunters who limit their pursuits exclusively to mature bucks should be especially interested in incorporating a complete scouting package into their hunting efforts. That's because it takes a very special approach to deal with the naturally suspicious, survivalist mentalities these creatures possess. More than 20 years worth of experience in dealing with such animals has taught me one very important lesson: Until you know every finite detail about every square foot of your hunting areas, you simply can't expect to realize any sort of consistent success rate on large-racked whitetails.

Mandatory: Topo maps & aerial photos

While there's no substitute for time spent studying your hunting areas first-hand, I believe it's important that you first become familiar with how those areas look from the "outside." The best way I know of accomplishing this is by thoroughly studying topographical maps and aerial photos of the areas concerned. Personally, I use my maps and photos to look for things like drainages (i.e., lakes, rivers, beaver ponds, creeks and/or swamps), funnel areas, natural clearings, fresh clearcuts and "break lines" caused by sudden and severe changes in elevation. I also use the maps and photos to pinpoint main and secondary roads, logging trails and any terrain features that could make it a bit easier to reach targeted areas.

Though most of my study of topo maps and aerial photos is done at home, I do carry copies of my maps and photos with me when scouting. There are two reasons for this. First of all, my

There's no substitute for time spent studying your hunting areas first-hand. It is also important that you study topographical maps and aerial photos of the area.

memory isn't quite what it used to be. But it takes only a brief look at a map or photo to remind me what my next step is supposed to be. Also, I like to make small notations right on my maps regarding what I find or don't find while scouting. That said, let's move on to the actual scouting process.

Post-season scouting

The vast majority of the deer hunters I know spend very little, if any, time in the woods during the post-season period. It's apparent these individuals have no idea how much you can learn, both about your hunting areas and the deer that reside within those areas, at this time of year. This is especially true for those people who live in a part of the country that normally has snow on the ground during the winter months. Not only is snow a tremendous asset when looking for sign, there even are sit-

uations when the presence of snow can help you determine sign freshness.

For example, the shavings from antler rubs that were only recently made usually will lay on top of the last snow fall. Also, you should be able to somewhat judge the freshness of any scrapes and large tracks you find simply by recalling the date of the most recent snowfall. And what's the benefit of all this? Well, finding an abundance of large, fresh tracks and a number of fresh rubs and scrapes is a fairly accurate indication that more than just a couple big bucks survived the recent bow and gun seasons. Conversely, a severe lack of buck sign could be a signal that buck numbers are discouragingly low.

The post-season is also a great time to search for preferred buck travel routes. This task isn't quite as difficult as some would believe either. Basically what I do is start out by searching for the beginnings of rub-lines near deer feeding areas. I then follow these rub-lines in their entirety. Ideally, I'll be able to follow the rub-lines to their ends, which usually are near the edges of bedding areas. My next step is to look for stand sites close to the bedding areas. After I'm done I'll turn and start looking for the beginnings of rub-lines that lead back towards the feeding area. All the while I'm walking these rub-lines I keep an eye out for likely looking stand site locations. By the way, those rub-lines where the rubs face toward feeding areas are morning travel routes. Conversely, the rubs on evening travel routes will face back toward bedding areas. (In case you're wondering, whitetails bucks will use the same rub-lines year after year.)

Along with searching for preferred buck travel routes and trying to determine buck survival rates, there's yet another reason why I so love to scout during the post-season period. This is the absolute best time of all to pinpoint the exact location of buck bedding areas. In fact, I make it a point to purposely walk through spots where I suspect some big bucks might be bedded down. Believe it or not, it's my intent from the beginning to jump these deer. From my perspective, this is the most accurate gauge for determining the exact location of buck bedding areas. Jumping bucks from their beds might also provide you with information regarding how to best hunt the area in the future. By the way, trespassing into buck bedding areas at this time of year will not have a negative bearing on your future hunting efforts.

Spring scouting

I love scouting during the spring. With no leaf cover to deal with and much of the underbrush gone and/or knocked down by winter snows, our visibility in the woods is as good as it ever gets. This makes it much easier to locate rubs, scrapes and well-used runways from the previous fall. Also, because it's so easy to get around, I'm usually able to effectively cover a great deal of ground in a relatively small amount of time.

Although I will already have pinpointed the exact location of several rub-lines during the post-season, I prefer to "re-scout" those rub-lines once the snow has melted completely. However, rather than searching for additional rub sign, I'm mainly looking for scrapes now. More specifically, I'm trying to figure which rub-lines played host to the greatest amount of scraping activity. My many years of experience in the matter have shown me that those travel routes that harbor good amounts of both rub and scrape sign usually are the most productive.

Also, the stand sites that I picked out on my post-season scouting forays will now get a much more thorough evaluation. If the existing sign indicates that they might well be in the right spot, I'll go ahead and prepare the sites for use at a later date. I'll also do whatever I need to do in the way of pruning and trimming to ensure that I'll have several clear paths for my arrows. I'd like to add that, even though opening day is still months away, I do only a minimal amount of cutting and pruning. Call me paranoid, but I prefer to not give mature bucks a reason to become suspicious — even during the off-season!

Some hunters have told me that they like to incorporate a bit of shed antler hunting into their spring scouting trips. But here's my personal take on the spring scouting/shed antler thing. Simply put, you must do one or the other. There's no way you can do an effective job of scouting if you're also trying to find shed antlers. And vice-versa. Why not? Because in order to effectively search for sheds you must keep your eyes riveted to the ground immediately around you. But in order to do an effective scouting job you must keep your head up

Spring is the best time to do any pruning and trimming around your stand sites. Even though the open season is months away, the author warns you to keep these changes to a minimum.

and your eyes constantly scanning the land ahead for buck sign.

Pre-Season scouting

Even though scouting during the pre-season period requires the least amount of time and energy, the information you gather at this time of year could prove to be the most beneficial of all. For instance, a certain aspect of pre-season scouting could provide you with the data you need to evaluate both the quantity and the quality of the bucks residing within your hunting areas. What's more, it's entirely possible that gathering this data might also help you figure out exactly where your early season stand sites should be located.

The aspect of pre-season scouting I'm talking about here entails nothing more than going out during peak deer movement times

Long-range observations during the pre-season can tell you much regarding both the quality and quantity of the bucks in your hunting areas.

...and watching deer. More specifically, it involves watching and learning exactly how big bucks relate to their most preferred late summer/early fall feeding areas. The best way I've found to accomplish this goal is by sitting back a safe distance from a known or suspected deer feeding area and using a set of high-power binoculars; simply watch what happens. In most cases it takes only a couple ...its before I've pretty much figured out how the big bucks are approaching the area.

I'll usually wait a few days, then come back ...uring the mid-morning hours and do an on-...oot scouting job. My observations have ...lready shown me where the bucks are walk-...g out of the cover and into the feeding area. ...'s now my intent to pinpoint the exact run-...ays the bucks are traveling and find stand ...tes that allow me to take advantage of these

patterns. In most cases, I'll find just enough rub and/or scrape sign to assist me when I make my final decision(s).

A word of warning here about scouting during the pre-season. Regardless of what you may have heard or read, this is not the time to attempt to completely and thoroughly scout your favorite hunting lands. For one thing, with the leaves and underbrush so thick, it's highly doubtful you'll learn much. More importantly, however, such invasions will tip off every deer in the area that something's up. The way I see it, it's tough enough to ambush a mature whitetail when that creature has no idea you're around. But that deer becomes virtually impossible to kill once he realizes you're after his hide. Bottom line? Tread lightly during the pre-season.

Scouting during the season

There have been hundreds, if not thousands, of articles written about spring and pre-season scouting. But for some reason, there hasn't been a lot of stuff written about in-season scouting. I find this downright discouraging, as it's extremely important that hunters continue to scout right on through the season. By the same token, however, it's vitally important that they scout smart. For as I've learned, there's a world of difference between the temperament displayed by whitetails during the off-season and the temperaments they display during the open season. Almost without exception these changes in temperament are caused by hunting pressure.

It's crucial that hunters use a very low impact form of scouting during the season. Personally, I prefer to do a good part of my in-season scouting while walking into and out of my stand sites. Along with checking every runway that I cross, I always keep my eyes open for fresh rubs and scrapes. And of course, I always pay especially close attention whenever I see some deer. More than anything, I strive to see if any of the deer are bucks. But whether there are any bucks or not, I still want to know why those deer were where they were when I saw them. Were they pushed into the area by other hunters, or were they merely traveling through? Were they on their way to or coming back from a food source? Or were they already at the food source when I saw them?

Thorough scouting can provide you with important information regarding exactly what the deer in your hunting areas are eating at specific times during the season.

The author does a good deal of in-season scouting while walking to and from his stand sites. Along with checking runways, he also keeps an eye out for fresh rubs and scrapes.

Whatever the case might be, I know that it's going to take some work to find the correct answers. But with the deer herd in a slightly more nervous and suspicious state of mind, I know that I won't be able to employ my normal scouting approach. Thankfully, I've developed a strategy that's perfectly suited to these types of conditions. I call this strategy speed-scouting. In a nutshell, speed-scouting can be a highly effective way to learn a great deal about specific areas, while at the same time expending very little time and energy.

I use the same basic approach on all my speed-scouting forays. I start out by studying topo maps and aerial photos of an area I've previously targeted. (I rely largely on deer sightings to help me select specific areas.) Then, waiting until the midday hours, I'll walk through the targeted area at a fairly fast

pace. I move fast for two reasons. To begin with, I'm looking to cover as much ground as possible in a small amount of time. And secondly, it's obvious that my fast pace sends no predatory vibes to whitetails. There have been numerous occasions where deer have stood and watched me breeze right on by.

Though I'm constantly looking for deer, my main objective is to find fresh rubs and scrapes. Once I locate some rubs and/or scrapes, I then start casting around in the immediate area to see if these rubs/scrapes are part of a line. If I find such a line, I'll follow it until I locate a suitable stand site. If the rubs and scrapes I find are not part of a line, I'll simply look for the greatest concentrations of sign and then establish a stand site within bow range of that sign. I used this exact approach to harvest a big buck during a recent archery season.

A bit of in-season scouting by the author and his daughter, Jessie, put Greg in position to harvest this big Wisconsin whitetail.

My daughter, Jessie, and I had initially found some sign from the mature whitetail while speed-scouting the area two weeks earlier. The greatest concentration of buck sign was located near a break in what was an otherwise tightly strung, in-woods fence line. Instead of looking around for a "better" spot, I immediately prepared a stand site within range of the fence crossing. The buck showed up several mornings later, and I arrowed him at a range of four yards.

The biggest perk of speed-scouting is that it allows you to continually find fresh stand sites during the season. The downside of the strategy, however, is that some of these stand sites are going to be slightly out of position. But instead of sitting on your stand and crying if a buck passes by just out of range, pay close attention to exactly where he walks. Why? Because there's a very good chance the buck will use that exact same route again on another day. Hopefully, you'll be sitting on a newly prepared stand site well within bow range of that route. (Far too many bowhunters are reluctant to relocate their stand sites once the season opens. Don't fall into this trap.)

Scouting during the four major periods can provide you important information regarding exactly what the deer are eating at specific times during the open season. Even more importantly, these constant scouting missions can tell you what travel routes the bucks most prefer to use when approaching and leaving those food sources. And it doesn't matter if your hunting lands are made up of 100 acres, 100,000 acres or something in between. The bottom line remains that you must have an effective game plan for hunting those lands. Incorporating a complete scouting package into your hunting efforts will provide you with just such a game plan.

CHAPTER 19

Common Sense Bowhunting

By Bob Humphrey

The setup was perfect. I was positioned at the top of a large draw with the wind in my face. Several trails, heavily rutted with tracks, crisscrossed below me. To top it off, it was a clear, crisp morning during the peak of the rut. As I sat on the hardwood ridge in the West Virginia mountains, I imagined a parade of deer passing below me. Suddenly my daydreaming was interrupted by the sound of footfalls on dry leaves. My pulse quickened as I turned to see a doe trotting quickly up the ridge to my right.

No sooner had she gone out of sight when a nice six-pointer appeared, nose to the ground, right on her trail. If he continued his current course, it would take him up and over the ridge, out of range. So I pulled out my grunt call and gave several loud tending grunts. The

buck slammed to a halt and stared in my direction. I gave several more loud calls and his ears shifted and his tail went up to half staff. "Now I'll really give it to him" I thought. I gave several more loud grunts and he made his move. If Detroit could match the acceleration of a whitetail deer, they could corner the world market on auto sales. In an instant, the buck turned and bolted straight away! As I sat the rest of that quiet morning I began to contemplate what went wrong.

The face of deer hunting has changed considerably over the past two decades.

Years ago, hunters went afield equipped with little more than a trusted rifle or a recurve, a moderate understanding of whitetail behavior—gained mostly through experience—and a generous portion of common sense. And they killed deer. Today, through the efforts of

This 10-pointer fell to common sense hunting techniques. There is no magic involved in successful hunting. Bagging deer consistently involves patience, attention to detail and a fair amount of common sense

Soft rattling simulates the early fall sparring matches of younger buck. Most encounters between bucks are not knock-down, drag-out fights. Most of the time the deer already have an idea of who is stronger and don't intend to do anything that will lead to serious injury. A huge fight may occur when two dominant bucks cross paths, but more often the sparring heard in the woods is between younger deer.

research supported by hunters' dollars, we not only have a lot more deer, we also have a much better understanding of their biology and behavior.

In the ceaseless quest to tip the odds in our favor, we have used this understanding to contrive innumerable new devices and tactics. Books, magazines, and videos are filled with them. But in some cases, hunters are afflicted with too much information on whitetail tactics. With the plethora of theories on rattling, calling, scents, and lures, they are overloaded with information and are confused in trying to assimilate all this into a successful and effective means for harvesting whitetails.

Many of these tools and tactics will work under the right circumstances. But it's important to remember they are supplements, not substitutes. You can't replace good old common sense. But, by taking a step back and relying on common sense first, hunters can apply some of these recent innovations to significantly

improve their chances for success in the deer woods. The reverse is also true. Success can also be achieved by applying common sense to our better understanding of deer and deer behavior.

Rattling

Antler rattling is one of those tactics hunters tend to rely on too much. While it is considered a relatively recent tactic, it has actually been around for centuries. Native American folklore contains many references to antler rattling. Though it can be effective, rattling may not always be the best tactic. Applying common sense will help you determine when and how best to use it.

The theory behind antler rattling is that by simulating two fighting bucks you can attract others. Like kids on a playground, two battling bucks will sometimes draw a crowd. In both cases, the onlookers are attracted by both curiosity and aggression. The toughest kid will charge right in, and may even intervene, while the more timid kids will keep their distance to avoid getting injured. Common sense tells us that the same should be true for deer.

What we now know about deer behavior also supports this. There is a dominance hierarchy among male deer in a particular area. It is usually sorted out before hunting seasons begin, but close rivals may continue to test one another, particularly as the rut approaches. As any fight has the potential to upset the established pecking order, it often draws a crowd. A dominant buck may perceive this as a threat to his rank and his approach may be motivated more by aggression than curiosity. But common sense also tells us that though rattling will attract big bucks, it may not work on the biggest bucks.

There's an old saw that goes: "It's not the size of the dog in the fight, but the size of the fight in the dog that matters." This doesn't just apply to dogs. Have you ever noticed how, in any group of guys, there always seems to be one or two who are the most aggressive, always spoiling for a fight? The toughest guys are not always the biggest guys either; in fact, they are usually the smaller ones. The big guys just want to be left alone. The same is true for deer.

The way bucks grow old, and big, is by avoiding dangerous situations, not seeking them out. As we have said, rattling exploits the aggressive nature of whitetails. They hear a conflict and some combination of curiosity and aggression prompts them to investigate. Smaller, subordinate deer tend to approach more cautiously than more aggressive, dominant deer. But those that approach hastily are placing themselves in potential danger, either

Lost fawn bleats are effective calling techniques for does. Despite what many people think, deer are very vocal and social animals. Adult female deer will respond to the vocalizations of younger deer very quickly.

from being thumped by a larger rival, or shot by a rattling hunter. Meanwhile, the old gentle giant will live another day or a year, to grow older and larger.

This doesn't mean you can't rattle up a trophy. Depending on the health and age ratio of deer in your area, some of those subordinates may sport some impressive headgear. Also, while aggressive rattling may draw in aggressive bucks, simulated sparring might just pique the curiosity of even the most timid deer. This is best imitated by soft tickling and meshing of antlers, not by loud smashing and grinding. Bucks do a lot more sparring than actual fighting. A real knock-down, drag-out fight is a dangerous proposition and could result in death or serious injury of one, or both combatants. Sparring, on the other hand is more of a wrestling match than a real fight. The bucks are testing each other for strength and endurance.

Common sense also tells us when rattling is most effective. Most sparring takes place before the breeding season, when bucks are still associating in bachelor groups. Just like kids on the playground, they wrestle and tussle to sort out who is the toughest. Sparring is a common occurrence and more likely to illicit curiosity than caution. Later, the bucks will disperse, but for now they are in groups. Thus, you have a much better chance of being heard by, and possibly attracting multiple bucks.

Calling

Our knowledge of whitetail vocalizations, and how they can be imitated, has increased considerably in recent years. When I started deer hunting, there were no deer calls on the market, and very few of my hunting companions had ever even heard (or would recognize) a deer grunt or bleat. Thanks to a lot of research, we are beginning to have a much better understanding of vocal communication by whitetails. Their repertoire of vocalizations goes far beyond what we once knew. There are greeting calls, tending calls and locating calls—all of which, when imitated, can be effective hunting techniques under the right set of circumstances.

Unfortunately, too many deer hunters take gadgets like calls at face value. They figure that all they have to do is blow, and deer will come. Furthermore, the old Americanism that more is better can be a real detriment here. Calling does work if it's done right. It just takes the application of a little common sense.

Deer hunters can apply a lot of what turkey hunters already know about communication. Aggressive calling may work in certain circumstances, but other situations call for more refined calling techniques. Just like humans and turkeys, deer are more likely to come when asked, rather than when told. A soft greeting call can be a lot more effective than a loud grunt. As I learned with that West Virginia six-pointer, a smaller buck certainly isn't going to go out of his way to approach a larger, more aggressive one.

This doesn't apply exclusively to bucks either. In fact, outside the breeding season, does are a lot more vocal than bucks. Much of the communication that takes place is between a mother and her offspring. Fawns can call their mother when hungry, lost, or threatened. Hunters can do likewise by imitating these calls. Again, applying a little common sense will make this tactic more effective.

Though a doe may respond to a fawn distress bawl more quickly than a lost fawn bleat, she'll likely be very cautious, tense, and alert, making for a poor archery target. A doe searching for a lost fawn on the other hand, will be more relaxed, and have her attention focused not on potential danger, but on finding her lost fawn. Timing is also important. While early in the fall a fawn bleat may draw in an adult doe, later in the season, her maternal instinct is not as strong and this call will be less effective.

If you're specifically after does, a buck grunt will probably scare more deer than it attracts. During the rut, does coming into estrus are being repeatedly harassed, chased, and prodded by potential suitors. Thus, a buck grunt will be perceived by a doe more as a warning than an invitation. A greeting call, on the other hand, will be an invitation.

Scents & lures

Probably the biggest area of recent innovation and marketing for whitetail hunters has been with scents and lures. In my early years of deer hunting, all we had was doe and fox urine. Today, you can buy doe-in-heat scent, buck lure, scent gel, scent tablets, tarsal glands; fox, raccoon, skunk, coyote scent; apple, fir, pine, acorn, and earth scent. There are products to neutralize any scent, including a breath neutralizer! (Believe me, if a deer gets close enough to smell my breath, it is because I have chosen not to kill it.) Just like calls and rattling, scents occasionally work when applied with common sense.

Whitetails use their sense of smell to communicate in a variety of ways. A dominant buck uses scrapes not only to tell does that he's looking for a date, but to tell other bucks that he's the top gun in these here parts. In most areas, by the time the rut begins, there is only one dominant buck, and nothing will rile him up more than a challenger. As already mentioned, one way to exploit this is with rattling. Another is with scents.

If you can artificially introduce a challenger, you may be able to draw the dominant buck out into the open during daylight. Applying commercial buck lures to a hot scrape is one way to do this. Another is by using the real thing. While there is usually one dominant buck in an area, over several areas, there are several dominant bucks. By taking soil from a fresh scrape in one area, and moving it (in a scent-free container) to a scrape in another area, you are issuing a challenge to the dominant buck there.

Deer use wind to alert them of approaching danger. To get a shot at a trophy like this you must consider the wind.

He'll want to know who this new upstart is and will come around often to find out.

Probably the most common application of lures is using doe-in-heat urine to exploit a buck's lust. Here, as with rattling and calling, timing is critical. Bucks use scrapes to help them locate hot does. But once the breeding period begins, the bucks are not checking their scrapes nearly as often. They're too busy tending does. Thus, the best time to hunt scrapes is before or after the rut, when bucks are actively tending scrapes looking for early- or late-cycling does. Once the majority of does come into heat (and in most areas it is fairly synchronous), bucks don't have the time, or need to tend scrapes.

The greatest obstacle to deer hunters, especially bowhunters, is overcoming a whitetail's keen sense of smell. Cover scents can work well to camouflage human odors. However, the scent you choose should be one that is familiar to deer in the area you hunt. Balsam fir scent will not work in the oak ridges of West Virginia, just as apple scent will be foreign to deer

in the northwoods of Maine. Your objective is to blend in with your surroundings, visually as well as by odor. Learn what aromatic vegetation or animals occur in the area you hunt and try to mimic them. When hunting in dairy country, I will often walk through a cow pasture, grinding my boots into cow flops, on my way to the woods. Foxes often travel on the same trails as deer, but they tend to occur in areas of mixed cover, not in large unbroken tracts of forest. Skunk scent is a powerful masking scent but if used in an area with no skunks, will frighten deer long before you are aware of their presence. It also may get you banished to the garage.

Wind

Another way hunters try to overcome a deer's olfactory senses is by using the wind to their advantage. Common sense tells you to position yourself such that you will be downwind of approaching deer. It seems fairly straightforward; yet this is a situations where hunters often mess up. They assume deer will be traveling mostly into the wind when the exact opposite is true, especially in field situations.

Think about it. Deer have three senses, sight, hearing, and smell, to rely on for detecting danger. When traveling into the wind, they are using both sight and smell to search in front of them, while leaving their rear vulnerable. When traveling with the wind, they can look for danger ahead, and smell for danger behind, which is where most of their natural predators will approach from. This is especially true for deer approaching fields. They will be able to see out into the field for some distance and can detect danger with sight alone. Since they are most vulnerable from behind, approaching a field from upwind is the safest route.

Much of this information is not new. Many of these tactics are well-known to hunters who read about them in popular outdoor publications then try them out in the field. In some cases, they even work, despite the fact the hunter really doesn't understand how or why. But by understanding the how's and why's, and applying common sense, you'll find these tactics working more often, and when you expect it.

CHAPTER 20

Still-hunting Whitetail Bucks

By Bill Vaznis

The Art and Science

It all happened so fast. I was still-hunting just inside a wood lot that bordered an alfalfa field when I first saw her. She seemed to be browsing nonchalantly in my direction, but her half-raised tail and stiff-legged gait told me she

Effective still-hunting tests all your skill and knowledge. Still-hunters need not only archery skills, but skills in woodsmanship, tracking and stalking as well. The end result is usually a memorable hunt. Any deer bagged while still-hunting should be considered a trophy.

was near estrous, and that meant a buck had to be hiding somewhere nearby.

I slipped to within 25 yards of her position, and knelt down for a better look when a Pope and Young eight-pointer sauntered onto the scene. He had been with her just over the ridge, and was now bird-dogging the doe as she slowly worked her way past me. I planned on taking him as soon as he stepped into an opening, but a smaller eight-pointer appeared from somewhere behind the ridge, and complicated matters.

The two bucks were oblivious to my presence, and squared off in front of me as soon as they spotted each other. I wanted the larger buck, but thick brush continued to conceal his vitals. When the smaller of the two bucks offered me a clear shot at 18 yards, I brought my bow to full draw, picked a spot and sent a full-length aluminum arrow tipped with a cut-on-impact broadhead deep into his chest. He bolted from the scene, but it was too late. He was dead on his feet.

There are no magic or mysterious forces at work when a bowhunter tags a buck by still-hunting—just good woodsmanship and a bit of common sense. You see, still-hunting is both an art and a science, and to be consistently successful you must practice both every time you head afield. Here's how to make your next whitetail buck the most memorable yet.

Camouflage

The ability to pick the right camouflage, then hide in plain sight is the sign of an experienced still-hunter. Why? Most bucks are taken at point-blank range. It is as simple as that. Of the white-tailed deer I have tagged while still-hunting with archery tackle, only three were taken past 25 yards. My closest, an unlucky and rut-crazed seven-pointer, approached within a mere three yards.

The more you still-hunt with a bow, the more you realize there is no such thing as too much

This is what you're after. If you can get this close to a relaxed white-tailed deer, you should have no trouble making a good shot.

camouflage. Your outer clothing, any exposed skin and all your equipment must be camouflaged in dull, earth-tone colors or you risk spooking the buck of your dreams before you ever get an arrow nocked.

In the early season, designer camouflage patterns with wide-open spaces seem to work best in disguising the human form. Tree bark patterns blend together out past 25 yards making a bowhunter look more like a solid, out-of-place blob than a natural part of the forest.

I am not a slave to fashion however, and right after the season's first frost I begin to mix and match my camo. That is, I match my upper body with what is above the forest floor, and my lower body with what is on the forest floor. For example, if I am still-hunting among light-skinned trees like beech and oak soon after they drop their leaves, I will wear a gray-based camouflaged cap and jacket with leaf-colored camo pants. If I am going to still-hunt an old apple orchard, a branch-pattern hat and jacket paired with shadow-based camo pants is often the ticket to success.

This technique of mixing and matching is also very effective a day or two after a winter storm when the sun and wind have knocked the white stuff off the branches. I then prefer to wear a 3-D snow pattern on my lower torso with a camouflage hat and jacket that best resembles the leaf-less brush.

You must also conceal any exposed flesh. Get into the habit of camouflaging your face, neck, ears with "war paint" rather than a head net. Mesh nets are fine in a pinch or if you only have an hour or so to hunt before work, but a cold cream-based face paint is best for extended periods of time. That's because face paint does not interfere with your ability to hear, or impair your peripheral vision like head nets are apt to do. And you can more readily determine changes in wind direction by simply feeling the air pass over your skin, something that can't be done when wearing a head net. Remember you want to "mask" your head, face and neck, not your primary senses!

Don't overlook your hands. Even in warm weather, you should apply camo cream to your hands or wear a pair of light cotton gloves. Try this experiment, and see for yourself. Have a friend stand on the edge of cover, and slowly wave first a bare hand and then a camouflaged hand in your direction. The bare hand will stand out like a neon light whereas the camouflaged hand is nearly impossible to see.

When it comes to camouflaging your archery tackle, don't overlook your arrow fletching. Bright, contrasting colors are designed to help you find your arrow after the shot, but they are detrimental when they interfere with a shooting opportunity. Indeed, a quiver full of brightly-fletched arrows can sometimes spook a buck faster than a fluttering white handkerchief!

I prefer red fletching and nocks on my shafts when I'm still-hunting eastern whitetails, but other dark colors, such as green, black and blue work just as well. If it is important for you to pinpoint the entry point of your broadhead, an acceptable compromise would be a light-colored cock feather or fluorescent nocks.

While you are at it, get rid of your hip quiver and attach a quiver to your bow. Sure, a bare bow may be more accurate under controlled conditions, but hip quivers (and back quivers to a lesser degree) tend to be bulky and noisy in the brush. They are also quick to give away your position. Here's another experiment. Have a pal sneak past you at 30 or 40 yards

Still-hunting in standing corn can be very effective on windy days. The sound of the wind masks the hunter's movements and corn provides outstanding concealment. Remember to move slowly and quietly.

with a hip quiver in place. See how his arrows bob back and forth like the pendulum on a clock? That unnecessary motion is what so often spooks deer.

Outer Wear

"If you want to sneak up on a big buck," an old-timer once told me, "you must learn to move like a deer, and let your shadow make all the noise." That advice is as good today as it was 35 years ago. Only today we have a much better choice of clothing and footwear to choose from. Here are three tips to help you still-hunt undetected through the forest.

The first tip is to learn to pick the right fabric(s). Before you buy any new garment, try running your fingernail across the surface. If it squeaks or scratches in the store, it will also do so whenever you encounter a twig or a branch in the field. Brushed cotton and Polar Tuff are two of the better "quiet" materials on the market, but wool is best. Not only is it incredibly silent, but it will also keep you warm in the field even when it is soaking wet.

Secondly, pay closer attention to your head-gear. Indeed, one of the most under-rated pieces of still-hunting clothing is the baseball style cap. Knit hats tend to snag on brush and do little to reduce eye fatigue, but a cap with three-quarters or full brim shields the sun from your eyes, keeps the rain off your face and protects your eyes from branches—especially in dim light. If you want a good excuse for a frustrating day afield, leave your baseball cap home. What is the best construction material? Well, wool of course!

The third tip involves boots, or should I say soles. Heavy-duty lug type soles offer protection from sharp objects and good traction, but they do not allow you to feel the ground as well as a thin sole with a ripple-tread design. Unfortunately, these thin soles are slippery when wet making for hazardous walking in the early morning dew or during periods of inclement weather.

The best outer sole for still-hunting white-tails is the Air Grip or Air Bob. This design has been around for nearly 20 years, but it didn't become popular with deer hunters until the early 90s. Its main features are hollowed black nipples that flex or "bob" up and down as you walk. This flexing action gives incredible stability in the woods, and unlike some other outer sole designs, keeps the traction relatively clear of mud and snow. Most major boot manufacturers now offer some type of Air Bob sole.

Special Equipment

One of the beauties of still-hunting is its simplicity. You don't need to lug tree stands, climbing poles, saws, bow holders and other stuff around the woods to hunt successfully. You need just three "specialty items."

Dave, Don and Rick Plant of Rochester, New York have tagged over a dozen whitetails by still-hunting, including several mature bucks. According to the family spokesman, Rick, a taxidermist, the most important specialty item is a pair of quality binoculars. "Good binocs gather light under low-light conditions," says Plant. "In addition, they let you peer into the brush for a private look-see and help identify those unusual objects up ahead that so often turn out to be an antler tine or the back leg of a whitetail. Next to your bow, binoculars are your most important tool."

Lean towards the top of the line mid-sized models, and buy the very best you can afford. You won't regret it. Stay away from the mini's. They simply do not have the light-gathering abilities or the field of view to be of much use to a still-hunter.

The second item I would not leave camp without is a grunt tube. Actually, I carry a couple of deer calls with me whenever I am afield, including a variable and at least one single-purpose model. Grunt tubes not only attract unseen deer, but they can be used to coax a distant buck into bow range. A moderately toned buck grunt, for example, stimulates a buck's territorial instincts whereas a doe bleat imitates a doe near estrous—a hot call for a rutting buck.

If I could still-hunt with only one call, it would be a fawn bleat. Not only will one attract rutting bucks, but it will also lure an estrous doe into bow range, an important strategy if she has the buck of your dreams in tow. More importantly perhaps, a fawn bleat camouflages my clumsiness in the deer woods. Whenever I snap a twig or stumble, I use my fawn bleat to

relax any nearby deer. Fawns are very noisy in the woods, and a couple of imitation fawn bleats will put the local herd at ease.

Finally, I always have a roll of fluorescent orange flagging tape in my pocket. I use it to mark the exact spot from which I shot before I begin to trail the deer. Unlike a tree stand hunter who can easily climb back into his stand to relive the path of his arrow, a still-hunter can easily forget exactly where he was when he shot. The flagging tape helps me return to the exact location from which I shot in case I loose the blood trail or can't find the arrow.

The Eyes and Ears Have It

The corner stone to successful still-hunting is seeing the buck before he is even remotely aware of your presence. If you can catch a

Read the signs. Deer sign has much to tell still-hunters. The buck that made this rub might still be in the area. Knowing how to read deer sign can mean the difference between success and failure while still-hunting.

Landowners are the best source of information when searching for deer. Using a map to mark reference points can put you right on top of great deer habitat.

mature buck off guard, you are halfway to filling a tag. Here are three tips to help you in that endeavor.

Mark Eddy, Adirondack guide and owner of the Moose River Company in Old Forge, New York advises his still-hunting archery clients to take advantage of available cover whenever possible.

"In essence, you want to plan a route that will allow you to see easily into the woods," says Eddy, "but where it is difficult for a deer to see you. That means sneaking along near the top of the ridge, not on the top where you are likely to be silhouetted. It means skirting the edges of abandoned beaver ponds where there is plenty of tall grass and alders to conceal you, not across the middle of the meadow in plain sight."

To follow Mark Eddy's advice properly, you must learn to walk with your eyes off the ground. Let me explain. One of the biggest

mistakes a still-hunter can make is to spend too much time looking where he is going. If you can teach yourself to look about and quickly determine where to put each foot, and then walk slowly forward with your eyes constantly scanning the woods for bucks, you will be more successful. Your goal is to spend at least 50 seconds of every minute actually looking for game.

Finally, you must learn to tune in your other senses in your search for wary bucks—especially your ears. Undisturbed deer make a lot of noise as they go about their daily routines. Your job is to identify these various tones and cadences, and react accordingly.

What sounds should you listen for? I key in on the soft "thump-twang-thump" of a deer jumping a barbed wire fence, the "clackety-clack, clackety-clack" of a deer crossing over a stone wall, the gentle "snip, snip" of a deer biting the tops off golden rod plants, the "crunch,

crunch, crunch" of a deer chowing down on acorns and a series of Urp's from a mature buck tending a hot doe.

How can you learn to recognize these sounds? That's easy. Try this exercise right now. Relax, close your eyes and list all the sounds you hear in your home. Can you identify the furnace blower, the refrigerator, what program is on television? Pay attention to what you hear in the woods, and you'll see more deer.

Killer Strategies

Each day's still-hunt must begin with a plan, and the details of that plan depend on such factors as wind direction, terrain features, previous sightings, time of day and the timing of the rut. Here's three killer strategies guaranteed to bring action your way.

The easiest way to learn how to still-hunt is to practice sneaking to and from your tree stand during legal shooting hours. You'll learn such basics as how to play the wind, when to hunt bedding grounds and travel routes, and how to pace yourself according to the availability of cover and the amount of deer sign. The anticipation of walking up on a buck in a known hot spot can be very exciting!

After hunting for years from a tree stand, the Plant family now still-hunts almost exclusively. And with their track record, why not? "My favorite technique," says Rick Plant, "is to be on the edge of a bedding area at pink light, and then, with the wind in my favor, work my way slowly towards a known feeding area. This can be especially effective early in the season before scrapes and scrape lines appear. I have been able to intercept a couple of nice bucks in this manner, including a fat six-pointer I arrowed at three yards!"

During the pre-rut, I prefer to still-hunt on the downwind side of an active scrape line. Examine nearby rubs, tracks and the direction the forest duff is tossed to learn when the buck is likely to return, and then be there at the same time. I've arrowed several bucks by still-hunting along these deer highways, including a dandy nine-pointer that grossed in the-mid 140s.

Later in the season, my favorite strategy is to pussy foot around the edges of bedding areas preferred by family groups of does and fawns during the rut, especially if there are abandoned farm fields of goldenrod and thorn apple nearby. You see, bucks like to check out these bedding areas and surrounding cover all day long for estrous does. In fact, you can sometimes catch a buck bedded in that goldenrod right in the middle of the day. I've nailed two bucks in their beds still-hunting these deer-rich pockets during the peak of the rut, including a wide-racked eight pointer I took at 21 yards.

Moment of Truth

The goal of every still-hunt is to first work yourself to within easy bow range, then shoot an arrow into the vitals of a relaxed, mature animal. The trick to pulling off such a shot is not pinpoint accuracy or even knowing when to come to full draw, although both are important. The trick is your stance. Let me explain.

The author looks over the rewards of a successful still-hunt. This bulky Iowa whitetail would be a trophy for any hunter. To bag a trophy like this while still-hunting takes exceptional skill and dedication.

Most whitetails, even a buck crazed with the rut, instantly recognize human silhouette. The average hunter stands 5 to 6 feet tall, is wandering the woods on his hind legs with a shiny face, no nose, tiny ears and two beady eyes placed close together. This image is not something deer normally see in the woods. It makes them nervous.

To distort that image into harmless contours, simply darken your face, and kneel down. It's amazing how often deer will look right past you when you are crouched low to the ground. They will ignore you at least long enough for you to pick a spot, and shoot.

Well, there you have it. Use these still-hunting secrets to help you bag the buck you'll brag about for years to come. All you have to do now is climb down out of your stand, and start sneakin' and peekin'. Good hunting!

CHAPTER 21

Stalking Mule Deer, Bow in Hand

By Jim Van Norman

So, you hope to get close with stick and string? Walking up on a mule deer is an "undertaking" not for the faint of heart or easily discouraged. Getting into position for a responsible shot at a mule deer takes the right equipment, planning, physical stamina, a flawless approach and nerves of steel. But, the rewards of a successful stalk on mule deer with archery equipment are more gratifying than almost anything you can do in hunting.

Stalking is a very effective way to take mule deer with a bow. By choosing your stalks carefully and following a few basic rules, your chances are increased dramatically. Here are some tips that have proven successful to me and my bowhunting clients now for many years.

One of the first important factors in successful stalking, believe it or not, is our choice of clothing. A great number of stalks are blown because of poor selection in this area. Wool is hard to beat for being quiet. It can be too hot and heavy for the early fall temperatures, but use it whenever you can. I always throw mine in regardless. The weather in prime muley country can be quite fickle. Other types of garments that I recommend are cotton, fleece, and saddle cloth. Pick your hats and gloves with the same idea in mind, stealth! Also, give some

...et him decide when to go. A relaxed mule deer makes a much easier target. Mule deer will often get tired of sitting ...n one spot, or the sun will shift prompting them to seek more shade. Either way, if you are in close let the deer ...ecide when it's time to move. This might not be a perfect shot, but if you can draw without being seen, this deer is ...ours.

The author poses with the fruits of a successful stalk. It takes skill, stamina and nerves of steel to get close to an animal like this. Once you're within bow range, there's no need to force the issue. Let the deer decide when it's time to move.

thought to how much noise the clothing underneath your outer garments will produce should you have to shed a layer or two while stalking. Also, quiet rain gear is a must.

Boot choice ranks right up there with being one of the most important elements in successful stalking. Support is important! Trading support, for a quiet pair of "floppy" tennis shoe-type stalking shoes, is a mistake. We seldom plan to go as far as we actually do when stalking mule deer but, we always end up two drainage's farther than anticipated. Some of the most painful and dangerous experiences I've had have been while wearing a pair of canvas stalking shoes hoofing it 6 miles back to camp after heading out on what I thought was a "1-mile stalk." If you have a pair of stalking shoes. carry them with you in your pack and change when you get in close. I will address this item later but, a pair of heavy, knee-high, wool socks are great for stalking when you get in close.

Buy the foot and ankle support you need, but take note of the type of material used on the uppers and their noise production. The key to quiet boots is mainly in the type of sole you pick. Choose a sole that has some flexibility. Soft rubbery soles that provide good traction and will mold around things you step on are good choices. Traction bars have a tendency to grind and break things under foot making considerable noise. So avoid the lug sole boots, if possible, for stalking mule deer. Rubber boots are hard to beat for being quiet if the weather is wet or it's not too hot.

Where are you headed?

Having chosen your boots and clothing properly, the next step is to evaluate the type of country you will be stalking in. This can be determined with a map or, better yet, when you arrive in a piece of mule deer country. I've learned, over the years, to pick areas that will present the best opportunities. In most mule deer areas there are two types of terrain – the "hard-to-stalk" type, with either heavy brush, heavy timber or wide open rolling hills and the "easier-to-stalk" type, containing canyons, draws, cut-banks, washouts, etc., with scattered vegetation.

Although there is nothing easy about stalking mule deer, the "roughest" types of terrain present the best opportunities. Stalking is tedious and very time-consuming, so don't waste your valuable hunting time in a hard-to-stalk area that your chances are obviously "slim and none"!

Note: If you're from the East, I'm sure most of the country out West—(short of the mountains)—looks like a person couldn't sneak up on a "blind sow" standing by a water fall! But, with a little experience you'll quickly be able to tell which country will present the best opportunities for you.

Shade is the best place to find mule deer. The roughest and most sparsely vegetated areas often have very little shade, therefore helping your odds of first, finding a bedded deer, and second, finding one bedded in a good site that will increase your chances of success.

The best time of day to stalk a mule deer is between 10:00 a.m. and 2:00 p.m. Mule deer at this time of day, are almost always found in the shade, they are stationary and sometimes sleepy. Shade provides mule deer with much-needed heat relief and cover. Now, mule deer will be found in their beds earlier and later than these specific times, but one of the keys to effective stalking is to get into position for a shot, as close to a transition period as possible. That is, mule deer get tired of laying in one spot for long periods and will eventually get up to change positions or the sun will cause their shade to disappear, forcing them to seek out a new spot. Bugs can also make them move. And that's when you want to be ready. Another notable transition period is an hour or two before dark, when mule deer generally get up and start their evening feed.

My point of view on stalking bedded mule deer differs from others in that I contend you must get into position and wait for a transition, instead of forcing the deer to stand up when you get there. Throwing rocks, calling on a predator call, whistling etc., works at times, but more often only provides a great view of the south end of a northbound mule deer. By letting the deer stand of his own free will, your chances for an opportunity to draw on an unsuspecting target are far greater. We will talk more about this philosophy later.

Even though the best opportunities for stalking are as described above, it is important to be out before daylight and in a position where you can glass a lot of country. I will assume you already know how to get into position before daylight, without being seen, and have the necessary skills and "skills with optics" to successfully find mule deer.

The reason to be out before daylight and in position is that you will have a chance to see

This is what you're after. The deer is standing still, looking away from you and providing you with a great shot at his vitals from just about 15 yards. If you had decided to toss stones or howl like a coyote once you got to checkpoint three, this deer would not be standing still when he got up to look around. Patience pays off. Once you get within bow range, sit still. Wait all day you have to. This is what you'll get as your reward.

more deer while they are out feeding, and may find several deer you would like to stalk. All that is then needed is to watch until each picks a bedding site and then determine which deer presents the best chance for success. Many stalks are unsuccessful because they were poor opportunities to begin with. Evaluating each stalk in terms of poor, mediocre, very good and excellent is one of the keys to being a top-notch stalker. I never (anymore) attempt a stalk unless I have a very good or excellent chance of being successful. Rating each stalking opportunity is critical for a bowhunter. The least amount of disturbance you bring an area in terms of "botched" stalks, the better your chances are of not spooking all the deer out of your area.

Your evaluation needs to be in-depth. Ask yourself, can I get into position for a responsible shot, can I draw without being seen when he stands up? If I have to wait a while for the deer to stand, is the wind variable or steady? What is the terrain like, what's the footing like over there, etc? By evaluating each aspect of a stalk, you can make an educated decision on whether to stalk or not, as well as maximize your odds when the decision is made to "go for it." If you find the buck of a lifetime and he is in poor or mediocre position for a stalk, "camp on him" until he moves to a better spot.

A note on wind: Wind is the main culprit in most unsuccessful stalks. It must be scrutinized carefully. If the wind is light and variable generally a stalk is not advisable. If the wind is steady or strong it has more of a tendency to remain blowing from a specific direction. But, don't forget that the terrain (surface interference) can and does change wind direction notably. So look the situation over carefully, making note of everything near the bedded mule deer.

Even though a strong wind is very annoying to both us and the deer, stalking in a big wind can be beneficial. As mentioned previously, a strong wind's direction generally remains constant. It also hides many other noises that would otherwise be easily heard by the acute ears of mule deer. Mule deer are very nervous during periods of strong wind but, will stay put better as they seem to associate inadvertent noises to the wind. Evaluating the wind, knowing when to attempt a stalk and when not to, is paramount.

Once you have made a decision to try a stalk, mapping your stalk mentally is the next critical element. Pick your route carefully, including three solid checkpoints. These should be prominent checkpoints that will guide you to a spot near the deer's location and are not easily mistaken. It is always amazing to me how different the country looks when you get over near the deer, as opposed to how it looked from where you spotted the deer. So, pick checkpoints that are unusual in nature and avoid objects that are numerous and could cause confusion. I can't tell you how many times I've neglected to pick prominent checkpoints or not picked checkpoints at all in my early years only to find myself in the wrong place when the deer bolted away. But, it only took once for me to "blow it" with a paying client staring down my neck, before this practice was engrained in my thick head forever.

Choose your three checkpoints backwards. Your third checkpoint (the one closest to the deer) is primary, so pick it first because it is the place where you are going to wait for a shot to develop. Do not use the deer's location as your final checkpoint. You should try to end up no closer than 15 yards and no farther than 30 yards from the deer, if the terrain and cover will allow. By getting no closer than 15 yards you create a little buffer in case the deer gets up and comes towards you. And by staying within 30 yards, you will still be close enough, should he get up and move away, for a responsible shot before he moves out of your effective range.

The second checkpoint should be chosen at about the halfway mark in the stalk—a point at which you can confirm the position of checkpoint three and the status of the deer.

The first checkpoint should be chosen as a mark confirming you have found the proper place to commence the stalk, after leaving your glassing site.

If you have a hunting partner, have him or her stay where you spotted the deer. Have a set of hand signals worked out ahead of time so he or she can not only direct you to the deer, but can also signal the status of the deer, (still there, standing up, alerted, gone, etc.) But even with your partner there to direct you, do not neglect to pick your checkpoints to confirm your route without the help of the spotter.

When picking your checkpoints try to pick them so the route is totally obscured from the deer. Keeping in mind that what the country looks like from your glassing spot sometimes

will be very different when you get there. You may have to make some minor adjustments. Depending on the surrounding vegetation to obscure you from view is not a good choice as a mule deer's ability to pick up the lightest movement is amazing. If you can't stalk totally out of sight you may need to wait or pick a better opportunity. In addition, pick a route containing as much shade as possible. "Camo" patterns are more effective in the shadows and movement is not detected as easily.

Having picked your checkpoints and route, glass carefully in search of hidden deer along that route. Adjust your route accordingly if there are other deer or determine whether or not the stalk is even feasible. But, even if you don't find any deer , always assume others are there, waiting to jump up and ruin your chances. If you don't consider the other deer you'll be "jumping stiff-legged" right along with the "party poopers" and the buck you were trying for! Also, use your binoculars during the stalk. It's amazing how much more detail you can pick up—detail that may alert you to the presence of another deer, a deer you didn't see initially.

Stalking is physically demanding and a hunter needs to be in fairly good condition. Taking slow, deliberate steps while bent over along the route is hard on your back and leg muscles. Even if you are in good physical condition, take an opportunity at the first two checkpoints to extend your legs and rest for a moment. It's tough enough to control the "adrenaline shakes" without adding cramping and severely fatigued muscles to the scenario.

Foot placement while stalking is obviously very important. Stalk with your feet farther apart than normal to avoid rubbing boots or pant legs together. To avoid this problem I stop at checkpoint two, remove my boots and put on an extremely heavy pair of knee-high wool socks, pulling them up over my pant legs. Wool socks will quiet the average stalkers step about 100 percent. You do however, have got to keep your eyes open for cactus, thorns and burrs, but the extra stealth is worth it. Broadleaf plants and seed pods should be avoided at all costs. Actually, avoid as many plants as possible. Learn to high step between individual plants and when that's not possible slow your pace two-fold. A good pace for stalking when closing the final distances is five steps and stop for 30 seconds. In extremely dry conditions, take three steps and wait for 30 seconds. If you accidentally step on something that makes a lot of noise, get down and stay put for two to five minutes. The longer you remain still, the better. The deer will focus in the direction of the noise until satisfied there is no cause for alarm, generally two to five minutes in my experience, and then go back to what he was doing. Checking the status of the deer after making a mistake is important before continuing. Wait the allotted time before checking! Note: When checking to see what the deer is doing at any point during a stalk, it is important to look only at a small piece of the deer that doesn't include his eyes. If you can see his eyes he can see you! A mule deer's peripheral vision is extreme and they will "bust" you every time, believe me! I prefer to check the tips of a mule deer's antlers as I can obtain more information about the demeanor of the deer than from any other body part. For example, you can always generally tell which direction a deer is looking by referencing to the antlers. If the antlers are rigidly upright and twitching back and forth rapidly, then you know the deer is getting nervous. There is a definite difference in "alerted antlers" and those moving back and forth simply fighting flies. If the antlers are drooping forward slightly and then jerking back to attention at fairly regular intervals, as you watch, there's a good chance your buck is having trouble staying awake. It will take a little experience to learn to read antlers, but mule deer antlers are my first choice for attitude reference.

If you can help it—don't check the status of your quarry after checkpoint two, unless you've made a major mistake as described above. Check to see what the deer is doing when you arrive at number two, but don't look again until you reach checkpoint three. More stalks are blown by what us professional hunters call "sneakin' a peek" than any other problem besides wind. It is tempting when you get in close to see what's going on. Don't do it! You know where the deer is in relation to checkpoint three, so there is really no sense in giving the deer another chance at "pegging" you. Concentrate on foot placement and staying out of sight.

Checkpoint three! "Ambush City!" It's a remote and exhilarating little town where adrenaline flows like wine! You have also entered into "Mule Deer Aura!" A chamber of mule deer extra sensory perception and acute

Sneaking a peak only gives a wily, old mule deer one more chance to get a look at you. Once you get past checkpoint two, stop looking at the deer. Any time you can see his eyes, you can bet he'll spot your movement and make tracks for the safety of the next ridge.

awareness where all bowhunters, having been there once, long to go again and again. It is the place that separates the men from the boys and the women from the girls. But, regardless of the outcome beyond this point, once you reach checkpoint three and are settled in, your stalk can be considered a success. The exhilaration and sense of accomplishment of shadowing, undetected, into the "personal space" of an ever-vigilant mule deer buck is ominous! And from this point until the buck rises from his bed and an arrow is sent to it's mark, is the best part.

Here are some ways to further enhance that success: As previously discussed, checkpoint three is the place all diligent bowhunters should wait for an opportunity for a responsible shot. Many bowhunters make the mistake of thinking they need to force the deer to get up and present a shot. More often than not, this action will cost you the opportunity to further enhance your success. You've taken the time and painstaking effort to make a perfect stalk, putting you within easy bow range and now you want to hurry things? That's not the most intelligent predatory tactic. Wait for an opportunity at an unsuspecting mule deer, no matter how long it takes! There is no sense in putting a mule deer on alert unless you have to. Note: There are a few instances however, where forcing something to happen may be an intelligent option. The first is if the wind begins swirling and is sure to give away your position. The second is if some poisonous vermin crawls into your space. The third is if your survival depends on it. A friend of mine and I stalked into position on a big buck, each of us covering his only exits from a rock pile. The wind swirled once and I'm sure the deer caught our scent, but he wasn't going to move until he pinpointed our position. After four and a half hours of waiting in the sun at 96 degrees, with the buck also laying in full sun panting like a hound dog, we finally forced the situation as a matter of survival. The big buck blew by my partner like a freight train passes a tramp! So, use your best judgement in similar situations.

Upon reaching checkpoint three, the physical position in which you choose to wait will make a difference in how long you can stay put. The longer you can comfortably stay put, the more the odds are in your favor. Pick a position that will allow you to move your legs slightly to restore circulation when needed. Shooting from a sitting position takes a little practice, but can be a good choice. Sitting with your legs tucked under you is not recommended. Being right handed, I most often sit on my left hip and rear end with both legs in front of me, bent at the knees, left thigh on the ground. It's a reason-ably comfortable position for a long period and I can easily shoot from this position or slowly roll up on my left knee, if necessary. Standing behind a tree, bush or rock is a good option, if available. When sitting or standing make sure you have some sort of a backdrop to break up your silhouette. Regardless of what position you have to take while waiting, your bow should be up in front of you, perpendicular to the ground, as you will want very little movement when it comes time to draw.

I know it's tough for people who come from areas where they have to spend all their hunting time waiting in tree stands, to be patient and wait, while out West when there appears to be a buck on every knob. But, as you will learn, many of the deer can't be stalked without "boogering" them clear out of the country. So, look at it this way, the average bowhunter will sit in a tree stand back home for hours, sometimes days waiting for an opportunity. In stalking, once you get in position (checkpoint three), there is no waiting for the deer to show up, he's already there! All that is necessary is for the deer to get up on his own accord and present a responsible shot—generally a much shorter time than the normal tree stand watch.

I also know that many of you are saying to yourself, "Man, this is too difficult, if I wanted a headache I'd have invited my mother-in-law along!" But, I guarantee once you are out there, these simple methods really help when it comes to getting in close for a shot. They also serve as a few remedies for lessons learned in the "school of hard knocks."

Stalking and waiting for the right opportunity is truly the essence of hunting. Stalking a mule deer with a bow is a combination, that once tried, will beckon you back year after year to the haunts and magical hideouts of these sorcerers of wit and detection. Best wishes for many successful stalks in the coming seasons.

CHAPTER 22

Common Sense With Scents And Lures

By John L. Sloan

Deer hunters today are faced with about as many scent and lure products as there are mosquitoes in an Alabama swamp. How do you decide what to use? What works? What doesn't?

Actually, the situation isn't as complicated as it first seems. Just remember a couple common sense rules. First, every product should carry the disclaimer, "WARNING: This ain't magic." And somewhere in the directions, users should be told that any product, used improperly, may produce adverse effects.

nder proper conditions and with proper use, bottled cents or lures can be as effective as the real thing.

Over the years I have hunted with the manufacturers of some scent products. Under their guidance I have experienced a wide range of results. Some animals showed no reaction at all. Others appeared to be reading the maker's script and still others did just the opposite of what we all expected. In most cases, it would be safe to say that the proper use of any of these products is better than using nothing. Sometimes it may be the key to slipping an arrow into that special buck or bull.

To begin with, let's understand the three categories of scent or scent control products. All products fall into three groups: There are those designed to eliminate scent, those designed to mask or cover scent and those that are designed to attract animals. Remember, none of these products—by any stretch of the imagination—is 100 percent effective. Any of them can, when used improperly—or even when used properly—fail. There is no magic.

Odor Eliminators

The odor-eliminating product is designed to do just that; eliminate human odor or odors picked up by human clothes. These products come in several forms from soaps and washes to sprays and powders. This category also includes clothing designed to prevent human odor from escaping into the air. In my experience, most work fairly well. I use some and am pleased with the results. But make no mistake, if an animal with a sensitive nose gets downwind of you, chances are pretty good it will eventually smell you. But without these products, it will smell you for sure. So use advantage odor eliminators provide.

If you're serious about odor control, it's important to begin with the naked truth. Start naked. Wash with an odor-eliminating soap. Wash and shampoo well. Dress in clean clothes washed in an unscented, odor-eliminating detergent and stored in a plastic bag or some other air-tight container. Your outer layer

It doesn't get much fresher than this. Now look which deer is paying attention.

should be clothing that is designed to prevent odor from reaching the air currents and your boots should be treated with some masking scent. In terms of controlling body odor, that is the best you can do. To be at peak efficiency, you would have to get dressed in the woods. Yes, it is a lot of trouble. Are you 100 percent odor free? No. You never will be. What about your bow, arrows, quiver, pocket knife, breath, tree stand, haul line, and safety belt? What about the sweat you produce and the natural bacteria you produce? It's easy to see that eliminating 100 percent of the odor is impossible.

But that is no big deal. If you can eliminate, say 80 percent or even 50 percent, you are ahead of the game. Now combine your relatively odor-free self with proper stand placement so that game is likely to pass upwind of your position and you have a workable situation. More importantly, you have an advantage.

Cover Scents

Have you ever wondered where hunter's minds were when a couple of once-popular, cover scents hit the market. Remember skunk

screen? How about coyote urine? I don't know about you, but I can't remember the last time I saw a skunk in the woods. And where I hunt, coyotes are running deer all over the place. If I was going to use an animal scent, I would want to use one that walked where deer walk, eat what deer eat and climb trees. I guess my first choice would be raccoon or squirrel. But I'd really rather not smell like an animal.

In today's marketplace, there are products available that smell nothing like animals. In fact, when properly used, they do not smell like much of anything. Isn't that the idea? A good cover scent should not have a strong odor. Some of the best ones smell like acorns, leaves and dirt or nothing at all. The scent you want on your clothes should not be a strong scent at all. Strong scents attract attention and that is what you are trying to avoid.

There are products that can be added to the clothes dryer cycle, products that can be sprayed on and one product that impregnates your clothes with warm, scented air. There are wafers, liquids and gels and just about every other method you can think of. All of these

For full scent control, even the stand is treated with an odor masking/eliminating product.

products have worked, but none are magic. If you have been wearing your clothes for a week, you are not going to cover up the odor with a spray. The key to good results with any of the products in the first two categories is to begin as clean and odor-free as possible and then try to stay that way. After all, what we really are looking for in a cover scent is just a bit of an edge. A little confusion for the animal's nose.

The two most important parts of the body to treat with a cover scent are the head, (hat), and hands. I've seen very few times a deer has smelled where I have walked regardless of what boots I wear. I wear rubber boots to keep my feet dry. No other reason. A few years ago, while making a video, I began using a popular cover scent. Because we had to trim more than the usual amount of branches to clear shooting and camera lanes, we left a lot of scent around. The first day of filming several does spooked when they smelled where we had touched branches. On day two, we sprayed our gloves with the cover scent. When the first deer to approach our new location turned out to be a wise old madam, I figured we were busted. Not so. She never lifted her head. To me, that was as close to magic as I need to get. I have used that product ever since and yes, sometimes it as failed. More often, it has helped cover my odor. It ain't magic but it is an edge.

Attraction potions

Within the realm of lures designed to attract deer, the most popular, by far, is some type of urine. Within the realm of urine products, probably the most popular is a doe in estrus urine. But to confuse the issue is the plethora of buck urine, dominant buck urine, little buck urine, matrix urine, big buck urine, combinations of buck and doe and water buffalo urine, freeze-dried urine and synthetic urine. Do they work? Sometimes they do. And sometimes they don't. Sometimes any of these products may bring the buck of your dreams to your stand on the run. Other times, one whiff of this stuff and the buck of your dreams is gone like a dime Coke. Do things correctly and you'll be giving yourself an advantage.

Sometimes you can top all of this information off with vanilla. Really, I have had some positive results with vanilla scent, peanut butter and oil of anise. But, these are just curiosity scents. Deer come to investigate out of curiosity but seldom are these deer mature bucks. Oddly enough, through the years, (more frequently as I get older), I have had great results using my own urine. I actually use it from time to time to freshen scrapes...a buck's, not mine.

A natural, masking or cover scent should be applied to both front and back of clothing and boots.

Sometimes it works quite well. I always feel better afterwards.

I would not dream of trying to explain or even understand the exact process of what delightful combination of smells will attract a buck every time. In fact, I don't believe there is such a recipe. Sometimes one thing works and sometimes another does. Recent research indicates that saltwater may be effective in making mock scrapes. Go figure. Personally, I believe it is the branch above the scrape that makes the difference and that would lead us into gland secretions and I won't pretend to understand all of that.

Okay. Let's look at this deer urine business. The hunter is smart to stick with three basic urine products: doe urine, doe-in-heat urine and buck urine. But what's what and why? Imagine a buck is sauntering along and suddenly this smell hits his nose. Is he going to go ballistic over the smell of a dominant buck intruding in his territory? Sometimes, you bet he is. Other times, he may ignore the scent or even leave the country at a high rate of speed. But if on that day he had smelled the heady scent of a doe in heat, he may have reacted...exactly the same way. You see, there is no foolproof way to know what a buck is going to do. If there was, we would have a lot fewer mature bucks in the woods and a lot more of them on the wall. But do not despair. All is not lost. It would seem that a little common sense would go a long way. A doe-in-heat product will likely be most effective just before and during the peak of the rut. Buck urine might work best prior to that period.

My thinking is that during the pre-rut and peak rut, a buck is looking most for a doe in heat. Prior to that time he may be inquisitive, or some might say protective, if a strange buck were to enter his area. A matrix urine, one that is a combination of buck and doe urine, could possibly work any time. But remember, this is not an exact science. There are probably no true experts when it comes to the use of attracting scents. There are some knowledgeable folks and the ones I have met all agree...sometimes it works and some it doesn't. But it always gives the deer some scent to think about besides yours.

An attracting scent, properly used, is an effective tool in your hunting arsenal. Proper use will take some research on your part. You may need to buy several different products and

A de-scented tool, such as this hammer is used to make a mock scrape under an overhanging branch.

try them to see which works best in your area. You may find that freeze-dried, then re-hydrated products work well. You may find that fresh urine is the best for you. I'm sure you are going to find that none of them work all the time. As you use them, you'll learn.

Here are a couple things I have learned in the 45 years I have been getting fooled by white-tailed deer. It's best to start a mock scrape in the spring or summer. Using plenty of urine is better than being stingy. Urine on branches can be effective and a drag rag, half the size of a bath towel and soaked in urine works well. And, what I find most important, whatever attracting scent I use, I don't want the smell on me. It's best to put the lure where you want the deer to look and walk. I have also learned it is not wise to enter a diner with my clothes soaked in skunk screen.

Drag rags should be large enough to hold plenty of lure and cords should be long enough to allow the rag to drag along ground without whipping around hunter's legs. Freshen the rag about every 75-100 yards.

Here are some basic rules to follow in scent and lure use. Only the first is carved in stone.

1. Pay attention to the wind. Wind carries all scent, that which you want the animal to notice and that which you don't. When you are working with scents, you are working the wind.

2. No matter what you do, start clean and try to stay clean.

3. Use a masking scent throughout the day to help cover odors that are produced as you hunt. Pay special attention to head, hat, hands and feet.

4. When using attracting lures, follow the directions and don't be afraid to experiment with your ideas. Pay attention to what the animals are doing and then try to imitate that.

5. Don't be discouraged. If at first something doesn't work, don't give up. It only takes one good buck to make the entire season a success.

6. Most of all, use some common sense with your scents. Skunks only spray when they are in danger and deer don't like coyotes. Both of those scents will likely put deer on the alert, removing some of your advantage.

CHAPTER 23

Big Bucks Like Small Clearings

By Jim Churchill

It seemed to take forever for the buck to graze along the trail from the top of the ridge to where I was sitting, bow clutched tightly in my hand. Buck fever gripped me after several minutes of waiting, and I started panting like a runner. This wouldn't do, I had to try to calm down or I would miss him for sure. I looked away and forced myself to remember how I happened to be sitting in this particular ground blind in the first place. It started in late summer, when I found one of this buck's unobtrusive lunch counters. Later, I built a comfortable stick-and-balsam ground blind in hopes of putting an arrow into this deer. Now, on my seventh day of hunting, the buck was headed my way.

A few years ago, before we began to recognize the importance of small food plots, my hunting partners and I would have walked right on by this spot in our northern Wisconsin deer hunting territory. Sure, four red oaks grew there within easy bow-shooting distance of each other but these were currently barren. Nothing here to bring a deer along the trail that led from the ridge top to the shoreline of the lake. We suspected, however, that the oaks and a nearby patch of lush clover indicated a small plot of uncommonly fertile soil. We called it a garden spot.

The author looks over a nice buck he bagged in an area that had recently been clearcut. Logging often provides internal openings in otherwise dense forests.

Ranging in size from a few square yards to as much as several acres, these small natural gardens are found in every northern forest. Created by natural recycling or deposits from the last glacier, they are like an oasis in a desert. Within their borders plants grow larger and are more nutritious than in the surrounding area. Bucks know from the taste, and maybe the odor, that these plants are uncommonly high in protein and minerals. Deer will visit these plots most regularly during the antler-growing and fat-building seasons. Logically, a buck will then lay out his territorial and scrape lines between several of these feeding locations and will continue to travel about the same route during the early rut.

Back to our hunt. We found fresh, big deer tracks, most likely buck tracks. Nearby, we found five small, but fresh scrapes. No question

hen looking for an internal edge, pay special attention to "garden spots" where deer seek out preferred oods.

this was one of the buck's favorite places. Besides the clover and barren oaks there were several other nearby foods that deer, especially bucks, commonly browse—red maple shoots, clover, mushrooms, and bracken ferns. Along the lake shore, a few yards east, white cedar trees grew, and in or near the water an assortment of aquatic and wetland plants clung stubbornly to life in spite of the frequent frosts.

The tracks and scrapes indicated that a big buck, probably the "boss" buck, visited this place when he was hungry. And now he was coming down the trail! I drew when he passed the stick placed at 35 yards and released when he almost reached the 25-yard marker. Still I misjudged slightly, shot high, and the arrow struck his backbone behind his shoulders. He dropped in his tracks, but required another arrow as a killing shot. He was a good, solid eight-pointer. His antlers now hang in my den.

Bucks utilize these small, remote food plots because they are "programmed" to do so. In the northwoods bucks seldom join does and fawns in eating rich food such as is found in extensive hayfields, large apple orchards, significant oak stands, and cornfields. I believe that large bucks instinctively avoid these places so they don't compete with the other deer. This is nature's way of saving the best foods for the does and fawns who need it for growth and gestation. Also, when not aggressively seeking does, the bigger bucks will stay out of the limelight and likely enjoy some level of comfort by feeding alone at these solitary sites. Bucks can do well by utilizing coarser fodder and small, scattered food patches. Their established territory is more dependent on a supply of good food than the availability of does.

But deer are often described as being creatures of the edges, and they are. Their food grows in openings and they hide in thick cover. Therefore, they spend most of their time where the two come together. Most every forest is continually evolving because of natural growth and events such as weather, fires, and logging. These changes regularly create new clearings and thus new edges. Consequently hunters can utilize these ever-changing deer hot spots if they know what to look for.

We once had an extensive jackpine stand in our hunting territory. Eventually the area was logged, and soon afterward a forest fire roared through the 10-acre tract. Remarkably, the next year it burned off again. At first, deer visited to lick the burned stumps for potassium and other minerals, but soon fireweed, mullein and bunchgrass appeared, followed the next year by clover and an assortment of tree seedlings. The rare opening created an internal edge in the deep woods that has attracted deer for several years.

Although this territory is small compared to the extent of the forest surrounding it, many of the big buck food tracts hunters should be looking for are much smaller. Even two or three large blown down trees can create a commonly visited feeding spot. High winds in cedar swamps regularly produce some excellent small food tracts. If two or three cedar trees are tipped over in a summer storm so that some of the trees roots are still in the ground the branches will stay alive and green. Bucks don't often eat cedar needles in the growing season, but about midway into the bow season they start utilizing browse and will visit such a location regularly. Such tracts are particularly attractive to big, reclusive bucks because they don't have to leave the security of heavy cover to utilize it.

Everett Stonehouse is a storm watcher and trophy buck hunter of my acquaintance who utilizes this phenomena extensively. All year he investigates the path of any severe storms looking to see where they cross swamps. If he can find cedar trees that have been blown down, he builds a ground blind nearby to be ready for the bow season. Stonehouse has found that bucks seem to be a little less cautious in thick cover and move right in to eat, providing, of course, they don't hear any suspicious noise or smell any man scent.

Tornadoes roar through the northwoods every year, and they can create miles of deep woods edge that is conducive to producing food for bucks. Trees are often flattened in a fairly broad corridor for hundreds of yards and in some cases for miles. Wherever the trees are knocked over so the sunlight can reach the ground, new growth of tree shoots and green plants proliferate.

In the first year the deer can eat the twigs of trees that have been blown over and in later years grass, forbs and new tree shoots will spring up. If this happens in a big buck's territory, you can be sure he will utilize it. Every serious deer hunter should keep track of such storms. The weather report can be a source of increased hunting opportunities.

This small backwoods clearing is likely one of this buck's favorite places to feed. Internal clearings provide deer with security and food. They are great places to set up a stand.

All big forests have natural clearings somewhere in their midst. Most of these clearings which produce food for deer are worth studying. It is easy to overlook them, but in spring and early summer grass and weeds (forbs) provide deer food and later in the season a dozen or more food plants such as new growth maple, aspen, dogwood, and wintergreen will proliferate. I have watched deer spend hours grazing in the edges of clearings feeding on the plants that are stimulated to growth by the sun's rays. In this situation the deer act as their own provider. The more they graze the plants down, the more sunlight that can reach the ground which stimulates other plants to grow.

A few years ago, in mid-October, I set up my tree stand near a small clearing in a deep woods stand of yellow birch and sugar maple trees. About an hour before sunset a doe and fawn walked into the opening, fed through it and disappeared. A few minutes later a small forkhorn came into the clearing, next a six-point buck, then an eight-pointer. The biggest bucks started half-heartedly pushing at each other. This frightened the forkhorn and he trotted away. The other bucks seemed to get a little more serious all the time and pretty soon they were vigorously grunting and clacking their horns. Distracted as they were, it should have been a good opportunity to get a shot, but antler to antler they worked their way out of the clearing and vanished.

It was a real eye-opener, though. Three bucks were using an opening that was so small it would have been easy to walk through with

Water and riparian areas provide deer much needed nourishment. Water also has an impact on deer movement making it a doubly effective asset when searching for a stand site.

out a second glance. There was no other opening, however, anywhere near that size within a mile. Thus, it had more edge than any other single location in this entire hunting area. Incidentally, I returned later and bagged the six-pointer when he walked right under my stand.

Disease and insects can also provide clearings and edges and therefore deer food. In drought years, when trees are already stressed by the lack of water, entire stands of a certain tree might be killed out. White birch trees were severely decimated a few years ago in some northern regions. When the trees died back grass and weeds grew up underneath them; this was followed by tree seedlings. Deer use of these areas increased incredibly.

Power line corridors can also provide miles of edge and opening that is attractive to bucks. The corridor is kept free of brush and trees, the sunlight can reach the ground and, therefore, clover and other grasses grow well. Along the edges new shoots of trees grow. In deep woods areas where there are few or no open fields these corridors produce food and also provide travel lanes and open areas for socializing. Rutting bucks often patrol the power lines. They make scrapes and rub their foreheads on the poles to pass on their scent. Interestingly, the males often stand on the highest ridges and look down the power line for other deer. If they see one they might investigate to see if it is a potential mate. Some hunters have gotten shots at bucks by placing deer decoys on power lines and waiting nearby for a buck to show up. My friend, Mack, bagged the biggest buck of his career using just such a method. He com-

monly followed the power line corridor as he walked to a heavily used deer trail that he was hunting over. Although the trail was productive, he had trouble finding a location where the deer couldn't wind him. After being detected by a succession of deer one afternoon, he gave up on his stand and decided to climb to the top of a nearby ridge where he could look down the power line for deer. That day a big buck came out of the alders on the north side of the line and started right up the hill towards him. He didn't dare move, located as he was right out in the open. The inevitable happened. When the deer got close enough it saw him and retreated down the hill to the same alders.

On a hunch, a week later, Mack took his deer target which, very closely resembled a deer, out to the pipeline and set it up within sight of the trail. He laced the ground around the decoy with doe "perfume." Within an hour a trophy buck came out of the trail, into the pipeline corridor. After studying the "decoy" closely for what seemed like 10 minutes, he arched his back and walked stiff legged up the hill towards the decoy. Mack was kneeling behind a clump of ironwood on the side of the corridor. When the buck got within 50 yards of the decoy it seemed to sense something was wrong, stopped and stared suspiciously. Then it turned and walked off the corridor. Mack thought it was gone until he spied it sneaking though the balsams on the side of the line. The deer was obviously trying to get downwind. It headed right at him and eventually placed itself, broadside, about 15 yards from the kneeling hunter. Even though Mack said he was shaking like a leaf, he released and heard and saw the arrow hit the deer. He didn't attempt to track him that evening but returned the next morning and found the big buck stone dead from a chest wound.

Interstate gas pipelines also stretch through many backwoods areas. Like power line corridors, pipeline routes provide plenty of open space, but pipeline clearings contribute to the deer's livelihood in another way also. The pipe is buried deeply, but the pressure inside the line generates considerable heat. This heats the soil directly over the pipeline so it seldom freezes or is covered with snow. This provides a rare location for deer to graze on green plants in winter when the rest of the landscape is covered with snow.

Railroad right-of-way corridors are also worth investigating. Most of the railroads where I hunt in northern Wisconsin have been abandoned but their right-of-ways still exist and they are worth scouting because of the potential of providing deer pasture. As always hunters should secure permission to hunt these stretches of land. It can sometimes be difficult to find out who actually owns abandoned rail lines.

Aspen clear cuts are produced when the aspen trees are completely harvested from a stand. They are attractive to deer for about 15 years or more after the cuts are made. Probably the 4- to 10-year-old stands are most productive. Deer eat the leaves of the aspen and the new shoots. Clear cuts are pretty well-known as good deer food producers and cover but many people don't hunt them, maybe because they can be misleading in the amount of sign that is obvious. Deer might not make trails in the stands since they can circulate through them almost anywhere. They usually follow any log skidding trails in the cut, though. Hunters can find out how many deer are frequenting the stand by digging up and spreading fresh dirt in the skidding trails. Deer are attracted to fresh dirt and, of course, cross it on their regular meandering journeys. A very accurate count of the local deer can be gathered by this method. We use this method regularly to find big buck tracks that would otherwise be impossible to locate in the vegetation covered forest floor.

Deer change their diet according to the seasons. This is useful information for scouting big bucks. Look on a topographical map for potholes or small lakes deep in the forest where aquatic plants will probably be found. In spring and early summer, bucks will visit these potholes to utilize the pond lily and other plants growing in the water. After their antlers start growing they will eat the scouring rush and the leatherleaf shrub, because both plants are high in minerals. Both plants grow in acidic mud close to water. Often the ground is soft around the water's edge and will imprint with the large tracks of the buck. Potholes, of course are another example of an internal edge, but they don't really provide much of an open area for hunting.

Hardy settlers once kept backwoods farms where many state and federal forests now grow. One by one, the farms were abandoned

Power line corridors are usually kept clear of brush ar undergrowth, providing deer with nice grazing areas. These corridors can be very productive stand sites fo bowhunters.

and the land annexed, but in some cases the forest hasn't completely reclaimed the area ye Apple trees, berry and cherry bushes and eve remnants of hayfields might remain. Hunters might walk right past the area without noticing, but probably some nearby whitetail buck is using the area as a favorite food plot.

Scouting for deer in a deep woods area of Fl rence County, Wisconsin I once found a long abandoned one-room cabin and single-stall barn made of pole sized logs. A clearing of about two acres surrounded the buildings. I couldn't believe my good fortune when I couldn't locate any sign that anyone else was hunting this tremendous hot spot. Later, Jim Jr. modified the cabin to use as a blind. I hunted out of the barn.

The first evening a buck appeared at the edge of the clearing but left without presentir a shot. A week later we set up again and within two hours the clearing seemed to be alive with does and fawns. They scattered, however, when a sturdy seven-point buck stalked into the clearing. Jim bagged the buck. We continued to hunt the "farm" for almost two decades until aspen reclaimed the opening and the buildings rotted down. By that time a timber sale had opened up several new internal clearings and we built blinds in the new locations. It always pays to look for the openings. Deep woods bow hunters can always find a good place to hunt bucks if they scout out the openings and hunt the internal edges.

CHAPTER 24

Use Ground Blinds for Big Bucks

By Jim Churchill

When I first moved to the northwoods and started hunting deer from tree stands, fawns and does would walk right under my stand. They were fooled so completely that I once had to drop a handkerchief on the back of a doe standing under my stand to move her out so she wouldn't, inadvertently, spook any buck that came by. Contrast this to what happened early in the 1998 hunting season. The incident made me lose all hope of getting a buck within range.

During a hunt in the Nicolet National Forest, a yearling doe came along the trail I was watching. This animal spotted me when it was still 50 yards away, carefully skirted my well-hidden, 12-foot-high stand and resumed its chosen path. Days later, a calm, mild-mannered old doe spotted me from another tree stand in my hunting territory and bolted like a racehorse.

It could just be the luck of the draw that both of these deer foiled my efforts, but I've come to believe that deer, after being hunted from tree stands for about 30 years, have rekindled an

Ground blinds can be very effective for late-season hunting. Check out the antlers on the buck that is entering the clearing from the left.

instinct that has lain dormant since the last mountain lion was killed off in the great Eastern forests. Deer once again remember to look up. They seem to know instinctively that danger can lurk in the trees.

What's to be done about this? The simple answer is to stay where you can't be seen so easily. Hunt from ground blinds. They have many advantages. They are warmer than tree stands, you can shoot more accurately because you don't have to shoot at an angle, few if any hunters have been badly injured by falling from a ground blind and, if made correctly, they help conceal human scent.

A few weeks after the incident with racehorse doe, I spent an interesting half hour building a ground blind near a small backwoods clearing where big tracks and buck scrapes showed in the forest floor. I fitted the blind with a folding chair, attached a peg to a sapling to hold the bow upright, and dangled a pair of turkey feathers from strings tied to limbs at hat height so the wind direction could be constantly checked. I washed the chair with a solution of water and bicarbonate of soda to make it as scent-free as possible and left it in the blind so I didn't have to carry it in and out. All I needed was favorable wind to be ready for a hunt.

The wind I was waiting for came up on a Saturday. It was during the height of the rut, a time when a hunter should spend as much time in a blind as possible. I took a lunch and drinking water and spent the day in relative ease, entertained by grouse, snowshoe hares, foraging skunks and coyote songs. I even read a small booklet that had quiet waterproof pages. When it was necessary to leave the blind for a short time, I noticed that it was easier and quieter than exiting from a tree stand.

In mid-afternoon a big doe, a yearling and two fawns fed through the opening. They were walking into the wind as expected. I was sure a buck would come by sooner or later, but he never appeared. The next day I went back to the blind again. The wind direction was still favorable. If I had spent the entire previous day in a tree stand I would have been suffering from muscle fatigue and assorted cramps and probably, wouldn't have wanted to hunt all day again.

In mid-morning, I saw antlers projecting above a rise in the clearing before I saw the deer. I rose quietly from my chair, picked the

Evergreen boughs offer total concealment and help to contain human scent. Notice how the bare face stands out. Always wear a face mask or camo face paint.

bow from its hanger and got ready. A tornado was whirling in my chest, and I stopped moving for a minute to let the excitement die down. The buck looked shaggy, unkempt and distracted. He was definitely in the embrace of the mating moon.

Nevertheless, he snatched a few mouthfuls of grass, then became more interested and started feeding in earnest. Luckily, he moved in my direction and was soon within bow range, but facing me. I waited as he slowly adjusted his feeding position until he was almost broadside. It was time to shoot. Half-afraid I would miss, I slowly came to full draw and found him in the peep. Then a doe walked into the opening, and he lowered his head and charged as if to gore her. She turned and ran and he followed at a canter, grunting excitedly.

I stood a long time staring at the clearing in disbelief, but then I heard bird-like sounds, and a doe trotted by my blind, so close I could see her eyelashes. She was bleating every few seconds. Sure that the buck would be right behind her, I got ready to shoot. Then, I heard him walking through the underbrush behind me. When I turned, he broke into a run and disappeared.

When the excitement died down, and the disappointment washed away, I stopped to consider what could be learned from the incident. First, the ground blind worked pretty well. Until the buck started air tracking the scent of the doe and circled behind me, the deer were not aware that I was anywhere around. This was a bad luck encounter, but not uncommon to bowhunters. Deer often approach within bow range without giving the archer a good shot. Still, I could have gotten a shot if the buck had not been able to get behind me so easily.

So, the first rule for placing ground blinds is this: Try to make sure deer can't circle behind you. Most deer will approach a specific feeding location from a downwind or crosswind position if they can. Some bucks, the big and the wary, often won't ever come into an opening in the daylight unless they can, first, circle downwind to scent check for danger. Therefore, locate the ground blind where it is impossible or at least difficult for the deer to circle downwind. A ground blind backed up by a pond, an open marsh, mature trees that have little underbrush, an open field, a logging road or most anything else that a wary deer would probably avoid definitely helps increase the chances for success. Don't forget the sun when setting up a ground blind. If you face east in the morning, a bright morning sun could be in your eyes, in late afternoon you don't want to look in a westerly direction unless the treeline will shade the sun. Conversely, if the deer has to look into the sun to see you, it probably won't see any small movements you make.

Wind directions can change regularly and make a certain blind useless. But this is also true of tree stand location. Careful scouting can point out where to set a second blind to compensate for wind shifts. It usually isn't as simple as locating a blind on the opposite side of the hunt location.

In one opening I hunt, the deer filter in from every direction but east. For years, I didn't hunt the opening except when a west wind was blowing. Then I noticed that very few deer actually walked into the north end even when a south wind was blowing. Instead they usually just walked around to the northwest corner before they came into the clearing. The blind I placed on the northern edge of the area was, sometimes, productive.

Such knowledge can only be gained through hours spent watching deer. Scouting from a distance to see where deer go, according to wind directions, can pay big dividends and is an excellent way to spend time if you can't hunt from your blind because of unfavorable wind. If you stay a minimum of 150 yards from their path and observe all the rules of de-scenting yourself, deer usually won't detect your odor.

This worked very well on a northern buck a few years back. I know of a food plot that is composed of a 1/4-acre or so of wild clover and red maple shoots. Four acorn-bearing oaks at the edge of the plot sporadically produce fruit. There's not enough food here to interest a herd of deer but it's all a lone buck needs for one of his scattered feeding area. I went to this location and built two ground blinds. One was located on the edge of a pond and the other was backed up by an open marsh. They were within 20 yards of the edge of the food plot.

I was extremely careful not to let the buck see me, and I didn't want him to catch my fresh scent anymore than was necessary. So, I backed off to the other side of the pond and watched with binoculars to see where the buck went. Normally, he waited until about a half-hour before dark and then cautiously made his way out to the edge of the opening to graze. He came out on the downwind side most of the time. When the wind was from the north or south he came out on the opposite edge of the field. The only chance to hunt for him was to occupy a blind on the east edge of the opening when the wind was blowing straight out of the west. It required as much patience as I could muster to wait for a favorable wind, but I eventually got a killing shot.

There are some very good deer hunters who never hunt directly at a food plot. They believe this tends to alert the deer that his lunch counter is mined with danger. They set up instead on trails leading to the food plot and, therefore, don't risk spooking the buck away from the location.

Because the buck might be bedded nearby, and hunters can get into and out of ground blinds very quietly, a low-level ambush can be far superior to a temporary tree stand for this type of hunting. The deer likely will follow about the same route from his bedding grounds to the food and sometimes will have a noticeable trail worn into the forest floor. If not, a few evenings spent watching the area from a distance with binoculars might reveal his actual path. The blind can be built alongside the trail

Of course, ground blinds are very useful for watching well-worn travel routes that deer use We hunt a cut where a logging road was bulldozed through a ridge many years back. The cut has grown up to saplings, but a plain deer trail shows through it. Blinds built on top of the ridge on either side of the cut have been

When putting together a framework for a ground blind, make sure there is ample room to shoot comfortably. It's best to do this early in the construction phase.

productive. A mile or so north, there is a location where two ravines, with well-worn trails, intersect. This, also, provides an excellent opportunity for hunting from a ground blind placed on the ridge above the deer.

Bucks in rut often sneak around in the thickest cover available because they know does might be hiding in the cover. Thick cover is ideal for ground blind hunting. A hunter in a tree stand probably can't even see down through the thick cover, let alone shoot through it. We look for a place where a shooting lane can be cut, or exists naturally before we build our blinds. In my experience, deer let down some of their caution in such areas also and point blank shots are possible. This is close work, however, and the archery tackle should be made as quiet and as smooth running as possible.

There is a phenomena that thick cover creates that is easy to overlook. Deer typically use thick cover areas to abandon their customary upwind movement when they want to head off in some other direction. A typical example is a point of short evergreen trees extending out from an evergreen thicket. Deer will often disregard wind direction to follow the point to reach another stand of thick evergreens or to enter a marsh or other areas where dense surroundings make it unlikely that they can be

seen even though they are moving downwind. A well-hidden ground blind in such areas will commonly produce deer sightings in good deer country.

Hilly country is a good place to use ground blinds because you can sit on a ridge overlooking a hollow or cut and be as well hidden as needed. If the wind changes you can just walk across the valley and set up on the opposite hill without the noise and effort needed to climb down from one tree and up another.

Building a ground blind

The construction of a ground blind from natural material is made much easier and you will get a better finished product if you plan it beforehand. I have built blinds in the center of downed tree tops, against the trunk of a single large spruce where the branches reach to the ground, in upland forests using dead tree branches for frame and cover and in an open marsh using dead wood for a frame and grass and weeds for cover. The very best ground blinds are built from cedar or balsam boughs; besides being good cover their strong odor covers human scent to some extent.

Fresh earth also helps disguise human scent. One of the best and most-utilized ground blinds in our hunting territory has a hole in the ground as a base. We found a nat-

The best blind material is often available closest to the site of your blind. Using dead wood from the general area is always the best option because you won't have to haul in materials.

ural depression in the ground and used a shovel to deepen and level the floor of the pit. When the pit was deep enough we drove a series of sticks into the rim of the hole to create a stable platform for building a fence a foot or two high. The fence was woven with cedar boughs. Most every time it is used we turn over some more fresh earth and weave in fresh cedar boughs to help hide human scent.

Where a natural start for a blind is not available, we build blinds by covering a framework of sticks with dead weeds, branches or evergreen boughs. The framework consists of six sticks about one to two inches in diameter and six to seven feet long. Alder and willow works well for the framework. The frame can be cut at the site if the shrubs are available. Where it is prohibited to cut any live material, framework poles can be cut elsewhere and carried to the site. Where we hunt, in a wilderness area, cutting green material is not allowed, so we cut the sticks elsewhere and let them dry out all

summer to lessen the weight. After the frame sticks are cut, the butt of the stick is sharpened so it can be pushed into the ground. The limbs are trimmed so a stub about six inches long is left on the stick. This helps hold the covering material in place.

The sticks are pushed into the ground about 2 feet apart to create a straight line about six feet long facing the expected deer sighting. Then material that blends into the location is woven into the framework to create a wall to hide behind. About five feet above the ground, depending on the height of the hunter, a rectangle about one foot wide and two feet high is created with short sticks found at the site. This framework is wired in place. It is not covered. This is the lookout and shooting port.

The front wall should be tall enough so the bow limb won't show above the wall when the hunter is standing up. Hunters that shoot from a sitting position can adjust the port and the wall accordingly, but keep in mind that you

The author looks over a nice buck taken during the 1998 season. A ground blind worked perfectly to trick this deer.

might want to stand up to stretch your legs once in awhile and you don't want to show above the wall and give yourself away. The remaining sticks are used to create side walls. Make the side walls about six feet long also, so you can sit down on a chair in the blind and still have space enough to stand up and shoot without having to create noise by moving the chair out of the way.

The result?

How good do these blinds work? The 1998 bow season proves the point. I had spent much time in late summer in a wilderness area in the Nicolet National Forest scouting for a buck I'd spied while walking into a remote lake for trout fishing. I fed mosquitoes and slogged swamps and puffed my way to the tops of ridges in pursuit of this deer. Finally I found two of his food plots.

I figured it was one of his favorite areas, and I was right. When mid-October arrived he made scrapes adjacent to the food plot. It was a long walk, so I only hunted afternoons. I sat in the blind several times before he came sauntering down the ridge adjacent to my blind. He never knew I was around until I released the arrow. It was all over in a minute or so. All over except for a long drag back to the truck, that is. He was well worth it.

CHAPTER 25

Let Instinct Guide The Arrow

Shooting a bow and arrow instinctively is a talent that everyone is capable of, and one that can be brought to the surface with a little time and effort.

By Joe Blake

Mastering the art of instinctive shooting will make you a better bowhunter, and will help you to enjoy the sport more by relying on your natural ability.

The evening sun was just touching the western horizon, signaling the end of another day. The woods around me had grown still. After seven long, cold hours in my tree stand, I relished the thought of getting moving and feeling the life return to my aching limbs on the long walk back out to the road. The afternoon had been an exciting one, with several whitetails moving in and around the old farmstead where I waited patiently, but the shot at the big eight-pointer that chased a doe past my ambush several times never materialized and now it was time to think about heading home. Or was it?

With less than half an hour of shooting light left, I began to pack up my gear because the doe and her suitor had seemingly left for parts unknown. I didn't want to get caught in my stand after shooting light failed. Planning to be back at first light, I was just about to slip out of my safety belt when the steady grunting of an approaching buck caused me to once again lift my 65 lb. Shadow longbow from its resting place and prepare for action.

The massive buck came trotting down the timbered ridge at a steady pace, nose to the ground and full of purpose. He coasted to a halt a scant 5 yards from my tree; unfortunately, try as I might I could find no opening to slip a heavy cedar arrow through. As the buck again began to move I knew I would have to make something happen.

As the big deer quartered past my location, I grunted loudly and watched as the trophy slammed on the breaks at 7 yards, head swivel-

ing back and forth while looking for the intruder who dared to crash his party. A dense tangle of branches again covered the deer's body, but as I began to lean out away from the tree and bend at the knees the view began to clear and a small opening showed itself. As my safety belt tightened, I bent double at the waist

Shooting at aerial targets or even fast-flying game birds is not only possible, but effective for the well-practiced instinctive shooter. Trying to put a sight pin on one of these will give most shooters fits, but natural hand-eye coordination makes it possible to hit moving targets without the aid of fancy mechanical sights.

The author's wife, Kim, removes a well-placed arrow from a rotten stump. Informal practice sessions such as stump shooting are great ways to improve your instinctive shooting skills.

and canted my longbow over until I held it parallel to the ground, and as the heavy bow tensed a baseball-sized opening came into focus and the arrow was on its way. As the two-blade broadhead struck the buck's rig cage and angled down and forward the big buck crashed away, back up the ridge from which he had come. He fell dead in the tall grass just over the crest. Another trophy animal harvested in no small part because of the advantages of instinctive shooting.

Instinctive shooting is certainly nothing new, but in this era of modern conveniences it seems that we often get caught up in the thought that "easier is better" instead of "better is better." And while I may well concede that it is easier to learn to shoot a bow with sights, I also firmly believe that instinctive shooting is the best

method of shooting a bow under the demands of field conditions. A bow and arrow is a simple, close-range weapon. So why burden it down with peeps, sights, and range finders? Learning to shoot instinctively is a talent we can all hone. If the idea of unlocking this potential within yourself intrigues you, read on.

The first question you might ask is, "Exactly what is instinctive shooting?" Well, simply put, it is the ability to send your arrow where you want it to go without the use an external sighting system. That sounds simple and it really is. Instinctive shooting is not some magical power that only a select few individuals possess, but rather a simple and effective method for shooting a bow and arrow that each of us is capable of. All it takes is a little time and effort. The basis for instinctive shooting is hand-eye coordination, that same hand-eye coordination that allows us to throw a baseball, shoot baskets, or even drive a car. There are no sights on a pitcher's arm or on a basketball player's hand or on the steering wheel of a car, so how do we accomplish these feats? With hand-eye coordination and practice through repetition, that's how.

As an instructor for the International Bowhunter Education Foundation, I get the opportunity and the privilege to meet with bowhunters of all skill levels, and one such meeting was a real eye-opener for the individual involved and I think it will be for readers of this article as well.

My partner Larry Benke and I were teaching a bowhunting class out in North Dakota. It was a good class except for one individual who was pretty sure he already knew everything. This high-school senior sat in the back of class and contributed plenty of information, although not always in a constructive manner. When another class member asked how Larry and I were able to shoot our longbows and recurves without using sights, this young man matter-of-factly stated that we used the "guess and by golly" method. "Just pull 'er back and let 'er go and hope you hit the target" was his take on instinctive shooting.

Well, his letter jacket betrayed the fact that he was a good athlete, so I picked up an eraser from the front of the room and asked him to throw it back to me, which he did. Then I moved closer and did the same; then further back and did the same; and finally I was jogging across the front of the room while he

Archer Dave Englund shows excellent instinctive form and concentration. Note how the arrow, bow arm and eye are all on the same plane at full draw.

threw the eraser to me with exceptional accuracy each time. After several minutes of this exhibition I'm sure that the entire class thought I was a few arrows short of a full quiver, but when I asked this individual how he was able to get the eraser to me each time accurately from a variety of distances and even while I was moving, the light bulb finally came on. Instinctive shooting isn't a hard concept to explain, but it seems to be difficult to understand or comprehend. I believe this is because we as human beings always seem to be looking for the most difficult answer, even when the best answer is often right under our noses. As a side note, the individual from the above story spent the rest of the week in the front of class and gained a strong interest in bowhunting and instinctive shooting from that day forward.

So now that we have a basic definition of instinctive shooting, and are at least intrigued enough to read on, why should we give this shooting method a try? Well, if you are willing to put some time into learning to shoot in this manner, I guarantee that you will find it to be the most effective shooting technique to use for bowhunting.

The main advantage to instinctive shooting is its simplicity. As mentioned previously, with no sights or other equipment to worry about you can concentrate fully on the task at hand, and this will make you a better bowhunter. Of course, without all this extra gear hanging on your bow you also don't have to worry about sights becoming loose or other such maladies that could possibly cost you the shot of a life-

time. You also don't have to be tied to your sights and knowing exact yardage, because the time you put into shooting your bow will allow your brain to make adjustments for you, automatically, without the need to know that "the buck is 24 yards away so I'll need to hold my 20-yard pin a little high or my 30-yard pin a little low." With practice and familiarity your "hair covered computer" will make these adjustments for you so that all you need to do is focus on the tiny spot you want to hit.

Another distinct advantage to instinctive shooting is its flexibility. The opening story illustrates this point perfectly. I would wager that few sight shooters could have pulled off that shot even though the range was only around 7 yards. Every sight shooter I have ever met sights in his or her bow while standing on level ground in a classic archer's stance, that is, upright with the bow held perfectly vertically. Throw in an unorthodox shot where you have to bend and twist and cant your bow and those sights will become virtually useless. But an instinctive shooter can shoot from nearly any position imaginable, even laying down, with exceptional accuracy. I don't know about you, but passing up a shot because my equipment isn't up to the task doesn't sit well with me.

After the simplicity and flexibility of instinctive shooting, I would have to list its quickness as a third important attribute of this shooting method. While most sight shooters must be very methodical in their shooting because of the nature of their gear, an instinctive shooter

The author's sons, Andrew and Nathan, remove a pair of well-placed arrows from a 3-D bear target. Such targets help to improve shooting skills by giving archers a realistic look at the game they might be pursuing in the woods.

Instinctive shooting lends itself well to archery hunting because of the variety of shooting positions that may be encountered. Bowhunters don't often get the perfect shot and instinctive shooting allows for a wider range of motion while lining up on a target.

lem. Also, instinctive shooting does not lend itself well to long range shooting, so it is unlikely that an instinctive archer will be able to keep pace with sight shooters at 3-D shoots where ranges seem to be getting longer every year. The problem here isn't with the equipment, or the lack of it in this case, because a bare bow can be shot with extreme accuracy from a machine; the difficulty is that the human eye is less and less able to focus on the tiny spot necessary for successful instinctive shooting as distance increases. However, bowhunting is and always has been a close-range sport, one where a person's skills as a hunter should far outweigh long-range shooting ability. Lastly, when you shoot instinctively you can't blame your equipment for a miss. No more "my sight pin moved" or "I couldn't see through my peep." A miss is just that, and most often boils down to the fact that the shooter didn't pick a spot and concentrate on it.

If you're still with me, you obviously are at least a little bit serious about giving this instinctive shooting thing a try, so let's take a look at a few basics so you can get out and give it a shot. Of course, the vast amount of information on instinctive shooting is beyond the scope of a single article, but I will offer a few basic thoughts and list some excellent book and video sources at the end of this article for those who want to dive all the way into this shooting method.

To begin with, any bow can be shot instinctively, but it is important to get the arrow down close to your bow hand. That makes an elevated rest a handicap. Because of this, and because of the fact that most compounds are not designed to be shot off the shelf, recurves and longbows are probably the best bet for the instinctive bowhunter. Not that compounds can't be shot instinctively, because they can, but if you want to continue to shoot a compound, do your best to lower the arrow rest as close to your bow hand as possible.

With your arrow down close to your hand, that bow hand becomes the "front sight" which will point your arrow towards your intended target. Your eye becomes the "rear sight" and your string hand becomes the line which connects the two. The most important thing here is to strive to have the entire apparatus, that being you and your bow working together as one unit, in the same plane. The arrow closely follows the line created by your extended bow

can get off a killing shot in a fraction of the time. This is very often a necessity while hunting. Plain and simple, deer and other big game animals seldom do the expected. A bowhunter who has long minutes to dial in the range, line up the peep, and get the sight pin steady on the target, all while in a perfect position for that classic, upright shot, is the exception rather than the rule.

Now that we have discussed instinctive shooting and some of what it can do for you, let's examine what it isn't. It is not a method that is well-suited for repetitive shooting, because the intense concentration required for each shot is something that few people are capable of duplicating over and over. Because of this, sight shooters have a distinct advantage when it comes to target shooting. But a bowhunter rarely gets more than one shot anyway so for the hunting archer this isn't a prob-

Proof positive. Although this buck was taken at less than 10 yards, the shot required every bit of instinctive shooting skill the author could muster. The unorthodox shooting position and heavy cover would have certainly kept a sight-shooter from bagging this deer.

arm and the string is brought back to a point close to and directly below the eye so that the entire system is lined up; then you simply focus every ounce of concentration that you can muster on the exact point where you want your arrow to go, relax your fingers to let the string slip smoothly free. Maintain a good follow-through, and watch your arrow hit right where you were looking.

As you start out on the instinctive shooting trail I would definitely recommend using a relatively lightweight bow. Over-bowing yourself will lead to sloppy shooting and bad habits so start out with a bow that you can easily handle. Also, to begin with, shoot at ranges measured in feet instead of yards. Get up close to a backstop with no target on it because your initial concentration should be on learning technique and form. Even after shooting instinctively for over 25 years I still practice form shooting regularly at close range in front

of an empty backstop to continually reinforce the "feel" of how I want my shooting to be.

An important part of instinctive shooting is being relaxed and comfortable as you shoot so experiment with what feels best to you. I prefer to have a relatively open stance, and I bend slightly at both the knees and the waist as I come to full draw; this helps me line up better and I think it helps me focus on the target. Try it yourself sometime, even without your bow in hand, by looking at something and then pointing at it as you bend slightly into the "target." In fact, this is an exercise that can be performed just about anywhere, at any time and place you have the opportunity, go through your shooting motion by picking a target, concentrating on a tiny spot within that target, and bring your bow arm up to point at that spot. The key to instinctive shooting is doing the same thing over and over until it becomes second nature to you. Then, when that monster buck steps out it will be natural and automatic for you to send your arrow where it needs to go.

As you start shooting, keep the ranges short until you gain confidence, but don't ever be afraid to move back into "spittin' distance" if your confidence wavers. Besides being good practice for form shooting, extreme close range practice is important if you like to get really close to game; like the mule deer buck I shot from the whopping distance of three feet a few years back. Also, don't ever shoot until you are fatigued to the point of getting sloppy. It is much better to shoot 10 good arrows a night than to shoot 50 marginal ones. Fatigue breeds poor habits so when you feel yourself getting tired hang your bow up for the night. Finally, have fun. There is nothing quite like making a perfect instinctive shot, one that relies on nothing more than your own God-given abilities to make your arrow hit its mark. So give instinctive shooting a try, I think that if you give this shooting method an honest try you will find that going Purely Instinctive will make you a much better bowhunter.

For bowhunters interested in more in-depth information on instinctive shooting I would definitely recommend picking up some of the many books and/or videos available on this subject. The number one collection of works on this subject, and what I consider to be mandatory reading and watching for any instinctive shooters is *Instinctive Shooting* and *Instinctive Shooting II* by G. Fred Asbell. These books, along with Fred's video on the subject, contain a wealth of information and will improve your shooting tremendously. I have a couple of well-worn copies of these books and I still read and reread them on a regular basis.

Another good source of information is the video *How to Shoot Instinctively Better than Ever*, which features well known bowhunter Dan Bertalan and a host of other successful instinctive bowhunters. This video also contains a wealth of information on the subject and translates this information into actual hunting situations through the magic of video. I would strongly recommend both of these sources of information, and both can be found at archery shops, through bowhunting mail order companies, or in the back of most bowhunting magazines.

CHAPTER 26

Fooling Mother Nature

Make and Use Mock Scrapes and Rubs.

By Bob Humphrey

As a wildlife biologist, I have spent considerable professional time designing and implementing wildlife habitat management plans. I have also devoted a fair parcel of personal time

When he encounters a rub, a buck will instinctively leave scent from their forehead glands on it. Other bucks encountering it will, in turn, do the same. You can bring bucks close to your stand by strategically placing mock rubs in the area you hunt.

to managing my own property for wildlife; and because I am also a sportsman, much of this management is devoted to benefiting game species and enhancing hunting opportunities.

One autumn several years ago, I discovered a line of rubs and scrapes in a grove of pole-stage aspens on my land. It appeared that a buck had staked this place out as his core area as I found fresh sign every couple of days. The problem was, there were no trees in the vicinity big enough to hang a stand. As I prefer to bowhunt from an elevated platform, I ruled out building a ground blind. I couldn't go to the deer, so I had to find a way to make him come to me.

I decided to implement some of what I know about deer behavior, and began experimenting with what were, at that time, unorthodox techniques—I created my own scrape line. Results were a bit slow at first. Then, just as I was beginning to get discouraged, it happened. I was able to pull the buck off his regular route and onto my bogus scrape line. He passed within easy bow range and one shot did the job. Since that time I have done more experimenting with my own techniques and those of others, with similar results.

Nowadays most experienced hunters are familiar with, and may even have used, some type of mock scrape. Biologists and hunters are also learning more about the significance of rubs, and how they can be used to the hunters' advantage. What follows are some of the techniques for creating artificial rubs and scrapes that I have found to be most effective.

Scrapes

Being effective at making and using mock scrapes first requires a little basic understanding of how natural scrapes work. Scrapes are like an olfactory dating service for whitetails. They usually begin appearing early in the rut when a buck paws away the surface duff and urinates on the exposed earth to advertise both his presence and dominance to other bucks in the area, and his interest and availability to the local female contingent. In areas with a balanced buck to doe ratio and light hunting pressure the dominant buck in an area does most of the scraping. Other local bucks may do some scraping but usually limit their activity around traditional breeding scrapes to scent-marking the overhanging licking branch. The dominant buck will continue to scent-check and freshen his scrapes periodically, until breeding begins.

Meanwhile, shortening day length is also having an effect on does. When she comes into estrus, a doe may alert the local bucks of her eagerness to breed by urinating in the scrape. This signals not only the dominant buck, but other potential suitors in the area that there is a hot doe in the vicinity and they'll stick close by, returning often in search of the source of that irresistible aroma.

So, how can you use this information to your advantage? During the rut there are two things that will cause a normally super-cautious mature buck to make mistakes: lust and competition. While older bucks do learn to avoid danger, most of their survival skills are instinctive, and by knowing how bucks react to certain stimuli, you can use mock scrapes to exploit both of these chinks in a cagey old whitetail's armor.

First, let's discuss competition. Through the summer, bucks often associate in bachelor groups, and older bucks are usually familiar with their peers. As the days of late summer grow shorter and testosterone starts to flow, they frequently engage in sparring matches so that by the time the rut rolls around, the dominance hierarchy has been pretty well established. The dominant buck knows he's the top banana in the bunch and he will tolerate no interlopers.

During the rut, however, bucks often range far outside of their usual domain. In doing so, a dominant buck from one area may encounter another dominant buck's scrape line. The interloper may return to his regular stomping

After making a fresh scrape a buck will usually urinate and may even defecate on the bare ground. Study natural scrapes to learn how to create mock scrapes that will trick deer.

grounds, or he may issue a challenge by urinating in the resident's scrapes. A big buck's dominance behavior can be exploited by artificially introducing a contender. The scent of an unfamiliar buck in an active scrape is a challenge no dominant buck can resist.

During the fall, mature bucks can become downright impossible to kill, staying in the deepest of cover and moving only at night. All this changes when the rut hits its peak. Bucks seem to abandon their wariness and may move all day in search of receptive does. These amorous daylight sorties have led to the demise of many a crafty old wallhanger. By signaling a buck that there is a "hot" doe in the vicinity, you can sometimes draw him out in the open.

What you use is less important than how you use it. There are numerous commercially available deer scents (both buck and doe-in-heat) and some work better than others. You may wonder how you can be sure the urine you bought actually came from a dominant buck or estrous doe during the rut. The truth is you can't. That's why the best stuff is the real thing; you can figure out for yourself how to get it. Otherwise, by experimenting, or talking with other hunters, you can find out which commercial scents are most effective.

Then, you need to decide where to apply them. You can apply scent to natural scrapes, but if those scrapes are not in a good location, as is often the situation, you'll need to make your own scrapes, or induce deer to scrape where you want them to.

Deer will use the same scrapes year after year, but they also open up new scrapes annually. While scrape characteristics vary from area to area, there are some common denominators. Scrape lines tend to be along well-traveled routes where many deer will have the opportunity to encounter them. They are also usually in the security of thicker cover, except for field edge scrapes, which are typically used at night. Keep these things in mind when creating a scrape line.

From his work in Michigan's Upper Peninsula, noted deer researcher Dr. John Ozoga found that an overhanging branch, approximately five to six feet above the ground is an important characteristic of a scrape site. When deer paw a scrape, they also rub and lick overhanging branches, transferring scent from the pre-orbital and forehead glands. In order to be

Most hunters know what a natural buck rub looks like. Finding a line of buck rubs is a good indication that a buck is nearby.

effective, mock scrapes should be made under such a branch, if you can find one.

Ozoga also found that bucks could be induced to scrape beneath human-positioned overhead limbs. If there is no licking branch where you want to locate your scrape, simply make one. This can be done by tying down a higher branch, or cutting a branch and tying or nailing it in place. It should be fastened well enough to withstand the sometimes vigorous thrashings of a rutting buck. Sometimes, simply tying a licking branch over a heavy trail is enough to provoke deer into scraping. But scraping away the duff and leaf litter, and applying doe urine is even more effective.

Elaborate measures should be taken to reduce human odors when working in, and around a scrape. Always wear clean rubber boots, rubber gloves and scent-free clothing. You're working in an area where a buck is going to spend some time scrutinizing odors. I

A natural licking branch hanging over a scrape. Scrape sites always include a licking branch.

One way to place a branch where you need it is to tie on a branch at your mock scrape site. Make sure the branch is 5 to 6 feet above the ground and securely anchored to the tree.

there's even a hint of human odor present, you can bet he won't be back.

From his analysis of natural and human-induced scrapes, Ozoga found other common characteristics of preferred scrape sites. The best places to position overhanging limbs is in areas of concentrated deer activity. Vegetation should be fairly open and the site should be on level, moderately dry ground; deer seldom scrape on wet ground because moisture dissipates the scent.

If you plan to hunt from a tree stand, you should locate your scrape upwind of a tree suitable for climbing. A buck will usually first scent-check a scrape by walking downwind of it. Density of the cover and effective range of your bow will dictate how far upwind of your stand to place the scrape; the farther away, the better.

There are several ways to apply scents to scrapes. Some methods work better than others at different times or in different locations. Again, it may take a little trial and error to find out which method works best for your particular situation. The basic concept is to fool a buck into thinking a doe in estrous or a contentious buck has recently used his scrape. The simplest way is to visit the scrape frequently and apply scent directly. But if your after a smart old buck, frequent visits to the site may alert him to your presence and spook him. Once he's detected your presence, the game is over.

If the tree offers a branch that is too high, use a piece of light rope to pull it down to the right height.

Scent drippers—containers designed to hold a larger volume and slowly release the scent—can be purchased, or fashioned. I use 35 mm film canisters. I put a small hole in the bottom and suspend it over the scrape with string. The hole in the lid, through which the string is passed, allows just enough air in so that the scent drips slowly out of the bottom. A nearly full container will drip for two or three days.

Make sure you hang it high enough so that a buck cannot reach it. I've had containers ripped down and stomped into the ground by rut-crazed bucks.

Another, better way to throw down the gauntlet to the local alpha buck is to introduce the real thing. To do this you need to hunt in, or at least be familiar enough with, several different areas that are at least 10 miles apart. Try to locate active scrapes in these areas. When you find a fresh scrape, remove some of the dirt and transport it to an active scrape in another area. You'll be amazed at how effective this little trick is. Again, it's important to pay extra attention to scent. Use scent-free containers—the plastic containers designed for food leftovers work great.

The number and location of scrapes can also be a factor influencing buck movement. If you have a specific location in mind for your mock scrape, try to envision that site as the hub of a wagon wheel. Mock scrape lines should then be set up like spokes on the wheel, all leading to your stand. You may want to avoid setting up a mock scrape line directly downwind of your stand. You don't want to funnel deer to your stand from this direction.

Rubs

While much is known about scrapes and their utility, there seems to be a lot less agreement among the so-called experts over the importance and purpose of rubs and rub lines. Still, there are some generalities that most agree on. Like scrapes, deer will often use the same rubs in successive years. In fact, rubbing on specific trees has been well-documented during the life-span of a single deer. Like scrapes, traditional rubs are usually located along well-traveled trails where many deer will encounter them, and thus they serve as communication centers.

Fresh rubs can mean several different things, depending on when and where you find them. Interpreting them is very important. An acquaintance of mine once related a story of how he had found what he called a buck's "core area." He described a patch of wrist-thick alders, all of which had been stripped of bark from knee to chest height. He hunted there for a week and never caught so much as a glimpse of the buck that made them.

He could have saved himself a lot of wasted time if he had understood what he was looking at. Those pre-rut sparring matches, designed to sort out the pecking order, are typically more of a shoving match than actual combat. But a lot can happen before, or instead of deer actually coming into physical contact. When two evenly-matched bucks encounter one another they usually do a lot of posing and parading for each other. If this fails to intimidate, they may take out their aggression on the local foliage. This is usually the cause of fresh multistemmed rubs. These rubs occur at random locations where the two bucks happened to cross paths, and mean little in terms of core areas or hideouts.

The territorial rubs of a mature buck generally occur in a consistent pattern. They're typically on single trees, often spaced some distance apart, and usually in a line. A line of regularly rubbed trees is a good indication you're in an area used routinely by at least one buck.

The size of the rubbed trees may be an important indicator of the size of the buck. Rubs on small trees don't necessarily mean small bucks, but only big bucks rub big trees. Larger bucks also tend to rub higher on tree trunks. The distance between rubs varies considerably but is often 100 yards or more. The direction of the rub line is key because it indicates a regular travel route used by the buck.

Making your own mock rub is easy, just carry a wood rasp with you. The exposed cambium on a tree is an important visual stimulus to bucks. A buck working a particular area will often show a preference for a particular species of tree and will ignore others of the same size. Pay attention and make your mock rubs on trees similar to ones being used in your area.

The exposed cambium on a tree is an important visual stimulus to bucks. When they encounter a rub, they'll instinctively leave scent from their forehead glands on it. Other bucks encountering it will, in turn, do the same.

Of what utility is this information? Research has shown that by mimicking the natural characteristics of rubs in a particular area, you can induce bucks to follow an artificial rub line. The more closely you mimic rubs in the area you are hunting, the better your chances of making this trick work. Note both the size, and species of trees being rubbed. Individual deer often show a preference for a particular species of tree and will ignore others of the same size.

The diameter of trees rubbed by an individual deer will also be fairly consistent, provided there are ample trees of that size present. Try to make your mock rubs on trees of similar diameter. If there are few trees of the right size present you have two options. You can make your rubs on trees of other sizes, or you can cut poles and stake them into the ground. Research has also shown that if an area lacks the preferred diameter rubbing trees, and you introduce them, bucks will actually leave their natural rub lines in favor of yours.

Creating rubs is actually a very simple process. First, try to locate a well-traveled trail. You will also need to know the predominant direction of travel on that trail. Once you have located, or placed poles of the right size, strip the bark from the side facing approaching deer. You should expose an area from approximately 18 inches to 4 feet above the ground. I know some hunters who apply scents to the rub. But deer rub their forehead glands on the tree and I believe they may perceive urine or tarsal glands to be a foreign odor on a rub.

I've found the most effective way to strip the bark is a coarse wood rasp. This not only strips the bark but the grooves create more surface area than a smooth scraper like a knife blade. This increased surface area, in turn holds more scent.

The number and proximity of rubs is more a reflection of an individual buck's personality than the number of bucks in an area. How many rubs you create is therefore subjective. If you can locate a trail between a known bedding and feeding area, make rubs along it close enough so that each successive rub is visible from the previous one. This will keep the buck on track and hopefully, lead him right past your stand. As with scrapes, your stand should be positioned downwind of the rub line. But you can position yourself closer than you would to a scrape line as the buck will usually be walking on the rub line, not downwind of it.

One advantage mock rubs have over mock scrapes is that they are effective over a longer period of time. Mock scrapes tend to work best only during the peak rut periods. Combining both techniques can sometimes be even more effective. First you persuade bucks to travel by your stand with rubs, then you introduce the mock scrapes. Voila! You've created a buck hot spot.

The most difficult part of creating mock rubs and scrapes is deciding how much is too much. You want to control the direction of travel of the deer without alerting them to your presence. This is especially tricky with older bucks. They got old by being conditioned to avoid humans. It may take a little trial and error to find just the right recipe. But once you do, your deer hunting success will increase significantly.

CHAPTER 27

Rattling, Calling & Decoying Bucks

By Greg Miller

The buck's reaction to my rattling sequence had been both immediate and quite obvious. He had strolled over to a nearby tamarack tree, dropped his head, and proceeded to send bark and small branches flying in every direction. After completing this apparent display of dominance the 10-pointer turned and glared in my direction for several seconds. The big deer then issued a loud, challenging grunt and began striding stiff-legged toward my stand site.

To make a long story short, the 10-pointer finally ended up standing within 13 yards of my position. Unfortunately, he was directly head-on at this point. But in the next instant the deer had swapped ends and was walking straight away from me. Convinced the buck was walking out of my life forever, I was pleasantly surprised when he suddenly turned broadside and started easing along an active rub-line. It was a relatively easy bow shot, and the big woods trophy made it a mere 40 yards before going down.

When done correctly, decoying can be very effective for luring big bucks into bow range. The popularity of this technique is growing, but hunters need to do it correctly.

Calling white-tailed deer has become an extremely popular tactic in recent years. However, hunters need to be aware that calling is a hit and miss proposition at best.

Making the statement that calling for whitetail bucks has become a popular tactic is like saying that Michael Jordan was a great basketball player. It's a virtual no-brainer. However, unlike Jordan's basketball skills, which were productive almost every time he stepped on the court, calling for whitetail bucks is a hit-or-miss proposition at best. And it can be totally unproductive for some hunters.

I've had the opportunity to talk with thousands of deer hunters over the past 10 years. As you might imagine, those conversations have encompassed a broad range of topics. But there's one topic that seems to have generated the most interest and discussion. That topic is calling. If my observations are anywhere close to accurate, there are one heck of a bunch of hunters out there who harbor totally inaccurate perceptions regarding the tactic.

Before proceeding, I'd like to set the record straight in regards to calling for whitetail bucks. Contrary to what you might believe, calling can be a deadly tactic just about everywhere whitetails are found. I've personally had success calling in mature bucks across a broad range of geographic locations. What's more, there's no doubt in my mind that even the largest bucks can occasionally be duped by a bit of rattling and/or grunting. In fact, my largest gun-killed whitetail to date, a 180 3/8 gross typical, was called in. And several years ago I called in what many people believe was a solid 190-class typical whitetail. (The entire encounter was captured on video.) I look at this as positive proof that calling can be effective on very mature bucks.

Many different methods of calling can prove effective for calling in bucks. And quite honestly, it's not my intent to attempt to educate hunters as to what sort of calling sequence might be best. Rather, I want to talk about the numerous and very costly mistakes that hunters routinely make when attempting to call in bucks. Of course, I'm also going to point out what hunters can do to keep from making these mistakes in the future and also discuss some things they can do to increase their "positive response rates".

Calling from the right spots is key

The number-one reason many hunters fail to call in bucks has to do with where they're calling from. Believe it or not, there are many instances when there isn't a buck anywhere within hearing distance of their set-ups. However, there are just as many cases when several bucks are well within hearing distance of the calling, but because of where the sounds are coming from, there's no way these deer would ever think about approaching those sounds.

The main problem here is with the way some hunters assess their calling set-ups. Put simply, these individuals are under the impression that any spot that looks good to them obviously has potential. But that's just not the way it works. Even though they may have hundreds of acres on which to walk, there are only a select few places across a mature buck's range where he feels safe, secure and confident approaching—especially during daylight hours. Though you might

Whitetail bucks establish their rub lines along those routes they feel most safe and secure using. These are excellent places from which to try to call in big bucks.

think otherwise, these places aren't all that difficult to locate either.

I firmly believe that the late pre-rut period is the absolute best time in which to attempt to call in big bucks. For one thing, the bucks are displaying much more protective and aggressive attitudes, which means they're more likely to respond to some calling. More importantly, however, at this time of year it's a piece of cake to figure out exactly where your calling stand sites should be located. This is possible because the bucks already have provided you with numerous, highly visible bits of sign that can point you in the right direction. I'm talking here about antler rubs. And more specifically, rub-lines.

Pre-rut bucks do the vast majority of their traveling along their rub-lines. Remember,

rub-lines are only established along those routes that whitetail bucks feel absolutely safe and secure using. Personally, I can't think of a better or more logical place to attempt to call in a mature buck. But a word of advice here. You can't set-up just anywhere along active rub-lines and expect to call in large-racked deer. It's been my experience that calling from stand sites located very close to bedding areas definitely will increase your big buck response rates. This "rule" would seem to hold true right up until the final two or three days of the pre-rut.

Timing is everything

Just like there are better places from which to call, there also are better times at which to call. Like many of my philosophies for hunting trophy whitetails, it doesn't take a rocket scientist to figure out this one either. About all you have to do is think about the precise time of day when you've seen big bucks moving. I'd be terribly surprised if the vast majority of this movement didn't occur during either the first hour of daylight or the last hour of daylight. (Some hunters I know simply refer to these hours as "prime-time".)

To be honest, though, the old "first hour in morning, last hour of afternoon" rule goes out the window in the days just prior to when the first does start coming into estrous. At this time you can expect to have bucks respond to your calling well after the first hour of daylight. The same thing applies to the afternoons. During the final stages of the pre-rut I start calling within minutes after arriving at my afternoon stands. The buck mentioned at the very beginning of this piece responded to an early afternoon rattling sequence. I arrowed that buck a full hour before the end of legal shooting time.

But regardless of what stage of the pre-rut I'm dealing with, I never call more than once per hour. This is mainly because I'm calling to bedded bucks. I know that those deer are hearing each of my calling sequences. In most instances, if they're going to respond they will do so right away. And if they don't respond right away, there's very little chance they're going to respond at all, regardless of how many more seductive calling sequences you go through. What's more, I've discovered that you can actually "burn out" a potentially productive stand site by over-calling from that site. Calling is definitely one of those strategies where a little bit is good, but more is not better—at least not during the pre-rut period.

But things change during the rut

Achieving high response rates during the rut means applying a totally different approach. To begin with, it's imperative that you relocate your stand sites away from active rub-lines and nearer to antlerless deer activity areas (such as food sources, bedding areas and the trails that link these two places). Also, it's okay during this time to increase the frequency of your calling sequences. In fact, I encourage that you do so. Personally, I go through a complete calling sequence every 20 to 30 minutes. I also call to every "cruising" buck I see. (These are deer searching for receptive does.) However, I never attempt to call in big bucks that are already tending a hot doe. It's a futile gesture, and one that can further educate deer to the whole calling thing.

Another very costly mistake hunters routinely make is attempting to coax in bucks that initially come charging in, but then "hang-up" just out of bow range. Hey folks, the reason that these deer suddenly stop is because they know they are within visual range of where they heard the buck fight taking place. But they don't see either of the bucks that were involved in that fight. While this certainly is cause for suspicion, the bucks also are still a bit curious about the whole deal. In many instances, their next move is going to be dictated entirely by what you do.

Dozens of experiences in the matter have convinced me that the best option is to do nothing at all. In other words, sit tight, be absolutely quiet and hope that the buck's natural curiosity gets the better of him. Contrary to what many hunters believe, additional calling at this point doesn't further convince mature bucks that they should come closer. In fact, it usually has just the opposite affect. Why? Because deer of this age have the ability to reason that if they hear another deer grunting or hear two bucks fighting right in front of them, they should be able to see those deer. The fact that they don't instantly puts them in a panic mode.

For most of the pre-rut period you'll realize higher response rates to your calling efforts by setting up along rub lines that are very near buck bedding areas.

Making your calling sound real

I'm not even going to attempt to describe the entire calling sequences I employ. I will tell you, however, that I've spent years perfecting my technique. The fact that I've been able to do this is directly attributable to one basic fact. I've paid extremely close attention each time I've seen two bucks do battle. Granted, the vast majority of these battles were nothing more than sparring matches. But some of those sparring matches had extremely intense undertones.

It's important that hunters understand that whitetail bucks don't run at each other from great distances and then slam their heads together like a couple of bighorn rams. In truth, there's usually a good deal of posturing that goes on prior to a head-to-head encounter. This posturing could include a bit of grunting, rubbing and/or scraping. For this reason, I begin my calling sequences with several subtle grunts. I then wait about a minute, and then go through a 30- to 45-second mock rubbing sequence. (I've had a number of bucks come charging in upon hearing the mock rubbing.) I wait a couple more minutes before going through my actual rattling sequence. How loudly and intensely I rattle is dictated by the time of year. Early in the pre-rut I'll usually only lightly tickle the antlers together. But I'll gradually increase both the volume and intensity of my rattling as the rut draws near. And during the rut I try to make all my calling sequences sound like full-blown, no-holds-barred buck fights.

Decoying big bucks

No single strategy for hunting white-tailed bucks has received as much attention over the past several years as decoying. There's good reason for this. Put simply, when done correctly, decoying can be a darn effective strategy for luring big bucks within bow range of your stand sites. With more than half a dozen years worth of experiences in the matter, I feel as though I know as much about the proper ways to decoy mature bucks as anyone. This isn't to imply, however, that I know it all.

The first and most important criteria for ensuring high response rates has to do with the decoy itself. More specifically, it has to do with the sex of the decoy. After countless decoy/deer encounters I've found that I'm almost always better served by using buck decoys. One reason for this has to do with our antlerless decoys attracting antlerless deer — sometimes large numbers of antlerless deer. Almost without exception, one or two of these deer would eventually figure out that something wasn't quite right. Either they became leery of the decoy or wound up "picking me off" in my stand sites. Whatever the case, they would then let every other deer within earshot know that something was definitely amiss in that particular spot. End of game!

Believe it or not, I was able to solve this problem simply by switching to buck decoys. One thing I noticed was that, while they do keep their distance, antlerless deer weren't terrified of buck decoys. Also, estrous does seemed extremely attracted to buck decoys. There even have been several instances where "hot" does that already had been sequestered by big bucks

Your best chance of calling in a rutting buck will come from stand sites located near antlerless deer activity.

approached buck decoys. Of course, you can just about imagine the type of response this generated in the buck!

Another positive aspect of using buck decoys is that it's entirely possible to lure a big buck away from a hot doe. I had just such an experience on a cold November afternoon a few years back. I'd placed my buck decoy near the back corner of a small, hidden soybean field. Approximately 30 minutes before dark a lone doe came trotting out into the bean field and stopped about 80 yards from my decoy. The doe glanced at the bogus deer, then turned her head and stared at her back-trail. Seconds later a big buck waltzed out of the timber. The stud 8-pointer took one look at my decoy and walked right away from the obviously hot doe. I sent a broadhead through his vitals just as he was preparing to smash my decoy.

Decoy positioning a key

We've discovered that it's entirely possible to get big bucks to walk exactly where you want them to simply by how you position your decoy. Mature bucks will almost always approach a doe decoy from the rear end. They do this because they want to get a sniff of the doe's rump. Obviously then, those hunters who prefer to use doe decoys should position their decoys facing away from them, 20 to 25 yards upwind of their stand sites.

Placing a decoy in the woods may actually reduce your chances of getting some big buck/decoy interaction. According to the author, bucks simply don't see decoys that are set up in the woods. Move the decoy to the edge of a meadow instead.

Conversely, big bucks will almost always approach a buck decoy from the head end. In fact, every one of the mature bucks that I've decoyed within bow range to this date have approached our buck decoys from the head end. Therefore, place your buck decoys 20 to 25 yards upwind of your stand sites, at either a directly head-on or slightly quartering angle. In almost every instance, the mature bucks I've decoyed ended up standing broadside somewhere between me and the decoy. Each of those deer were so preoccupied with the decoy that I was able to draw my bow undetected and take the time necessary to ensure an accurate shot.

Calling & decoys

There's no question that incorporating a decoy into your calling set-ups will dramatically increase your positive response rates. Remember, anytime you can fool two of a big buck's senses, you stand a much better chance of having him approach those last few crucial yards. In this case, your calling sequence has fooled his sense of hearing and draws him toward your stand site. And, once there, the decoy fools his sense of sight into believing that there is, indeed, a reason for him to take a much closer look.

Whether I plan on doing some calling or not, I use the same basic decoy set-ups. All these set-ups, by the way, see me placing my decoy in open areas. In heavily forested areas, I'll place my decoys in first-year clear cuts or grass swamps. In farmland regions, I like to place my decoys in alfalfa fields, picked corn fields or cut or standing soybean fields. I never, repeat, never place my decoys in the woods. I've seen too many instances where rutting bucks walked quite close to a decoy placed in the woods and never saw that decoy. They do, however, see decoys that are set up in the open. And in case you're wondering, rutting bucks do spend an enormous amount of time cruising around in open crop land, grass swamps and first-year re-growth areas.

It's entirely possible that you could see some big buck/decoy interaction by placing your decoys anywhere in an open area. However, you can significantly increase your big buck/decoy interaction rates by searching out and setting up in specific spots. I've personally had the best results by placing my decoys near the very back edges of fields, in the narrows between two points of thick cover and along thick brush lines. From what I've been able to gather, even though a big buck might be thoroughly convinced that your decoy is a real deer,

This photo shows an excellent spot for a decoy set-up. There are a couple different attractants and a distinct corner situation created by the intersecting brush lines.

he still would prefer to approach that "deer" while remaining close to cover.

As I stated earlier, rattling, calling and decoying can be extremely effective strategies for taking mature whitetail bucks. But even in the hands of the very best, these strategies are never a guaranteed deal. In fact, it's my honest opinion that hunters can expect to realize a five-percent positive response rate at best. No doubt that number seems depressingly low to many hunters. However, you must remember that we're talking here about mature whitetails. Anything you can do to increase your chances for success even the slightest on these creatures should be viewed as a blessing!

CHAPTER 28

Bowhunting Barometer Bucks

By Peter Schoonmaker

It had been a long, arduous bowhunting season for Iowa outfitter Steve Shoop. His 9,300 acres of prime whitetail habitat is home to many of the outstanding bucks the region is noted for. It had been a warm, almost sultry, bow season from the October 1 opener until the January 10th finish. But Shoop's food plots, managed agricultural lands, and deep oak bottoms, still produced 14 Pope & Young bucks, most taken during the corpuscular periods of dawn and dusk. Mother Nature can play an

utting bucks during the post-storm period will be trolling their turf and reopening scrapes.

important role in the outcome of a six day hunt. Weather fronts are often welcome as a sign of whitetail activity. But the weather during the week of November 7 to 14 was so oppressive, both the hunters and the whitetails were unable to function. First came 4 inches of snow, then 4 inches of rain whipped by 62 mph winds. For the first time in Shoop's guiding experience his hunters were camp bound for two whole days.

Pennsylvania bowhunter Dan Musser arrived at Shoop's southern Iowa operation as the storm-laden week wore down. Musser and his three hunting companions naturally inquired about the whitetail activity as that week was the known peak rutting period for this region. Unfortunately, outfitter and guides had little to report. During the week before the severe weather rutting activity was on the rise. But during the week of wind-driven snow and rain, the rutting was stalled, and deer sightings were few. Musser is an experienced bowhunter who has taken several fine bucks in his home state, as well as a 137 P&Y in Montana. No matter how well-honed a bow shot you are, or how accomplished a tree stand hunter you have become, unless the deer are motivated to move, a tree stand can be a lonely perch in the whitetail woods.

A Call To Action

It was 33 degrees and the stars glistened on the calm morning of November 15th. Musser was boated across Sundown Lake in the pre-dawn and put ashore at the base of an oak ridge. A line of reflective dots led him uphill to a treestand that, until now, had only been a tack on a map back in camp. Musser had no sooner climbed into the treestand, harnessed in, and hauled up his bow, when he realized the oaken slope was alive with the sounds of moving deer. At first light, 10 does scurried past at a brisk pace. Next, a grunting, basket rack buck, chased a doe up over the ridge. That buck

Barometric pressure is the key to whitetail activity and hunter success. Knowing how deer will react to changing weather conditions will put you in position to bag the buck of your dreams.

of this deer was obvious. Musser grunted, but the oblivious buck ignored the call and walked on. As the big deer approached the last visible shooting lane, Dan literally yelled out, "Whoa Buck." The immense whitetail stopped, quartering away, at 25 yards. Musser already had the bow sights aligned and unleashed an arrow with an 85 grain broadhead. The compound bow with a 75-pound draw drove the projectile completely through the deep-chested deer.

Musser watched the whitetail take 4 or 5 steps and let out a big wheeze. The bowhunter knew his shot was good. The awesome buck trotted about 30 yards, stumbled, and fell over dead without even a kick. The hunter sat down and collected himself. It was only 8 a.m. After 5 minutes of watching the still deer he climbed down and inspected his post-storm trophy. The buck was impressive, all bulked up from rutting. Massive, thick antlers carried 12 main points, with several smaller ones. (Dan Musser's incredible Iowa buck gross scored 182 5/8, and netted at 175 2/8 inches of antler for the Pope & Young record book. Two of his hunting partners also scored on that action-packed morning with one of the bucks a 146 inch 10-pointer.)

Musser wasn't going to be picked up until 11 a.m., so he climbed back into his treestand. The show wasn't over.

At 10 a.m. another 10-pointer walked up to the dead buck, sniffed him over and took off. Dan then moved down to the lake shore, ate a sandwich, and pondered his morning experience. While he thought about all of the intense whitetail activity, another rut-worn 8-pointer popped out of the cover 20 yards away, and got a drink. The rut was certainly in progress, but what actually initiated the whitetail behavior on this specific morning?

The Silent Signal

It was the weather.

Humans feel winds change, see clouds gather, and sense a pressure change upon their body. Whitetail deer have a "built-in" barometric sensor that triggers their behavioral patterns. This is why deer habitat that has routine travel from bedding to feeding areas suddenly sees a high level of traffic, one to two days prior to the arrival of a storm as the barometer falls. Often times, even before precipitation begins, whitetails bed up and hold

no sooner went out of hearing when a high, wide, 10-pointer appeared, walking briskly just below the skyline. Dan called to the patrolling whitetail with a grunt tube.

The handsome buck stopped and looked in the direction of the hunter. Musser was hoping to coax the buck into bow range when suddenly, there was a crash behind him. Dan peered behind his tree to see the biggest buck he had ever seen in his life, running downhill right at him. The buck's flanks were heaving and his tongue was hanging out. This buck was definitely making up for lost time. The rutting buck paused from chasing does and confronting challengers just long enough to get a drink out of a creek. At 35 yards the buck circled behind the bowhunter through some thick whips. Although obscured, the body and antler mass tight as the barometer bottoms out. Once the barometer begins to rise again, even if rain or snow is still falling, deer become active again having been signaled the end of the storm.

Whitetail activity is definitely triggered by the rise and fall of barometric pressure. Illinois biologist Keith Thomas found the highest amount of whitetail feeding and movement occurred when barometric pressures were between 29.80 and 30.29. The National Climatic Data Center has on record the barometric pressures that led to Dan Musser's success in southern Iowa. The pre-storm pressure was 29.15, then it dropped to 28.29, then it rose again to 29.94 on the day Musser arrowed his magnificent buck during a flurry of whitetail activity. Meteorologist Scott Stevens at the N.C.D.C., in discussing the strong November storm front in terms of barometric pressure stated, that it was "...significant millibar movement."

Understanding Barometric Pressure

Barometric pressure indicates that air has weight.

Fronts are the boundaries between cold and warm air masses. The boundary lines on a weather map are called isobars, lines of equal pressure. The difference in barometric pressure on each side of the isobar will determine the "high" and "low" pressure. Pressure measurements are essential for the plotting of isobars over the earth, and determining the movements of fronts. Millibars are a direct measure of pressure, like pounds per square inch, but in the metric system. Since the measurement is in the metric system, 1,000 millibars equal one bar. A bar is a force of 100,000 Newtons acting on a square meter, which is too large a unit to be a convenient measure of Earth's air pressure.

Inches of mercury, the number used for surface air pressure in the U.S., is not a direct measure of pressure. Instead, inches of mercury tell you how high the pressure pushes the mercury in a barometer. The use of direct pressure measurements goes back to the late 19th century when the Norwegian meteorologist Vilhelm Bjerknes, the leader in making meteorology a mathematical science, urged weather services to use direct pressure measurements because they can be used in the formulas that best describe the weather.

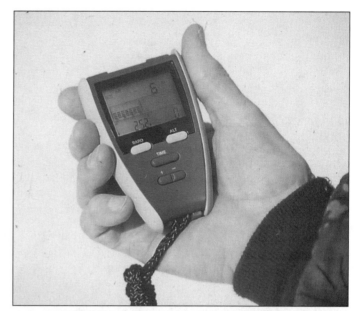

A hand-held weather monitor, like this one from Lab Safety Supply, will tip you off to whitetail movements.

Air pressure is caused by the force of gravity acting to pull molecules of the gases towards the center of the earth. Since barometric pressure differs with elevation, the pressure at the point of measure is referred to as station pressure. Barometric pressure at mountain tops is less than at sea level, regardless of positions of highs and lows, thus, all pressure readings are converted to what they would be if the readings were taken at sea level. This allows for accurate mapping of pressure readings anywhere in the world. As casual weather observers, we should recognize that barometric pressure is divided on weather maps by isobars, calculated in millibars, and reported to us in inches of mercury, the most accurate form of measurement.

Leading Indicator

Barometric pressure is one of the leading indicators for forecasting weather. Fair weather is associated with a steady or rising barometer. Stormy weather is associated with a steadily falling barometer. The telltale sign of a falling barometer is a ring around the moon. Weather after a storm will find the barometer rapidly rising as the cloud cover breaks and the sky clears. Storm severity is often determined by how fast the barometer drops. Barometric pressure signals significant weather changes 18 to 48 hours prior to its arrival. For reference, one of the lowest pressures ever recorded

Pre-storm activity finds whitetails traveling with the emphasis on food.

was about 27 inches of mercury in the eye of a hurricane. One of the highest was over 31 in a high altitude pressure dome.

We associate fair weather with a prevailing westerly breeze and a clear sky, often streaked with thin cirrus clouds. The progression of a storm front will find the wind has shifted to the southeast as a low pressure slips under a high pressure. Puffy layers of altocumulus clouds gather on the western horizon as a storm front becomes visible. Dark, rolling squall lines will pass over the countryside as precipitation falls to earth. As a storm advances, the wind shifts back to the west and north, the ceiling begins to lift, and the uniform cover of stratus clouds will begin to separate. The prevailing westerly breeze again makes its presence known as high pressure resumes with clear skies and fair weather.

Well-Acquainted

Humans know barometric pressure usually through discomfort. Hunters have wondered

for years if the same weather changes that made their joints ache, had any effect on the deer. The old wive's tales of bunions foretelling impending weather weren't far off. The University of Pennsylvania School of Medicine was one of the first to prove the effects of barometric pressure on humans. Thirty arthritic patients were put in sealed, room-sized climate chambers, and exposed to simulated storm conditions. Dropping barometric pressures and boosting humidity levels produced stiffness and swelling in the patient's joints. Reversing the conditions brought immediate relief. Sinus pressure and pain brought on by changes in barometric pressure are proven and referred to as "cluster headaches" by the American Council for Headache Education. Most of the population feels the effects of barometric pressure near sea level where the air is the heaviest. But higher altitudes have pressure problems of their own as the weight of the air decreases. We have come to know "jet lag" as a form of fatigue as the result of an extended pressure

Peak storm conditions will find the deer bedded.

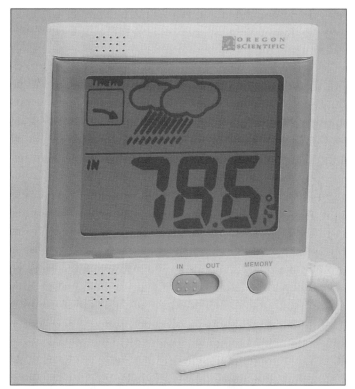

This compact weather meter from Cabela's shows barometric pressure and weather patterns as well.

change. Food requires greater time to cook in boiling water at higher elevations because of the lack of pressure, or "thin air." Today, doctors use hyper/hypobaric chamber treatments for the "bends", a medical condition caused by rapid diving and flying ascents, and for problematic wound healing.

Folklore No More

Outdoorsmen have always had a special take in tomorrow's weather. As a result, for thousands of years forecasting was a folk art practiced primarily by sailors, farmers, hunters, and fishermen. They studied the clouds, felt the air's dampness upon their cheek, noted a shift in the wind, felt a certain tingling to their head and an aching to their joints, checked it with the behavior of animals and birds, remembered pertinent sayings of their grandfather's weather lore, and came up with an "educated" guess.

The first meteorological surveys began in the early 1800s as U.S. Army hospital surgeons were ordered to take regular observations. By 1853, weather records were filed daily in 97 different Army camps. Today's satellites and computers have taken the folklore out of weather forecasting and accompanying barometric pressures.

Whitetails Under Pressure

There are three periods of whitetail activity associated with storm fronts. These periods are not controlled by daylight or darkness, but dictated by the fall and rise in barometric pressure. Pre-storm activity includes a period of deer moving with a falling barometer. One to two days prior to the storm's arrival will find the deer's emphasis on food. At this time, stand placements should be concentrated on seasonal food sources and their access trails. As a storm front closes in and the barometer drops further, whitetails begin retreating down the same trails to bedding areas.

Peak storm activity will find the barometer bottoming out and the whitetails bedded down. The severity of the storm will dictate the density of the cover taken for protection, and for the conservation of energy and body

Dan Musser with the incredible Iowa buck he arrowed during the post-storm, rising barometer period of whitetail activity. (Photo courtesy of J&S Trophy Hunts.)

heat. A severely sinking barometer, and a weather map with closely spaced isobars indicates a period of high wind. This will find whitetails bedded right out in the open, safe from the same deciduous and conifer trees that protect them from rain, snow, and cold. Still-hunting through bedding areas, or calling from stand locations, is the only way to see these immobile deer.

The post-storm period will find the whitetails leaving their bedding areas to feed and resume the rituals of autumn on a rising barometer. Pre- and post-rut deer, bucks and does alike, will be feeding heavily to build their body reserves. The does in estrous, and the bucks in rut, will be working at a fevered pace to make up for the "down time" of the storm. Bucks will be frantically reopening scrapes and patrolling their turf. The post-storm period, like the pre-storm, will see a noticeable increase in white-tailed deer activity for one to two days. This is a prime time to stake out a proven point of travel bordering a food source, or a known scrape line. Whereas pre-storm hunting gets a lot of notoriety, and rightfully so, the post-storm period is often overlooked. These days are top producers for rutting whitetail bucks.

Barometer Bowhunting

You have found prime, active habitat. You have scouted and patterned a buck. And your tree stand locations are selected. But no matter how much homework you have done, you will still find your best whitetail days afield are going to be determined by Mother Nature.

Bowhunters have long been aware that changing weather is directly associated with whitetail behavior. The question has always been why? Extremes in precipitation, wind, and temperature, will produce a defensive reaction from whitetails. But what informs them days in advance of changing weather? What tells them when to feed, when to seek shelter, and when it's safe to resume activity? It is the whitetail's built-in barometer.

If your deer is using a barometer, then you should be using one, too. Or at least closely watching the pressure patterns in your area.

Barometric pressure is the key to the behavioral patterns of whitetail deer. To pay attention to this you will need a barometer. A column of mercury that stands 30 inches tall and exerts 1016 millibars of pressure is the standard for measurement. At 14 pounds this system is rather impractical for field use.

There are liquid barometers for basic readings, and aneroid dial barometers that work on vacuum, that are common for home use. But for whitetail hunters today there are also compact weather meters. One that gives exact barometric pressure and shows weather trends as well is Cabela's compact, 4 x 4 inch, Jumbo Weather Forecaster. Lab Safety Supply offers the Pocket Weather Monitor that records barometric pressure for 12 hours and accurately forecasts for another 24.

By spending some time patterning the barometric pressure that accompanies weather fronts you will know without a doubt when deer will be moving. This will allow you to put in quality time at the peak periods of whitetail activity. Become a barometer watcher. Plan your hunts according to big changes in the barometric pressure. It will greatly enhance your bowhunting success..

Other Game

CHAPTER 29

Getting Your Point Across To Spring Gobblers

By Mike Roux

The gobbling was not constant, but it was regular. The bird, which I figured was a 2-year-old, sounded-off about every two minutes. He was directly behind me, to the east, across a small, bright-green wheat field. The sun had just begun to cast a rosy hue farther east of him.

he results of a good plan and a bit of tom foolery. Mike oux approaches the big gobbler he bagged on a Mississippi River levee. Proper decoy location was the key bagging this bird. Photo by Kevin Brunstein.

My blind, made out of cedar branches, faced straight west at the base of a Mississippi River levee in Hancock County, Illinois. The property is owned by John and Sue Caldwell and they call their place "THE BREAK." It got its name from a huge flood in the '80's that caused the levee to break right onto their farm.

Bowhunting the levee for spring gobblers is an incredible experience. Because it is located in the largest river bottom on the continent, there is no other high ground for miles in any direction. Knowing a mature gobbler's passion to "own" the highest point of real estate, you can see why the levee attracts big toms like an outlet mall attracts shoppers.

This particular stretch of levee is famous for producing larger than average birds. Hunting these wise old toms with a bow is no picnic. As you can imagine, there is not a lot of cover along the levee—making the use of a blind almost a requirement. And, a correctly constructed blind conceals the bowhunter while he draws, anchors, aims and shoots.

There was plenty of light now. I could hear two or three birds fly down across the wheat field. There was no need to turn and face the gobbling turkey. I knew that sometime that morning he would come to the levee to check-out my decoys. That is precisely when I planned to take my shot.

When the two-year-old gobbler hit the ground his calling increased. I had still made no calls to him. I needed to see which way he went around the wheat field first. He was gobbling a lot now. He had not yet come out in the field when another gobble came from the south end of the wheat.

This single, long gobble shut my bird down like someone had cut his throat. He shut-up immediately and I did not hear him again. It was obvious that the tom to the south was the boss and the other gobblers in the area were

Hens and jakes make for a convincing decoy arrangement. No tom worth his salt will stay away if he thinks a jake is moving in on his harem. Decoy placement also allows hunters to get the tom in the perfect position for a shot. Photo by Greg Nixon.

his subordinates. Now it was time for me to enter the morning's conversation.

If I intended to put a broadhead in that ole' boy, I would have to get his attention to my decoys. I ran off a series of hen yelps on my box call. He did not respond. I waited five minutes, then repeated the calls. Still the bird did not respond. I waited again and a few minutes later he gobbled.

He had moved only slightly from his original position. I called again and then shut-up. In the next 20 minutes he only gobbled two more times. I had made no calls. He had moved about 100 yards closer to the levee, about 250 yards south of me. He had not yet seen my decoys.

Calling to a tom while bow hunting is done a bit differently when hunting with archery gear than with a shotgun. You not only have to talk the bird into range, but you must quite often hold the gobbler at less than 20 yards until he presents you with a perfect shot. This can take quite some time.

I like to fire a bird up with hen calls. I try to get him to the point that he is answering every call. He most likely will not come to the hen calls, but all you need to know is that he knows there is a hen there. Gobblers do not like coming to hen calls. They would much rather have the hen come to them. However, the effectiveness of my gobbler calling strategy is dependent upon the tom believing there is a hen in the area.

Springtime bowhunters should know that wild turkeys do not think and reason, they merely react instinctively to stimuli. The normal reaction of a gobbler to a calling hen is for him to stay put. He will gobble and strut, expecting the hen to seek him out for breeding. If she is ready to breed she will quickly come to him. If she is not ready, why should he waste his energy chasing her? A tom's natural reaction to a hen call is to wait.

Now is when the turkey hunting archer out thinks the old tom. After your hen calls have him excited, shut-up. Stop calling and let him wonder what is going on. He may gobble to try to coax you, the hen, into making another call. He may even gobble more, after you stop calling. He is trying to vocally guide the hen to his position. He just cannot figure out why she will not come to him.

At this point you need to nock an arrow, get your bow ready and get back into the conversation. Only this time you must give the big tom positive stimuli to which he will react. You must now make the calls of a male turkey. That's right, you now become a gobbler with your calling. An educated tom may not come to a hen, but he will certainly come to defend that hen if another male infringes upon his territory.

There are two main calls that spring bowhunters can use to reproduce gobbler calls.

The author prefers concealment in a natural blind while bowhunting for turkeys. A good natural blind usually don't make the wary birds any more suspicious. Photo by Kevin Brunstein.

The first is the yelp of the jake, or immature tom. These calls are best made with a box call and are much louder and more coarse than hen yelps. These calls trick the old tom into believing that a young male is now with the hen. He will instinctively move to intimidate the youngster and run him off.

The other very effective call is the gobbler cluck. This loud, sharp cluck is a common noise made by gobblers and is often used when one male challenges another. The gobbler cluck is by far my favorite turkey call to make. It can be made with the box call, slate or diaphragm call. I like using a diaphragm call to make my clucks. This leaves both hands free to handle my bow.

By now the dominant tom was on top of the levee a couple hundred yards to my south. I watched him with binoculars as he strutted in a tight circle on the sand ridge. No other birds were gobbling now. The king was obviously on his throne.

I picked up my call and ran off a series of very seductive hen yelps. He was quite some distance away, but I knew he could hear me. I watched through my binoculars as he turned to look my way. Because of a slight bend in the levee, he could not yet see my decoys. I needed to coax him north about 50-yards to bring my foam flock into play.

The bird responded twice to my hen yelps. I put the call down and looked at my watch. If the gobbler stayed on the top of the levee I would not make another call for at least 20 minutes. If he started to move south, or off the levee, I would again fall back to the hen calls to keep his attention. For the next half-hour he did not move more than six feet.

The sun was fully up now. It was a bit after 7 a.m. He had gobbled many times in the past 30 minutes, his last call was about five minutes earlier. I picked-up my box call and gave him three loud, crisp yelps to imitate a jake. He did not gobble but spun in my direction like he was on a peg.

He raised his red head on a long neck, straining to see up the levee. He had folded his strut to half-mast and appeared to be ready to come north. I hit him again with three more gobbler yelps. This did two things; it put him back into full strut and it put him on the move.

As he came around the levee and saw my three decoys, he hit the brakes. My decoy arrangement for bowhunting spring gobblers has proven extremely effective. I have found that you need to fool both the ears and eyes of any gobbler you hope to bag with a bow. I think decoys and decoy placement are the most important factors in getting a gobbler close enough and to keep him close long enough for a good bow shot.

Early in the season my set-up is always the same. I put out two hen decoys and a full-strut jake decoy. I have tested and used many different turkey decoys from several different manufacturers. My experience has led me to a huge preference for Feather-Flex foam decoys. My entire flock can be folded and carried in my hunting vest. Also, these decoys are so light that the slightest breeze gives them natural, life-like movements. Just like the pirouettes the gobbler did on the levee for half-an-hour. These are, by far, the most effective, practical decoys a turkey bowhunter can use.

As I said, I like to use a strutting jake and two hens early in the season. Later on I will replace the strutting jake with a regular standing jake decoy. Late season toms are usually more nervous from hunting pressure and less likely to pick a fight that could be noisy and attract attention. Of great importance to the bowhunter is the combination of having your bird hear gobbler calls and then see a strutting bird as he approaches. The picture just feels right to him.

Decoys provide the right diversion, keeping birds interested in something besides the sounds made by the caller. Position your decoys so the tom will have his backside facing you for the best shot. Photo by Mike Roux.

The big bird stood there on the sand, eyeing my small fake flock. He gobbled a challenge at the jake, never folding down his stiff strut. Under natural circumstances, a live jake would have become intimidated by the presence of the alpha tom. He would have folded his strut and would have gotten off the levee. But these were not natural circumstances.

The adult gobbled again, warning his subordinate to vacate the premises. Not only did the defiant jake not run off, but I slowly placed the diaphragm call in my mouth and made the jake offer a challenge "cluck" to the old tom. This served to make the mature male furious. He puffed-up even more as he quickly cut the distance between himself and my decoy.

My decoys are placed in a very specific fashion. Even though the wind can move them enough to make them look natural, I do not let them move enough to adversely affect me getting my perfect shot. Decoy placement is directly related to what shot you want your gobbler to ultimately present you.

In the spring a tom's instincts are focused on two topics; breeding and fighting for the right to breed. A bowhunter needs to be sharply aware of these behavioral traits to be successful. These traits determine how the bowhunter will place his decoys.

Distance of the decoys from the hunter is a matter of skill and performance. You must realize that your shot will come as the tom is engaging one of your decoys. Which decoy is the turkey's choice. If he would rather breed than fight, then he will engage one of your foam hens. If he is in the mood to fight, then he will approach your jake. Either way, all decoys should be positioned so that the gobbler will turn his back to you while in full-strut.

To correctly set your hen decoys, place them facing directly away from you. In the spring, the "business end" of a hen, for a tom, is the rear. The male will strut around behind the hen, hoping she will lay down to be bred. He will usually stay in full-strut until he actually mounts her for breeding.

Conversely, your jake decoy, whether strutting or standing, should be placed facing toward you. When the tom approaches a jake to intimidate or to fight, they begin by being eyeball-to-eyeball. A mature bird will never fold his strut in the presence of a strutting jake. Both the hen and jake, set in this fashion, will present you with your best shot.

It was very obvious that the huge, black, strutting bird on the levee had no time whatsoever for the two hens. His full attention was focused on the stubborn jake that would not give in to his scare tactics. The closer he got, the madder he became. He was now spitting and drumming. He was about 50-yards from the jake who continued to defy him.

I had plenty of cover in front of me in my blind and had not yet raised my bow because experience told me it was way too early. Too much can happen at this point to delay things. I decided to give my big tom one last supreme insult. I took the new Lohman "Spit-N-Drum" call from my pocket. The sounds from this call very accurately reproduce this close-in gobbler noise. As soon as he heard it he marched, in full-strut, right to my jake decoy.

As planned, the tom came face-to-face with the foam jake almost immediately. With this move he put his huge tail-fan between his head and me. With his fullest attention focused on his sparring partner and his fan covering my movement, I raised my bow and came-up on one knee. My target was the small area where all of the tail-feathers from his fan converged. He was about 12-yards from me.

To make a lethal shot on a wild turkey with archery gear you must put your broadhead in one of two places. You must either break the bird's spine or virtually eviscerate the gobbler by cutting every vital organ in his body. The shot I like best is the one my entire set-up plans for. With his back toward me, in full strut, a broadhead right up the tailpipe will dispatch the tom in short order. I call it "The Texas Heart Shot".

When the gobbler made his first "swat" at my decoy, I drew my bow. I anchored, aimed and released as he recovered and came back to full-strut between the decoy and me. The arrow sailed through the bird, burying half the shaft in the sand levee. The tom jumped straight up into the air when he got hit. He flopped for only a very few moments before coming to rest among the decoys.

Taking a spring gobbler with your bow is one of the most challenging hunts you will ever attempt. To get a bird that can see as well as a turkey into bow range, then raise, draw, anchor, aim and shoot without being detected is a very difficult proposition. But it is not impossible if you consider the following factors:

Concealment

The bowhunter must be extra careful when it comes to camouflage and overall concealment. Your average shot distance will be closer than that of shotgun hunters, therefore your target has a greater chance to detect your presence. Make sure everything is camouflaged and be sure your camo pattern matches the natural backgound color.

Decoys

Turkey decoys are the most valuable tools at the bowhunter's disposal. They should be used in high-visibility areas such as open timber or field-edge set-ups. Be sure to put your decoys well within your effective range. Place male and female decoys so that a gobbler engaging either of them will present you with a perfect shot.

Calling

Bowhunters must approach calling a bit differently as well. Getting the bird into bow range is only half the battle. You must then manage to keep the tom interested enough to stay close long enough for that perfect chance. Remember to fire him up with hen calls, then close the deal by changing to male turkey calls like jake yelps and gobbler clucks. Be sure to never, under any circumstances, use the gobble as a call. It is just too dangerous.

Shot Placement

All your efforts as a spring gobbler bowhunter are focused on getting the tom to turn his back to you while in full-strut. This shot is always fatal. Shooting at the base of the wing, on a tom that is not strutting, will break the spine. You can also break the spine by putting your broadhead between the wing bases on a non-strutting tom facing away from you.

By applying these factors along with your skills as an archer, you too can be come successful with your bow in the spring. You will get a sense of satisfaction and a great deal of personal gratification when you take this toughest of all archery trophies.

CHAPTER 30

Sign Language:
All Bears Are Not Created Equal

By Bill Vaznis

All was quiet. Then, the snap of a twig from the edge of the swamp grabbed my attention. I turned my head a little to the right just in time to see the body of a huge black bear slip out of the shadows, and pass behind the stand. Then all was quiet again.

Half an hour before dark, the boar reappeared circling the bait and sniffing the air for signs of danger. Once he was satisfied all was safe, he committed himself to the setup, but when he reached the cribbed offering he suddenly jerked his head around and looked right at me.

The 400-pound bruin didn't lower his head one-inch as he closed the distance between us. He quickly climbed a log, stood up on his hind legs and looked up at me with his beady brown eyes. Then he woofed—twice. I hid behind the

Learning to read bear sign is the first step to a successful black bear hunt. Knowing what you are looking at helps you to choose a good stand site and bait location, that can mean the difference be taking a record-book bear or no bear at all.

riser of my compound as best I could, and tried to stop from shaking.

If I could have taken one step away from the tree, and then raised my bow over my head, I know I could have cold-cocked that old boar right then and there. Instead, I sat still and held my cool. When the bear returned to the bait site and turned broadside, I picked a spot low and behind his shoulder, slowly came to full draw and released an arrow at his vitals. The shaft hit with a resounding WHACK, nearly knocking the Pope and Young bruin off his feet. He turned to run, but his efforts where to no avail. The record-book bear fell dead less than 10 yards distant.

An hour later, outfitter Bob Heyde and his uncle Jake arrived at the bait site. They knew I had tagged a good bear just from the look on my face. "Boy, we were right," said Bob when he flashed his light on the big bruin, "he is a Pope and Younger for sure!"

And that he was. But how did we know there was a book bear at that particular bait? We read the sign. Many outfitters just drop their clients off at a stand giving them little or no say-so as to where they will sit for the evening. But you can just as easily book with an outfitter who will run a bait line for you, and then let you decide where you want to hunt each day. By learning to read sign and telling your outfitter you know what you're looking for, you can increase your chances of bagging a trophy bruin.

Here's a series of scenarios to think about before your next trip afield. Keep in mind that almost all record-book black bears are boars.

Making The Choice

The first tree stand is situated along a wilderness stream that abuts an open hillside. The bait has been placed in a lush meadow just inside the woods where you can see quite a ways up the hill. Your guide tells you the bait is being devoured nightly, and he is sure you'll see a bear the first night you sit in the stand. Indeed, there seems to be plenty of bear sign around, and the grass has been knocked down all around the site. The bait however has been scattered about in a wide circle. In fact, it is such a mess the site looks like it has been hit by a run-a-way garbage truck. There are no well-defined exit or entrance trails.

Bear tracks are a great indication that a bear has been visiting the area. Not only do they tell the size of the bear and the direction of travel, they can also tell you the frequency of the animal's visits to your site.

The second tree stand is on a peninsula that juts out into a remote wilderness lake. There's not much ground cover near the bait, but the outfitter assures you there's a trophy bear in the vicinity. An experienced bear hunter the previous week watched a big black circle the bait on two occasions, but the bear refused to expose himself during legal shooting hours. Although the hunter was able to sneak out of his tree stand each evening without spooking the bear; the outfitter blames that hunter for not getting a shot because he was too fidgety in the stand.

The third bait is situated at the foot of a narrow ridge that rises out of a large, impenetrable swamp. The spruce trees are so thick here that little daylight ever reaches the forest floor. It's a scary place, even in the middle of the day. According to the outfitter, the tree stand is a long walk off the tote road, so you won't be picked up until well after dark. He offers you a 12-gauge shotgun as "back up", and tells you to be sure you take a head net, plenty of insect repellent and a spare flash light with you to the stand. The bait is only being hit once or twice a week, but almost all the bait is taken on each visit. There are no well-defined trails leading to or from the bait.

Which of these three stands would you choose, and how would you hunt it? Well, the first tree stand sounds like the ideal black bear set-up, but it is not. Unless, that is, you have never seen a bear before or all you want to do is take pictures. A sow and cubs—not legal targets in the Canadian provinces and not ethical targets anywhere—are probably hitting it. The cubs knock the grass down and scatter food all around like a bunch of first-graders at a food fight. To confirm your suspicions, simply walk around and check the immediate vicinity for small tracks and droppings about half an inch in diameter.

The second bear is bait-shy because of the lack of adequate cover near the bait. With no nearby cover the bear only hits the bait after dark. This is the outfitter's fault. Although you don't know for sure just how big this bear really is, it might be worth your effort to move the bait and/or tree stand closer to cover, and wait for the bear to become accustomed to the new setup before you take the stand.

Stand three is the best of the lot. Any place that scares you or the outfitter has big bear written all over it. Big old bruins are extremely solitary, except during the mating season, and there's no better place to be left alone than an impenetrable tangle out in the middle of nowhere. In addition, that ridge is a natural highway in and out of the swamp. That doubles your chances of a sighting. I would hunt this stand in the absence of big bear sign simply because of the topography.

Timing is the key however. Don't sit in the stand until you fully expect the bear to show. If he is hitting the bait every second or third night, hunt elsewhere for a night or two. Your best chance of tagging this bear is on the first night you hunt it. Wait for all the conditions to be in your favor before you climb aloft.

Book Bears

Here are three more choices.

The first tree stand is a chip shot away from a cribbed bait hidden along the edge of a large swamp. There are two trails the bears seem to be using to enter and exit the baited area. It is one of the outfitter's favorite sites as his clients have tagged many record-book bears here. He tells you the bait is being hit sporadically by a bear with 61/2-inch front pads. Lately , however, it seems when a bowhunter sits near the bait, all he sees is mosquitoes. A few report hearing twigs snap downwind of the stand right around prime time. Two or three nights after the bowhunter abandons the site, the bear returns and hits the bait again, leaving impressions of his big pads all around the bait site.

A good elevated stand is just as important for bear hunting as it is for deer hunting. Choose a location that gives you a good field of view while affording adequate concealment. Bears working a good bait station will learn to ignore the stand, as long as it doesn't smell like there's a human up there.

The second tree stand is adjacent to a new bait located in a wooded hollow. The ground around the bait is spongy, and the source of much new spring greenery. The outfitter tells you the bait is being hit every second night now like clockwork by a bear with a 5-inch pad. This bear takes the same trail to the bait by placing his feet in the exact same tracks each time he visits. Then he circles the barrel, squeezes through a tight thicket, steps just over an 8- inch log, and approaches the mouth of the barrel using the surrounding brush to his advantage.

The third tree stand is located in an overgrown pasture 100 yards from an oat field. The outfitter has baited the area with oats, honey and plenty of meat by-products. The farmer

A trail timer can give you accurate readings on when something passes it's sensor. Some models include a camera that will tell you exactly what animal tripped the shutter.

tells you there's plenty of bears around as they are gorging themselves on his crops. As you approach the field for the first time, you see a very large bruin feeding in the oats not far from the bait. You watch him as he eventually takes the path that leads to the bait and your tree stand.

Where should you hunt? Obviously there is a record-book bear on the first set-up, and well worth any effort you might extend. The bear is bait-wise, but is attracted to the goodies nonetheless. Over the years, he has probably been here many times. What the bear is doing is circling downwind of the tree stand before committing himself to the bait. If he smells a stinky human, as he has apparently done in the past, he simply wanders elsewhere. If the coast is clear, he approaches the bait along one of the well-worn trails. The snapping of twigs

should give you a clue as to the bear's patrol route. Check it out early in the next morning by looking for bent vegetation and fresh depressions in the soft turf. One trick is to set up a second stand downwind of this route, and wait a few days for the bear to start hitting the bait again. Don't wait too long. As soon as this bear finds another food source; he'll likely abandon the site altogether.

The second setup is, in all likelihood , attracting a big bear. Although, the spongy earth my lead you to believe the track is bigger than it really is. He is very cagey and very cautious. And I say "he" because the odds are this bear is an old boar. Why? A sow generally steps over a log with little concern, but a boar is much more cautious, preferring to place his front pad only an inch or so past the edge of the log when he crosses.

Stink baits used as an attractant can bring bears in, but the bait must be used correctly.

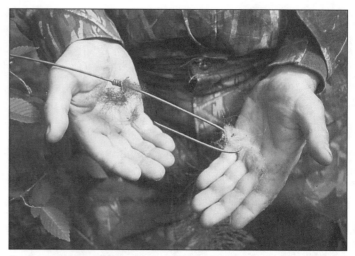

A great way to learn the color of the bear that's using your bait station is to locate bits of fur on fences and in the underbrush.

How big is he? Look for a "bear bed" at first light. A bruin will often lie down to feed near the bait . Look for bent and broken spring growth for a better idea of his body size. What color is this bear? That's easy. Stick your hand inside that thicket and pull out a few body hairs that invariably get stuck there. Another good place to look for bear hair is at the base of nearby trees.

You have an excellent chance of bagging this bruin your first night on stand if the wind stays in your favor. Remember, he's not expecting any trouble so wait for the bear to get to the barrel and turn broadside or quartering away before you shoot.

The third stand is ripe for the picking. The outfitter and his crew have done their job and now it is up to you to wait for the perfect shot. Wear rubber boots to your stand and do not

walk on the same trail as the bear. It may take several days for a big bear to return, but he will be in the area as long as there's plenty of food nearby.

Last Night

It's the end of the spring season, your last night in camp and you still haven't gotten your bear. The outfitter gives you three choices. He has one stand that's being hit nightly, but by half a dozen sows and yearlings. There isn't a big bear in the lot. There are however claw marks greater than 7 inches on a nearby tree that appear to be two or three weeks old.

His second bait has not yet been hit even though it is situated near the confluence of a creek and a small river. However, a very big bear was seen near the site last week when the outfitter checked the bait. The brush covering the barrel appeared to have been disturbed, but no bait was taken. Other than that, the setup was a letdown for the outfitter.

The third bait has been hit a couple of times. The last hunter to sit over the bait saw a very nervous 200-pound boar early in the evening, but elected to pass because the bear droppings left on one of the entrance/exit trails were the diameter of a Pepsi can. The bait has been stagnant the last three or four days because of high winds.

What choices. Now, if this were early spring I would choose the second stand over the first. Big boars often scout out a bait carefully before committing themselves. That the bear was seen in the vicinity is enough to hold my interest. However, since it is nearly mating season, I would choose the first bait over all three simply because of the number of sows and the big claw marks. Boars travel widely looking for sows in early summer, and there is no better bait than half a dozen female beauties. I sat on such a bait a few years back, and saw the biggest spring bear of my life—a boar that had to tip the scales at 675 pounds. His attention was riveted solely on a 150-pound sow. She came to the bait and left, taking him with her. I never had a shot.

The third bait held another record-book bruin that, as far as I know, is still padding about the Alberta wilderness. Next to an actual sighting, the best big bear sign is the diameter of his droppings. Big boars seem to leave their scat on trails as a form of territorial marker. Unless profoundly disturbed, bears will return. The nervous behavior of the 200-pound boar should tell you the big bear is still in the neighborhood.

As you can see, bowhunting trophy black bears over bait is no "gimme." To be successful, you must learn to identify preferred habitat, understand bear body language, and, above all, interpret big bear sign properly. The only way to acquire this kind of knowledge is to book with a reputable outfitter and ask a lot of questions—or run your own bait line!

The author shows off a fine Alberta black bear. Knowing what to look for made this hunt a success.

CHAPTER 31

Luring Elk Into Bow Range

By Brian Robbins

Looking through your peep sight to find the 20-yard pin your chess game is about to end.

The trophy elk you have been chasing for the past two days has just crashed through the brush and is bugling in your face a mere 15 yards away. The bull turns, exposing his rib cage, as he tests the breeze. Checkmate. The arrow finds its mark and your hunt is now a memory.

This scenario sounds easy, but the last 15 seconds of any project is a snap compared to what bowhunters sometimes go through trying to get a bull elk within bow range. Year after year many successful elk hunters fill out their archery tag after something similar to this occurs. Granted, some tags are filled by luck alone, but Lady Luck is usually cruel and more often than not it is preparation, practice and patience that allows the bowhunter to fill out an elk tag.

The sound of a bugle is a challenge to a bull elk. When the bull responds he will be looking for a fight. An archer needs to be ready to make a good shot.

Champion elk caller Chad Schearer lets loose with an elk bugle while trying to locate a bull in the nearby foothills. Schearer said one of the secrets to good elk calling is to not try to sound like a big bull. Bigger bulls will respond to calling if they think the challenger is smaller and weaker.

Chad Schearer, 1997 Pro Division Champion of the Rocky Mountain Elk Foundation World Elk Calling contest says calling is just one of the things an archer must understand in order to pull back on an elk. Schearer has a deep understanding of elk, their actions and vocalizations. It is his understanding of the elk's language that enabled Schearer to join the Knight and Hale Game Call Company's Pro Staff where he provides input on their lineup of elk calls. He spends nearly 200 days a year outdoors and when he is not hunting or guiding, he is appearing at speaking engagements to promote the products he uses, the sport of elk hunting and the outdoors.

Hunting elk is no easy task and archers need to be prepared before hitting the woods. First,

you must be a consistent shot. Elk make big targets but that is no excuse for long-range shooting or sloppy marksmanship. Schearer knows many hunters can consistently hit their mark at 50 yards but he recommends shots of 35 yards or less. Calling is also important. Since, like people, every elk has a different voice, callers need to concentrate on learning the correct rhythm. Sounding good with the correct rhythm is what every caller should strive for, but sounding bad with the correct rhythm is far better than sounding good and speaking elk gibberish.

Various forms of calling are used to locate and then draw in an elk to bow range, but calling is just one intricate piece of a much larger puzzle. Without all the pieces you are going to be disappointed. When the pieces all come together it makes a beautiful picture. Surprisingly, elk hunting and turkey hunting are very similar. A hunter must first locate the animals, set up and try to call one within bow range. There are, however, differences and variables that separate the two. The most obvious is that not too many people come walking out of the woods with an elk slung over their back.

Schearer said the most important thing to keep in mind in elk hunting is that the wind plays a crucial part in elk calling. The most important rule is to always keep the wind in your face when setting up and calling to elk. "Hunters need to constantly check the wind direction. Elk rely on their sense of smell and if an elk gets downwind of you he can easily make you out and move out of bow range. Bowhunting elk can be summed up in three words; location, location, location," Schearer explained.

Hunters attempting to locate a bull should not stand in the middle of a clearing. An elk's bugle is his call to challenge others. Good cover is a must. Keeping below the skyline of a ridge or just inside the forest edge is almost as important as checking the wind.

Once a hunter has established a good location, it's time to start making noise.

The first call should be a small grunt using 2 to 4 tones, said Shearer. If there is no immediate response turn up the volume without getting too aggressive.

"The biggest mistake people make when using a bugle call is they try to sound like a big bull by making a long call with a lot of chuckling at the end. All this will do is intimidate the

Elk are big animals living in big country. Bugling is the best way to locate bulls as they roam the foothills in search of cows.

medium and satellite bulls in your area. You want to sound equal to or lesser than any bull that is out there," said Shearer.

The whole purpose of the bugle is to issue a challenge. No elk in his right mind would answer a challenge knowing that its opponent is bigger and stronger. The bugle is the means by which elk size each other up. If a hunter sounds like a huge bull, no elk is going to take the challenge. Sounding like a young bull is just what a big bull will look for, a fight that he feels he will win.

The standard bugle call is made from a long piece of plastic tubing, adorned with camouflage cloth and has a carrying lanyard. A mouth diaphragm is used in conjunction with the tube to mimic the lovesick sound of a bull. While this is not a complicated instrument every hunter is bound to make a bad sound.

Relax, advises Schearer "Everyone's voice sounds different and cracks once in a while. During the peak of the rut a bull will sometimes seem like he is stopping in the middle of a bugle. This is their vocal cords giving out, so do not stop calling if you hit a bad note."

The whole reasoning for bugling is to get a bull to answer the challenge, thus giving away his location. It is at this point that a hunter will need to "Take the bull's temperature" as Schearer likes to call it. If the bull fires back and keeps getting closer, you know he is by himself and you stand a good chance of calling him directly to you. If the bull is really hot and gets after it with his vocalization, then you do the same.

A bull that is answering your bugle but moving away from you is with cows. You need to get him away from them by engaging in what is known as "The Annoying Game." You are to mimic every sound he makes as he makes it. If he waits 5 minutes to answer, then you do the same. If he blows twice, you blow twice. Irritate him until he comes looking for a fight, said Schearer.

Once a bull is responding to the calls it's time to set up for the shot. Experienced hunters know how to look for an advantage. The area should offer plenty of visibility yet provide ample cover. When moving to this area do not worry about making a little noise. Elk are big

Chad Schearer poses with the cape of a nice bull that responded to bugling. This bull came in looking for a fight and got more than he bargained for.

animals and won't spook at the sound of a snapping limb or rustling underbrush.

After moving to within 300 yards of the bull, find a good area to make your ambush and check the wind again, says Schearer. If it is not in your favor, move or adjust your position. Then take a second to do the few little extras that could make the difference in getting a shot or going home disappointed.

"I like to use a good quality cover scent. I spray the urine around my set up area and into the air from time to time. This scent covers your odor and reassures the bull that there is an elk in the area and he just needs to find it," said Schearer

Bow hunting for elk requires good shooting lanes in a few different directions. A pair of pruning shears will come in handy for this task. Do not worry about building a blind. Many times a good shot is ruined by brush in front of the shooter. Instead, select a tree or a pile of brush and get in front if it, much like you would while turkey hunting. Let your camouflage do its job.

With the setup complete, start calling the bull. This could take minutes or hours depending on the bull's temperature. If he is responding to the bugling, keep it up. Sometimes the bull will respond to teasing and taunting. Make him think there is another bull in the area after his cows or challenging his presence. This should be enough incentive to have him come running looking for a fight. Keep listening for his advances and his calls.

If the bull hangs up and refuses to continue forward do not panic, all hope is not lost. Just switch tactics a little. The most important thing is patience. The bull may be headed in and just stopped bugling because he is trying to sneak upwind of his latest rival.

"If you do not hear him, then he is looking for you so keep calm and keep still. If he keeps bugling out of range and you are positive he is hung up try coaxing him in with a little soft cow talk," said Schearer. "Hopefully the bull will forget about fighting and go looking for love."

Sometimes when hunting pressure is high or it is near the end of the season bulls won't respond to bugling. It is then time to go to Plan B. This plan still requires a bull, but this time a cow call is used to lure the big brute. The best call to use for this is a single-reed mouth diaphragm. A diaphragm call will give the volume needed to send a message where it will be heard. All the other rules still apply, but this time the call sounds like "Nee Yaaa." Repeat it three to four times then listen for a response.

Schearer believes most cow calls that you blow into are excellent for short-range work but do not produce the volume necessary for a locator call.

Schearer also advises not to get too aggressive with your cow calling. By sounding too aggressive with a cow call you will let a bull know something is not natural and out of place.

Bulls will sometimes even hang up when responding to a cow call. This is to be expected from time to time. Again, keep your cool and relax. Schearer has a solution.

"As you make a cow call, slowly start turning your head and call in the opposite direction, away from the bull. Then, call again in this new direction. This gives the illusion that a cow is leaving the area and may just be the ticket to make that bull stop thinking and react," he said.

Another highly effective tactic on elk is buddy calling. The caller sets up 50 yards behind the shooter in order to cut down the distance the bull must travel. This may also keep the bull's attention on the caller and not the shooter. The best thing about using the buddy system is that each person can concentrate on a designated job.

Hunting elk is challenging enough, but using a bow makes it even more difficult. Schearer's proven methods and tricks will help to call an elk into bow range. The rest is up to you.

Elk make noise as they move through the brush. Don't worry about sneaking into shooting position. Once an elk is responding to the bugle, find some cover and get ready to shoot.

CHAPTER 32

Radical Elk Hunting

By Mike Lapinski

On my knees behind a small spruce tree in the Colorado high country I nervously pulled in several deep breaths. I had good reason to be nervous. Somewhere, just out of sight, lurked half a ton of lust-crazed bull elk—and I was about to insult him.

I raised the elk bugle to my lips and let out a call that began with a low, menacing intensity and ended in a high-pitched scream. With bated breath I waited. The forest became hushed, almost foreboding. The only sounds were my ragged breathing and the wild beating of my heart. Then, it came.

A furious bugle ripped through the thin mountain air with such power and fury that I instinctively shuddered, causing the arrow to clatter from its rest. I bugled again. Within seconds, the bull bellowed back a reply.

Branches snapped and hoof beats thudded, and then a huge set of antlers appeared above the oak brush and began moving towards me. I barely had time to raise my bow before the elk's huge head appeared in a small opening 18 yards to my right.

ou can quickly locate rutting elk in the vast western mountains by hiking briskly along a high ridge and listening r bugling elk.

A rutting bull elk that hears a sudden bugle nearby will usually stomp forward to investigate the source of the calling.

I picked a spot behind the bull's shoulder and quickly drew my recurve bow. The arrow zipped forward and sliced deep into the elk's chest. The bull immediately spun and bolted back into the brush, while I slowly sank to the forest floor. My entire body trembled with a mixture of relief and excitement as I listened to the distant crashing as the bull ran off.

Half an hour later, I took up the blood trail and easily followed the huge crimson splashes. The bull had gone only 70 yards before piling up against a small tree. He was a dandy 6-point bull that I later scored at 270 Pope & Young points.

That big bull was not a fluke kill. Thanks to a new, radical elk hunting strategy which I've employ, 32 bull elk have fallen to my bow and arrow. The good news is that other archers who had been frustrated and unsuccessful for many

years, have begun harvesting big bulls regularly using the radical elk hunting strategy.

It wasn't always this way. Back in 1970 when I began elk hunting with a bow, I was totally frustrated by my inability to bring bull elk into bow range. I wasn't alone. Few elk were killed by archers in those days, and just about everyone, myself included, had an inferiority complex about their calling ability.

Back then, the accepted theory for bugling went something like this: If you could fool a bull into believing you were an elk, he'd come right in. Consequently, most bowhunters believed that the key to successful elk hunting was to perfectly simulate a bull's bugle. Hit that perfect note, and any bull would come waltzing right in.

I began to see many inconsistencies in this theory. My bugling was only average, yet I'd lured two bulls into bow range and killed them. But for every bull I called in, there were a dozen bulls that came in only part way, or not at all. My great love for the sport of bowhunting elk drove me to search for a better understanding of how bull elk acted during the rut.

Radical Elk Hunting Is Born

Actually, I discovered the radical elk hunting strategy by accident one fall while photographing bull elk in Yellowstone National Park. A particular meadow had four bull elk bugling from timbered pockets hundreds of yards apart. If bull elk did indeed respond to genuine bugling, why weren't these bulls converging on each other? As I pondered these issues, another bull came over a low ridge and passed by a thicket where one of the bulls was holed up. When the trespassing bull bugled, the resident bull went berserk! He bellowed several furious bugles in rapid succession and came stomping forward to challenge the trespassing bull, who ignored him and continued on.

I thought, "Could it be that bull elk are territorial and protective of their domain?" During the next two days, I slipped close to two bugling bulls and then "surprised" them with my sudden bugling. Each time, the bull stomped forward to investigate my calling.

I'd discovered a great way to attract bulls, but the proof of my radical elk hunting method would be if it worked during a hunting situation. A few days after I returned from Yellowstone, I hiked onto a high ridge in the Idaho backcountry and quickly located a bugling bull on a low ridge about 500 yards away. Three times, the bull responded to my bugling, but he stayed put.

I stopped bugling and quickly moved forward. The bull bugled twice as I moved in, helping me to pinpoint his position above a large patch of alder brush and young trees off the brow of the ridge. I guessed that I was within 80 yards of the bull, and I dared not advance any further. I hid behind a small bush and bugled. Immediately, the bull bugled back, and a few seconds later I heard him pushing through the alder brush.

I barely had time to nock an arrow before the bull entered a small opening 10 yards away. The bull spotted me and stopped. At that time, I was using a compound bow, so I put the 20 yard sight pin low on his chest. The arrow buried deep in the bull's chest, and the startled elk bolted and ran a short distance. I couldn't see him, but I twice heard him cough about 50 yards away. Suddenly, there was a loud crash, and I knew the elk had gone down. As I basked in the glory of this tremendous 5X5 bull lying at my feet, I thought, "Have I stumbled upon a radical new elk hunting strategy?"

It had worked once, but the test for this radical approach to bowhunting bull elk would be its consistency in bringing elk forward. I didn't have a long wait to try it again. At that time, I was hunting both Idaho, which opened a week earlier, and my home state of Montana. The next weekend, I located a bugling bull at first light on opening morning in Montana and slipped to within 60 yards in dense brush and bugled a challenge. That bull ran forward to find the adversary who would dare invade his domain! And again, I barely had time to nock an arrow before the bull was standing in front of me. This time, my arrow zipped clean through the elk, and a half hour later I located the big 5X6 bull lying in a brush thicket 80 yards down the mountainside.

How To Locate Rutting Bulls

Elk are not evenly distributed through the western mountains. Instead, they tend to congregate in isolated pockets of prime elk habitat where the best water, food and shelter are found.

A bull elk usually responds quickly to a radical challenge, so a bowhunter should have his ambush site ready and an arrow nocked.

A bowhunter doesn't have the time to seek out these scattered pockets in the endless western landscape. Many visiting bowhunters who are unaware these pockets exist spend their entire dream hunt in a fruitless search for elk, and it's not unusual to hear horror stories about three men hunting hard for seven days without seeing or hearing an elk—even in prime elk country!

The key to locating the pockets where elk live is to cover lots of ground while listening for bugling bulls. I usually climb to a high ridge and hike briskly along while bugling off both sides. That way, I can bugle into several square miles of elk habitat in one morning or evening. If no bulls are heard, I'll move to another ridge until I locate rutting bulls. It is not unusual for me to locate several bugling bulls during one of these hikes. I then examine the terrain and

The key to radical elk hunting is to move in close and exploit a rutting bull elk's tendency to be territorial and possessive of his domain when you bugle nearby.

wind direction, and plan a hunt for the bull that offers the best chance for success.

Timing Is Critical

Timing is critical when confronting a rutting bull elk. It is not unusual for a challenged bull elk to bugle out his frustrations and tear up a bunch of trees. Feeling satisfied, the bull then stomps off. For that reason, it's vital to move in quickly on a bull that responds to your bugle. Don't waste an hour bugling back and forth with a distant bull, hoping he'll leave his domain and come half a mile or more to you. If the bull bugles back twice, he's interested, and you should stop bugling and charge forward to surprise the bull with a radical challenge at close range.

Of course, you can't expect the wind to always be perfectly blowing from the elk to you as you move forward. If the wind is wrong, simply circle the bull's position until you get the wind in your favor. Don't bother sneaking

through the woods. Remember, elk are big animals and make a lot of noise, so they aren't alarmed to hear heavy footfalls nearby.

Pick The Perfect Ambush Site

An elk will come forward quickly to investigate your sudden bugle nearby, and you won't have much time to pick an ambush site. In fact, the time between my radical challenge releasing an arrow at an incoming bull is often less than a minute. For that reason, you should pick your ambush site and have an arrow nocked before you challenge that nearby bull.

The good news is that the closer you get to a bull, the less travel corridors he has to get to you. This is a big problem, and one of the major causes of failure, for the bowhunter who brings in that one bull in 20 from a long distance. There are just too many avenues for the bull to take. I've had long distance bulls come in, but pass by 80 yards away. They then caught my scent and crashed off.

You can quickly locate rutting elk in the vast western mountains by hiking briskly along a high ridge and listening for bugling elk.

After I've slipped forward as close as I dare to a rutting bull, I quickly survey the terrain and look for an obvious trail, opening or crease in dense cover that an elk would pass through. Expect an incoming elk to travel the path of least resistance, just as you do in the woods.

If there's an opening between you and the elk, don't set up your ambush at the far end because the oncoming bull may step into the opening and then look around for his adversary. If he doesn't see an elk, he may become suspicious and move off. Or the bull may walk directly at you, offering only a frontal chest shot, which should never be taken. Instead, you want to be positioned so that the bull passes by your ambush site, offering a broadside shot. I usually advance to the side of the opening nearest to the elk, and look for a small tree or bush to hide behind on the downwind side which offers about a 15 yard shot.

Proper Elk Bugling Technique

Many new elk calls have appeared on the market in recent years with outlandish claims of bringing in any bull elk like the Pied Piper. Don't fall for this hype! All you need to lure a bull into bow range is a simple elk bugle. And you don't have to create a perfect simulation of a rutting elk's bugle, either.

I use a Lohman mouth diaphram and hollow grunt tube which amplifies the sound and gives

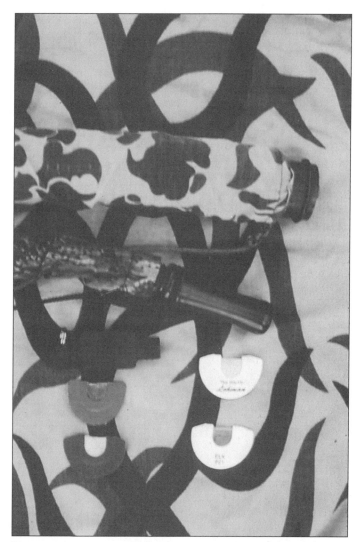

You can use a mouth diaphragm and large hollow grunt tube to simulate a bull's bugle. If you can't use a mouth diaphragm, try a reed-type elk bugle that you just blow into.

it a hollow tone. Some folks can't use a mouth diaphram because it makes them gag. In recent years several elk bugles with internal reeds, which work very well, have appeared on the market. You just blow into them to create a decent elk bugle.

The next time you locate a distant bugling bull, don't hide behind a bush, hoping you'll get lucky and hit that magic note with your call that will bring the bull in on the run. Instead, take the radical approach and move forward for a close-range challenge. You'll not only have a thrilling elk encounter, but you may also end up with a dandy bull for your trophy room.

CHAPTER 33

Calling Mid-Winter Coyotes

By Mike Roux

The air I inhaled as I crossed the frozen field felt like cockleburs inside my nose. Thankfully I had dressed for the brutal conditions presented that February morning.

What great desire would push a man into these harsh conditions? Was it heavy-beamed Midwestern bucks? That would surely do it, but on this day I had coyotes on my mind.

This wild canine has seen huge increases in both its range and population since the decline in fur prices and the elimination of the bounty system over the past decade. The number of coyotes dwindled in the 1920s when bounties and fur prices flourished. But today these animals are flourishing and often causing problems for farmers and ranchers. Some areas are now facing an overpopulation issue. Because of this, this otherwise wild creature is now becoming a crossbred pest.

Not everyone realizes that the coyote and the domestic dog have begun to interbreed. "Coy-dogs" are very common in some areas. Whether pure-bred or mixed, the coyote or "Canis latrans," needs to be hunted as the only current means of controlling their exploding populations.

Coyotes will either maintain a home range or will travel aimlessly from place to place in search of food and companionship. Some experts say it is the wandering marauders that do the most damage to livestock herds. Estimates are that, in 1994, coyotes killed almost 285,000 sheep, lambs and goats in the U.S. Those animals were valued at over $13 million.

Coyotes will eat virtually anything. And they are lazy, feeding on whatever is easiest at the time. Mice are easier than deer when the ground is dry. If the snow is too deep for mice to get out and too deep for deer to run in, then deer are easier. If sheep, or hogs, or calves are penned up, they are easy, too. These scavenger/predators will eat the pet food off your patio and then they will eat your pet.

There is a reason coyotes are called wily. What I have discovered, and what people in the western part of this animal's range have known all along is that these instinctive and opportunistic canines are a first-rate and thrilling challenge for bowhunters.

The stuff of legends. The haunting call of the coyote should be enough to stir any hunter into action. If you can mimic the call of coyote, you'll likely be able to bring these predators in close. Photo by Nan Ryan

Snow cover causes coyotes to hunt during the daylight hours, providing bowhunters excellent opportunities to call them in. Coyotes are opportunistic predators. They respond well to rabbit distress calls, believing they can find an easy meal. Photo by Nan Ryan

That's why I could not help but be excited as I made my way across the field to the hill where I would set-up and wait for daylight. At my chosen location I faced north, backed into a snow covered cedar tree and took up a position overlooking a fence row and an unplanted, 75-acre field.

Calling all coyotes

At dawn I began a calling sequence. I have a special routine for coyotes, and in January I don't usually vary the sequence very much. I begin just at daylight with about a half-minute of howling. This alerts the coyotes in the area that another dog has trespassed into their territory. This alone is often enough to bring them to bow range.

I then follow the howls with the squeals of a wounded rabbit. This call imitates the panicked cries of a bunny caught in the clutches of a predator. I squeal for a full minute, and then wait and watch for movement. A minute may sound like a short time, but if you are blowing into a rabbit squealer, it is about all you can endure. If nothing shows within a couple of minutes, I squeal some more and then wait again.

Staying in one spot for more than 10 to 15 minutes is usually not productive. In most cases if coyotes are in the area and they are going to come in, they will come in fast. Many times I have had shooting opportunities within 60 seconds of my first calling sequence. Understanding how coyotes react to calling

Calling and camouflage proved to be a deadly combination for this coyote. Author Mike Roux displays the reward of a mid-winter hunt that proves coyotes can be called well within bow range. Photo by Brian Dralle.

saves me a lot of time and gives me the chance to call from five or six different locations in one morning.

This morning, however, was a February morning which meant modifying my plan slightly. Overall I have found that calling coyotes is more difficult in February, but not at all impossible. February is the breeding season for these wild canines. I use this to my advantage as I play their territorial instincts against them. Now when I howl, I do not follow with rabbit squeals immediately.

During the breeding season a mature coyote is very aggressive towards outsiders, and a big male will often come directly to a howling intruder. His instinct is to challenge any other males and to breed any females. I have no idea if I howl like a male or a female coyote, but I do know that howling works.

If a couple of howling sequences fails to produce an angry male, I then fall-back to the rabbit squealer. Hungry coyotes of either sex, at any time of year, have good reason to investigate this call.

I had a good idea that coyotes would be active on this snowy Saturday in February. Lifting my dependable Lohman Model 281 Howler to my mouth, I produced an opening sequence of howls, hoping to grab the attention of unsuspecting coyotes and trigger an aggressive reaction from breeding-ready males. The plan worked.

Less than two minutes from my first howl, a coyote appeared in a brushy fence row about 75 yards west of me. With a prevailing westerly wind, I was in great shape. The beautiful, heavily furred coyote stood motionless and scanned the field for movement and, raising his nose, tested the wind. After a minute or two, he turned and headed toward me, using the brush in the fence row for concealment.

He was 30-yards from me when he stopped. I could see only his tail through the brown switch-grass. Having already raised my bow into shooting position, I slowly drew and anchored my single pin on the coyote's location. I was not going to take this shot but wanted to be ready when he stepped into the open.

The big male made quick lateral jump out of the fence row and trotted out into the field, 15 yards from me and my cedar tree blind. I followed him with my sight, and the split-second after he stopped, my arrow was in the air. The big canine went down rather quickly.

It is no simple task to fool these wary predators consistently, and because of the close-range characteristics of archery gear, calling seems to be the most critical aspect of the sport. However, gear choices and hunting clothes are also very important. Your deer hunting gear will likely do the job. I prefer a quiet, comfortable, fairly fast bow capable of making a close, quick shot. My bow is a Golden Eagle Ultra-Evolution and I launch well-matched carbon arrows.

When a coyote gets in close, full camouflage and the right background are extremely important. Most bow shots at coyotes come at 10 to 25-yards. For winter hunts I'll don Realtree snow camo and back up against a snow-covered cedar tree where a coyote cannot make out my outline. Coyotes are nervous animals with keen senses and you must be at the top of your archery game to put a broadhead into one. Even if you are not purposely hunting coyotes with your bow, you should always be prepared…just in case the opportunity arises.

A recent deer hunt drove the point home. The afternoon was cloudy but not too cold. Actually, for November it was really pretty nice. The peak of the white-tailed rut had passed, but bowhunting was still good. I was still hunting that evening. Slowly, quietly moving from place to place, rattling and grunting. This method allows me to not only hunt several spots but to drastically increase my odds of seeing animals. This is a good way to see lots of wildlife, not just deer.

The afternoon slowly ticked away, and at about 4 p.m., I sat on a ridge overlooking a cut cornfield. This ridge is a good staging area for deer entering the field to feed after dark. I had just completed a short sequence of grunts when movement below me caught my eye. Something was moving slowly just inside the woods, right along the field edge.

Focusing my binoculars, I could see the distinct outline of a coyote. It was not sneaking, but was moving too fast to be hunting. I quickly found my mouse squeaker and gave the dog a couple of calls, hoping to lure it up the hill toward me.

At the first squeak the coyote stopped and perked its ears, but then continued down the trail, seeming to ignore my follow-up calls. Through my binoculars I watched the coyote go out of sight.

With no deer activity on the ridge, I moved down the slope, closer to the field. The coyote, and my concern about it, had long since passed. I knew it was too early for deer to be in the field, so I set up to watch some trails leading out of the timber.

Again I saw the subtle flash of movement. This time it was up on the ridge, close to where I had been a short time earlier. And again I spotted a coyote through my binoculars. This time the wild canine was stealthily stalking up the ridge. "That's the same coyote," I thought to myself.

As I watched the hunter at work, I could see it was sneaking up on my recently abandoned position. The mouse squeaker had worked, but it was not patient enough to be there for the shot. The experienced predator had circled downwind of its prey before starting its approach.

I glanced around quickly and, not seeing any deer movement, launched a full-fledged assault on the coyote. Slowly adjusting my position, I called again. This time the coyote stopped in mid-stride, motionless, looking like a bird dog on a crouched point. Its ears were stiff and erect and its tail was low, almost between its legs. This is a typical attack posture for coyotes.

I now had a clear look at this fully mature coyote. It had a broad head, long muscular legs and a thick coat highlighted with long silver hairs. It looked like a statue, 65-yards away.

"Should I call again, or should I wait for him to move?" I wondered. I was sure that if I made any sound or movement he would see me in a split second. The predator too knew the advantage of waiting for its prey to become fearful, nervous and try to escape.

Luck was with me. At that moment a gray squirrel chased its mate around an aging oak tree, causing a racket about 15-yards to my left. The coyote reacted to the noise by barreling down the hill toward the commotion.

It hit the brakes as the squirrels reversed their course and ran back up into the safety of their den. The coyote was only a bit over 20 yards from me. It had stopped behind on old blow-down, and I could see its hips and tail but its head, shoulders and chest were behind the tangled brush. It would have to take three or four more steps to give me the shot I wanted.

Moving slowly I quietly placed the mouse squeaker in my mouth, leaving the barrel exposed between my lips. I then raised my bow, came to full draw and anchored, ready to shoot.

I took a deep breath and bit the call to produce a squeak. The coyote twitched but did not move forward. I waited, seemingly for hours, and then bit the call again. Again the canine flinched but still did not move. "Get ready for the shot," I told myself. I was sure the coyote would move from its cover at any moment.

Suddenly, as though recognizing its dilemma, the coyote bolted into the open and I released, sending a razor-sharp broadhead through its vitals. Surprised that I had won the battle of nerves, I was thrilled that the coyote had not outwitted me a second time. No, I did not get a deer that evening, but I still enjoyed one of bowhunting's greatest challenges.

The Future

CHAPTER 34

Encouraging Women & Kids

By Ron Tussel

Statistics show that hunting license sales in many states are showing a gradual decline. There is, however, hope for increasing the shooting and hunting population. The number of women and children involved in bowhunting and archery is growing. The interest paid to this group by the archery and bowhunting industries is beginning to show results.

This interest is being fueled by increased press coverage and by the fact that almost every major manufacturer and organization is welcoming, indeed embracing, these two groups of shooters. In a nutshell, it is now the "in thing" to be involved in archery and that spills over into bowhunting as well.

On the manufacturer's end, you can see almost every supply catalog now offering complete lines of products designed with women and kids in mind. From clothing and footwear, to bows, releases, tree stands, broadheads and more, bowhunting is no longer a "one size fits all" activity.

backyard target and a guiding hand begin the steps to getting kids started in archery and bowhunting. Patience ays off as does making the activity fun for youngsters. The future of bowhunting is in the hands of the next generation of hunters. What we do today will build that foundation.

Along with all the new gear, there are many new programs designed to help teach those with an interest in archery and bowhunting how to get involved. The "Becoming an Outdoors Woman" programs have been conducted across the country, signing up thousands of women to weekends of hands-on instruction. These types of programs are designed to create a friendly "don't be afraid to ask" atmosphere, where women can express their desire to learn and need not feel intimidated by their lack of knowledge. This hands-on approach has proven very effective, drawing new members to the archery community each year. To get involved in such a program, start by contacting your state's game and fish department. Local archery clubs and even individual instructors or shooters are also good places to look for information. Many will hold special events to try to answer questions, provide opportunity, and share knowledge. All of these efforts are paying off, and as the number of women in the sport increases, it gets easier to keep the momentum going.

Bringing more women into the sport, is also creating more young archers. Today's dearth of dual-parent homes often leaves mom also playing the role of father. With dads traditionally being the ones to inspire the interest in hunting and fishing, some youngsters are left out of the sports simply because they have no one to introduce them. Now, when mom returns home from her weekend event with a wealth of new knowledge and interest, we can believe that at least some of it will find its way to the children. If mom is out shooting her bow, there is a good chance that the youngsters may be inspired to join in.

The long-term results are potentially profound. Not just because of increased numbers of hunters and archers at such important places as the voting booths, but because of the dollars injected into the industry. Each new inductee is likely to spend at least some money on new gear, clothing, league or competition fees, accessories, hunting licenses or any other of a long list of commodities. More money in the industry helps make it stronger. Some of those funds are bound to be diverted to help preserve and promote the future of both archery and bowhunting.

You are holding one of the most comprehensive collections of information about bowhunting currently available. This small portion of

the book should be used as a primer. It will provide basic information for newcomers to the sport and should not be considered comprehensive. Other areas of this book will go into more detail about specific aspects of bowhunting. This is the chance for those who think they may be interested in getting started to read something that's not brimming with unfamiliar terms and overwhelming references to obscure subjects.

It is uniqueness that draws many people to bowhunting. Every person who takes a bow into the woods has different reason to do so. Almost all will make some reference to the fact that hunting with a bow puts them one-on-one with the game that they hunt. As such, the equipment follows suit. Bows are designed to fit an individual, and are set up with accessories to match. In other words, if you are a petite 5 feet, 2 inches tall, and weigh 110 pounds, you cannot be expected to successfully shoot a bow which is set up for a person who is 6 feet, 3 inches and weighs in at 220. It just won't work. It is imperative that you begin your quest for bowhunting gear with a properly fitted set of equipment. Your local pro shop is probably the first stop you should make to get started.

Selecting a Bow

The bow is, of course, the heart of your bowhunting equipment. Your body size, strength, and experience level will help determine the proper bow for you. There are bows available for almost every budget, but keep in mind that most times you do get what you pay for. A less expensive bow in your size range may prove to be much heavier and harder for you to hold than one a step or two up the price scale. The secret is to get your hands on several different bows before you plunk down your hard-earned dollars. An important first consideration is weight. Not the draw weight, as in how much strength is needed to pull the string, but actual overall weight of the bow. Most new shooters think that drawing the bow is the hard part. New shooters often find out that holding the bow at arm's length also proves to be quite a challenge. Lighter might be better for inexperienced archers.

Nearly all modern archers take to the woods with a compound bow. Not merely a "stick and a string," the compound bow uses wheels or

A recurve makes a great starter bow. The bow's light weight and ease of use makes archery easy and fun. Recurve bows are also inexpensive and provide a good foundation for shooters to build on.

Draw length is very important. Holding a yard stick at the base of the throat while extending both arms will give an accurate reading of your draw length.

cams to release some of the tension from the bow string when the bow is held at full draw. This makes it easier for the hunter to hold the bow while waiting for the perfect shot.

Traditional recurve bows can be good tools to use when getting started in archery. But making the move to hunting usually means archers switch to a compound bow.

Draw Length

Choosing a bow to match your "draw length" is also very important. Draw length is determined by the shooter's height and arm length. Most bow shops will have a bow there, which you can use to actually measure your draw length. A light weight recurve style bow that draws easily is used, and you draw back a shaft with measured increments on it. Another way

to determine your draw length is to use a yard stick. Place one end of the yard stick against your throat, and hold the other end between your hands held at arms length. The distance measured at your finger tips is the correct draw length for you. Most compound bows allow you to change the draw length simply. When you select a bow set for your draw length, stand with your feet pointing at a 45-degree angle toward a target and draw the bow. When you find your anchor point, look at the string to be sure it isn't resting against your chest. If it is, you may want to go an inch shorter on the draw length to ensure that the string does not slap your arm or clothing upon release. The anchor point is where your draw hand will come to rest every time you draw your bow. Consistent anchoring is a key to shooting a bow consistently. Some people use a knuckle to the back of the ear, some use a "kisser" button installed on the string. Whatever you find and feel comfortable with, make sure you determine an anchor point, and then practice to ensure that this point is used at every draw.

The Draw Weight

For hunting purposes, most states impose a minimum draw weight of about 45 pounds for game the size of white-tailed deer. For those just starting, you have much range time to put in before you go hunting, so starting out at a lighter draw weight is OK if you have trouble pulling back your bow. You want to start with a draw weight that is comfortable. One that you can pull back time after time will help form a good foundation for consistent shooting. Building your muscles used for drawing, holding and releasing is a big part of that foundation. Select a draw weight on your bow that will allow you to spend time on the range, shooting a couple dozen arrows without pain or discomfort. As your muscles build and develop muscle memory, you can turn up the draw weight on your compound bow. Muscle memory and consistent anchoring are two important things required when hunting. The more you practice, the less you will have to think about when game is spotted. Your instincts and body take over based upon your many hours of practice.

Fingers Or A Release?

There are basically two choices for grasping, drawing and releasing the arrow: You can use your fingers or some type of mechanical release aid. Some shooters prefer to use fingers, others prefer a release. It is a matter of personal choice. I like shooting with a release. I find that I am able to draw more weight with a release, and also my shot groups are much smaller and more consistent. Using only your fingers can allow variations in release form from shot to shot. Basically, you wrap your fingers, protected by a tab or glove, around the

Most release shooters use a shoot-through rest. The arrow rest guides the arrow while offering very little resistance. A release aid and a good arrow rest can really improve accuracy.

This is a typical shooting release. Most archers using compound bows use a release to improve accuracy. The release clips on the bow string and the weight of the pull is taken up by a strap. The lever on top is the trigger. Pulling on the trigger releases the string with very little disturbance.

string and pull it back, anchor, aim and release. The string rolls off the fingers, and this forces the arrow one way or the other, causing it to oscillate. This is normal. The rest upon which the arrow sits, is designed to help correct at least some of this oscillation. A plunger or flipper rest is most often used when shooting with fingers.

Releases are mechanical and can fail like any other mechanical device. They are most often a set of jaws, held by a strap, which wraps securely around the hand or wrist. The jaws grip the string, and when a trigger of some type is hit, the jaws open simultaneously releasing the string with very little disturbance. Oscillation is minimized. The arrow rest designed for release shooters is normally some kind of elevated prong, which allows the arrow's vanes or fletching to slide through with

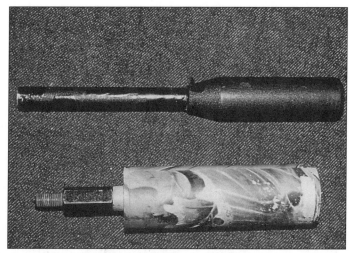

A stabilizer can reduce recoil and bow noise, and tighten an arrow group. Select a size and style consistent with your bow and strength ability.

Any quiver you choose should have a hard plastic guard covering the broadheads of your arrow. To be truly effective, broadheads must be razor sharp. If they are not covered, a slip or fall could result in a nasty cut, or worse.

little or no contact. The result is a very straight release. Beginners will likely see better results faster if they choose a mechanical release.

Accessories

The physics of a bow are such that it is designed to release its energy when the string is drawn and released. Sometimes, especially with compound bows, and even more so with shorter bows with radical cam designs, this release of energy causes tremendous recoil to the bow. This can result in excessive noise and inconsistent shooting because the bow moves prior to the arrow completely leaving the rest. A stabilizer can be added to the front of the compound to help with this. In the past, stabilizers were molded steel pegs. Today, stabilizers can be had with spring-filled pistons, hydraulic fluid and much more. The idea is to reduce recoil, absorb vibrations, and reduce noise. All of these things will improve accuracy and make you a more consistent shooter. Choose a stabilizer that is light enough not to fatigue your arm. Yet still heavy enough to perform its job(s).

Hunters have to carry arrows. Quivers can be mounted directly to the bow, worn on the hip, or be a part of a back pack system. Whichever style you choose, keep safety in mind during your purchase. Any quiver, especially one that will carry broadhead-tipped arrows, MUST have a very hard cover on the broadhead end. This will help to prevent cuts, or worse should you fall. If you decide on a bow-mounted quiver, be sure to practice with it

attached to your bow as it would be in a hunting situation. A quiver full of arrows can do interesting things to your accuracy.

I also recommend that you add a sight to your bow. Some shooters do not use sights, relying instead on instinctive shooting to get the arrow on target. A sight will improve your shooting rapidly and help you to stay consistent. There are too many sights on the market to evaluate them all, but suffice it to say that some sort of pin sight mounted on the riser of the bow can help. Think of this as the front sight on a gun. Advanced shooters often use a peep style sight fitted to the bow string. Together these two sights create a longer plane of sight across which to aim. The result is improved accuracy.

Arrows and Broadheads

Here, too, the selection is almost endless. Choices for arrow shaft material include aluminum, carbon, combinations of aluminum and carbon, graphite composites, wood and fiberglass. For the high energy of a compound bow, don't use wood. Arrows are selected based on the draw length of the shooter, draw weight of the bow, and weight of your practice tips and broadheads. Again, the pro shop will have a chart or computer program that will combine all of your data to help you select the proper shaft. Many arrow shafts are sold without feathers, fletchings or vanes. This gives you a little bit of personal input, but for the beginner I recommend plastic vanes. Vanes will fly a little faster, are quieter, and are virtually impervious to weather. Feathers appeal to the traditional shooter and perform quite well. They are much more forgiving upon release because of their ability to lay flat and then return to flight position should they come into contact with the bow or rest. Wet weather however, can render an untreated feather useless. Vanes come in different sizes, short, long, low profile, etc. and can be applied to the bow in either a straight or slightly helical position. Remember the purpose of the vane is to stabilize the arrow in flight. The smoother and straighter the flight, the more accurate the shot. This effortless flight also results in maximum delivery of energy, which when hunting, can mean a lot. Select a vane or fletching size that will work effectively with the head weight you have selected. I shoot 100-grain practice tips and broadheads, and my broadheads are of the cut-on-contact style. That means they have full-length cutting surfaces. The more surface area on a broadhead, the more area you have to catch air, or fly. A large, heavy, broadhead matched to tiny little vanes can result in very unstable flight. I use a 4-inch, low-profile vane, mounted with a slight helical or twist, to counteract the broadhead's desire to fly. The result is a very straight flight with maximum penetration and energy delivery. The last sentence should be the goal of every bowhunter.

Of course selecting broadheads is another project. I have already mentioned cut-on-contact. There are chisel point, two-blade, three-blade, four-blade, mechanical or expanding, fixed-blade resharpenable, replaceable blade etc., etc. The game you are going to hunt can help determine what head you choose. For larger animals such as elk or moose, many hunters prefer a cut-on-contact head. Those after medium-sized animals such as deer, might shoot a chisel point or mechanical head. The mechanical heads have come a long way in recent years and most available are quite adequate. The big advantage to this style of head is that it has minimal flying surface. There's not much there to throw the arrow off course. This makes the arrowhead more forgiving of slight imperfections in bow tuning or equipment match. Many shooters find that they must re-sight their bows when switching from target points to broadheads. Mechanical heads often eliminate this problem. No matter what broadhead you select, it is imperative that you sight-in and practice with that head on your arrows before heading after game animals. Also, never use broadheads for hunting which you have dulled by target shooting. Re-sharpen or replace any blades you've used for target shooting before hunting.

The Importance Of Practice

Archery in general and bowhunting in particular are learned activities. Expertise is gained through establishing a strong foundation in the basic elements of good shooting and repeating those steps as often as necessary to achieve consistent results. Those new to the sport would do well to take some lessons. Most

Youth archery events are becoming very popular. The are a great way to keep kids interested in the sport an they can be important teaching and social events as well.

Full bodied 3-D targets provide realistic shooting for young archers. They also help teach about shot placement and deer anatomy, both very important subject to the ethical bowhunter.

archery shops have indoor ranges. Local archery clubs often have members who are willing to provide instruction for a small fee. Look to these people to help you establish the basic form needed for good shooting. Then, put in a few hours at the range every week. Before long, you'll be a confident capable shot and you'll be on your way to bowhunting success.

In The Woods

As you enter the woods with your finely tuned equipment, you basically have two choices. You can hunt game from the ground, via stalking or sitting in a ground blind, or you can take to the trees. For many, bowhunting from trees offers the chance to get above the animal's usual line of sight, and sometimes even offers the advantage of removing your natural human odor from the deer's sensitive nose. Modern, portable tree stands offer the chance to be mobile, following the game as their patterns might dictate. They are also safe, stable platforms from which to hunt. Portable tree stands come in two basic formats, either a two-part climbing stand or a more permanent, hanging style. Climbing stands can be set up quickly, and move you up the tree via a stand up-sit down motion. With a hanging style stand you'll need to climb the tree, haul the stand up and put it in place. That usually requires the use of tree steps of some type (these are really big screws you crank into the tree), climbing sticks, or a ladder to gain access to the semi-permanent stand. There are advantages and disadvantages to both types of stands. I use climbing stands especially early in the season, and then later in the rut, to be able to quickly pull stakes from one location and set up in another where the deer are moving. One hundred yards can make a big difference to a bowhunter!

Climbing stands can be cumbersome to carry, especially for a smaller-framed hunter, and some of them are a bit noisy while climbing. The hanging stands, once in place, are faster to get into, and can be quieter. Many hunters often have at least one or two of each style to provide the best opportunity to stay on top of the deer action.

Safety First

No matter what style of tree stand you choose to hunt from, safety must always be your first concern. Any time your feet leave the ground, the chance for injury increases. Statistically, tree stand accidents account for more archery hunting accidents than anything else does. A safety belt must be worn anytime you are off the ground. As inconvenient as it can be, I recommend that you complete the climbing portion of the ascent and descent with safety belt attached as well. Most tree stand accidents occur during what is known as the transition stage. This is the time when we leave our ladder, sticks or steps, and climb over onto the stand. With your belt already attached, this lessens your chances of hitting the ground.

A word of caution here, do not assume that because you are wearing a safety belt that you cannot be hurt by a fall. Quite the opposite, an improperly worn belt may keep you from hit-

A full-body harness is recommended over a single strap or rope for tree stand safety. Should you fall from a tree stand, the harness will distribute your weight and prevent suffocation. In all cases, it is much better to play it safe. A fall from 15 feet in the air could be fatal.

ting the earth, but it may cause you to suffocate as it crushes your chest while you dangle from your tree. After much study of statistics and talking with fellow bowhunters who survived tree stand mishaps, I have switched from wearing a simple belt to a full harness. A harness that wraps around the upper thighs, waist and over the shoulders is best. A large "D" is attached to the center of the harness in the upper center of your back. This attaches to a strap which holds you to the tree. Should a fall occur, the harness distributes your body weight evenly, and does not cinch. Another added attraction is that you can attach a strap to your tree when you put your stand up. As you climb

your ladder, you can connect your harness to this strap before making the transition to the stand platform. Reversing the process when you descend reduces your chances of a fall during transition or while in the stand. Tree stand safety cannot be over emphasized. Don't think, "It won't happen to me." No one is immune, and the consequences are permanent.

Where to Hang it

Once you have your stand and safety harness, the question becomes where to hang the stand to increase your chances for a successful hunt. There is no substitute for hands-on scouting for bowhunting. Misplacing a stand by 20 yards can mean the difference between watching deer pass by and filling a tag. Since most archery seasons begin early in autumn, deer are usually still going about their daily routines, undisturbed by the rut and hunting pressures.

Keying in on food sources is a good bet. Apple orchards are my favorite hunting spots this time of year, followed by oak ridges or flats. Once you find areas with food, you'll want to look for fresh droppings or marks in the leaves to indicate that deer are feeding in the area. Among the acorn ridges, look hard for bits and pieces of acorns that escape the deer's crunching. Fresh sign indicates current use and you need to look for a place to set up. I always try to figure out which way the deer are coming to and going from these feeding areas as they enter and leave their daytime bedding areas. I prefer to hunt the trails in between these areas, rather than chance spooking deer directly from a feeding area. Set up your stand downwind from the trail or area you hope the deer will pass by. Getting the stand 15 to 18 feet off the ground should be plenty high enough to get above the deer's normal line of sight. Anything higher can result in arrow trajectory variances. In other words, you might not hit where you aim because of the steeper angle of the shot.

As autumn progresses and the rut begins, bowhunting takes on a whole new flavor. This is the time when you can break out the scents and rattling antlers, dig mock scrapes and try your best at calling in a mature white-tailed buck. Hunting during the rut is a subject of its own and will be covered in more detail elsewhere in this book.

Find a mentor

Buying a bow. Learning to shoot. Hanging a tree stand. All are just parts of the bowhunting game. You can delve as deeply as you want to into this sport, but you can speed the learning process by finding a mentor.

Experienced hunters can help newcomers in many ways. While it's possible to learn all about field dressing a deer by reading it in a book, there is no substitute for having an experienced hunter standing over your shoulder telling you where and where not to cut. Field dressing a deer can mean the difference between great-tasting venison and a horrible culinary experience. It's not something you want to do incorrectly.

The same is true for care of a game animal you may want to preserve as a trophy. There are books about the subject and a dedicated hunter will read them, but nothing helps like the voice of experience.

Looking for a mentor is a lot like searching for a friend. You've got to find someone who fits your style. Join an archery club. Attend the functions. Volunteer your time and introduce yourself to people. Sooner or later you'll strike up a conversation with someone who will help you become a better bowhunter. Who knows, it may be one of the best relationships of your life.

Pass it on

Whether you begin bowhunting for the solitude, personal challenge, long seasons, chances at big trophy antlers, or gourmet meat for the table, you must begin the quest with an open mind. Count each outing and experience as a chance to learn. Hold on to and appreciate your personal convictions. As you learn and enjoy the great challenge we call bowhunting, take on the responsibility to share your newfound knowledge, and recruit yet another member into the ranks.

Practice really pays off. There is no magic formula to bowhunting success. Anyone who takes the time to learn the basics and practice can achieve success.

CHAPTER 35

High-Tech Hunting

By Bob Humphrey

The term bowhunter encompasses a broad spectrum of individuals that range from self-bow shooting traditional archers to compound shooters equipped to push the limits of arrow speed. In between are a whole lot of us who are merely willing to take advantage of whatever technology is available to make us, not necessarily better, but more efficient hunters. While I have no qualms with traditionalists, my attitude is "If the technology's there, why not use it?" Bowhunters have chosen to hunt with archery tackle rather than firearms, so any argument that technological innovations in archery gear offer an unfair advantage is moot.

If you're among those of us who welcome innovations to the sport, there's a lot to be excited about lately. In recent years the progress in archery-related technology has been nothing short of revolutionary. Much of this is owed to advancements in electronics and computers, the latter are becoming more and more an integral part of our daily lives. If you haven't already done so, it's time to come out of your cave and take a look at what's out there.

Rangefinders

Among the plethora of new devices, some are quite novel, while others are merely improvements on existing tools. One example of the improvements is with rangefinders. I've always had trouble judging distances, so a dial-in coincidence rangefinder was, until recently, an essential item in my archery pack. This item uses mirrors and beam-splitters to produce a pair of identical images. Adjusting a dial merges the images into one. Then, a corresponding scale in the viewfinder shows the approximate distance to target. These have been around for some time.

More recently, several companies have come out with laser rangefinders. They work by emitting infrared pulses, which bounce off a selected target and back to a receiver. The rangefinder then converts this electronically to a digital readout of the distance between the receiver and the target. The advantages are obvious. There's no more guessing ranges, which can lead to misses or poor shots. Also, you get an instant, more accurate reading than with the old dial type.

While there are models that will calculate range up to 800 yards, bowhunters may want to choose from one of the less expensive models, with an effective range of 5 to 70 yards. Some models allow you to switch the readout from feet to meters, and have different settings for ranging in inclement weather (rain, fog, snow), or in dense, brushy cover. This sounds like a bulky piece of equipment, right? Somewhat surprisingly, they are roughly the same size, and lighter in weight than most binoculars. Incidentally, laser rangefinder binoculars are also available.

Trail Timers

High-tech scouting opportunities have never been better. Thanks to the magic of computers, motion sensors and fully automatic cameras bowhunters can now find exactly what time of day or night animals are using a trail.

Some of the newest gadgets in this arena will snap a photo of anything that passes in front of the camera. Others will simply record the time that something wandered through. The photographic models are more expensive, but they clearly provide more information.

There may be bigger names on the market, but one of the best units available is Buckshot 35A made by Foresite. This infrared game scouting camera is completely automatic and can even be programmed using most home computers. Best of all, the camera can be removed from the unit and used when you're not scouting.

The Buckshot 35A is one of the best infrared game scouting cameras on the market. Using such a camera can tell hunters much about what's happening in their hunting area.

By placing a camera unit along the trail, hunters can get a look at deer in their hunting area and determine the best times to be on the stand. This is a big help, especially if the trail timer shows deer continually moving through the area at times other than legal shooting hours.

Night-Vision Gear

Another relatively recent technological innovation that can be used as a hunting aid is night-vision optics. They work by electronically amplifying photons of light. Obviously, they should not be used under actual hunting conditions (except under specific conditions where legal). They can, however, be of considerable benefit to the bowhunter in other ways, one of which is scouting.

My pre-season scouting usually begins by driving around at dawn and dusk trying to locate concentrations of deer. Once located, I can size up the year's crop. However, many of the deer, particularly the big bucks, may not be coming out in the open until after dark. One way to overcome this is with a spotlight. But the deer in my area tend to be skittish. Stop-

ping and lighting them usually sends them fleeing back into the woods before I get a good look. Night-vision optics afford me an opportunity to look over undisturbed deer after dark.

Night-vision optics can also enhance your ability to travel in darkness, for instance, walking to and from stands. While I'm a bit skeptical, some folks will tell you flashlights spook game. With night-vision optics, you won't need lights. They can also be used to look around before leaving your stand at night, and thus avoid spooking nearby game that might otherwise not be seen.

GPS

By now most hunters are at least familiar with it; but for those who aren't, GPS stands for Global Positioning System. Simply stated, GPS units receive radio signals from several of two dozen satellites that orbit the earth approximately every 12 hours. These hand-held units then translate the signals into a reasonably precise geographic position on the earth.

This space age technology is actually an enhanced version of the old LORAN-C system, which transmitted radio signals from stationary towers located in coastal areas. Unlike LORAN-C, which has limited capabilities and range of coverage, GPS works anywhere in the world, 24 hours a day and under virtually any weather conditions.

Understanding how it works is less important than knowing how it can work for you. First, and perhaps foremost, with a GPS unit,

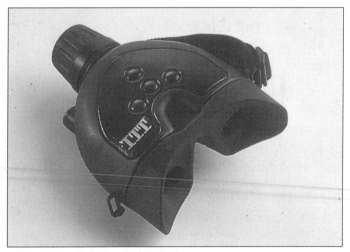

Night-vision gear, like this unit made by ITT Night Vision, can assist bowhunters with scouting and traveling to and from stand sites in the dark. Night-vision gear should never be used to aid in actual hunting situations.

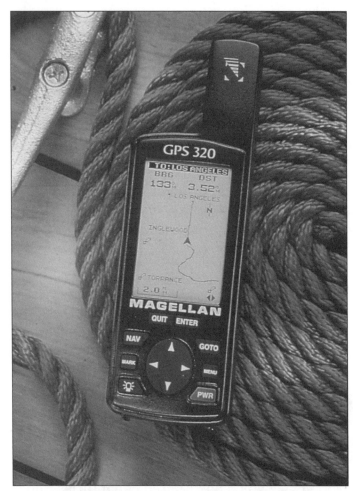

The hand-held GPS unit lets hunters record favorite hunting locations and can provide directions to and from the truck or cabin. These units are becoming more and more common. They can now be used with electronic maps to create even more accurate charts.

Then, when you want to leave, simply follow that route back out. You can also plot waypoints along a route.

GPS is a great tool for scouting too. You can save the positions of potential stand sites, buck sign, or deer sightings. Later, by using the GO TO function and calling up that location, your GPS will lead you right back to it. This function is also valuable if you have to leave a downed animal in the woods and go for help. While this might not be a problem hunting small woodlots, it can be a serious consideration for something like elk hunting in remote wilderness areas. In either case, the woods look a lot different after dark. A GPS will show you the quickest, most direct route in and back out.

E-Maps

Topographical maps aren't new or high tech, but what's been done with them is. Several companies now offer U.S.G.S. topo maps on CD-ROM. You can buy a CD or set of disks that cover an entire state for just a fraction of what it would cost to buy every map. The CDs take up considerably less space and are a lot easier to handle too. Simply insert a CD into your computer's CD-ROM drive, and with a couple clicks of your mouse button you can view any quadrangle of the state. Then, you can print out a map, or portion of a map. Any decent color printer will render a product that is virtually indistinguishable from a real topo map, unless of course you take advantage of the program's customizing features, which allow you to zoom in or out to change the scale, and add notes, markers, or boundaries.

Topo maps are a great tool for pre-scouting an area. Locally, I do a lot of driving the roads looking for deer. Once I've sighted a nice buck, I begin to learn as much as I can about the area, and this usually starts with maps. In the past, I would have to pull out a map index, determine which quadrangle I was interested in, then order it from the U.S. Geological Survey. In a couple of weeks, I might have my map. Now, I can be viewing an "E-map" in minutes. Studying the maps can reveal important clues to things like topographical funnels and pinch points, which concentrate deer movement.

These map programs also give me an edge when traveling out of state. Many hunters are hesitant to travel to new areas because they

a map and a compass, it is virtually impossible to get lost. The GPS unit will give you coordinates that show exactly where you are on the map. If you then enter a destination, the GPS will show you how to get there by displaying a compass heading.

In many cases you may not even need a map or a compass. Let me give you one example. You drive to a remote area and park on the side of the road. Using your GPS, you log your vehicle's location as a "waypoint." Then you can head into the woods and wander around all day long. When you're ready to leave, use the "GO TO" function to call up your vehicle's location. Most GPS units offer several display options for this function. One shows your direction of travel relative to your intended destination, literally pointing the way.

The GPS can also be used to plot a route. For instance, you can plot the route you traveled on your way in to a particular stand.

don't have the time to do any advance scouting. They are resigned to stick around home or hire a guide. With a full set of topo maps available at your fingertips, you can pick an area and study it, or study several areas and pick one.

I've done this several times. On one occasion I was traveling out of state with only three days to hunt a new area that I was totally unfamiliar with. I used these maps to choose my destination—a narrow bench along a steeply sloping ridge. I presumed this area would be the path of least resistance for deer traveling through the area. With a couple hours of scouting on the ground I found a suitable stand location and at 9:30 the next morning I shot a nice 10-point buck.

E-map programs are indeed handy, but imagine if you could interface them with GPS. At least one program, MAPTECH'S Terrain Navigator, allows you to do just that. You can plot intended destinations on your E-maps, download them into your hand-held GPS, and guide yourself directly to them. It also works in reverse. When scouting an area on foot, save the locations of scrapes and rubs in your GPS. Later, download them into the E-map program. Then, by viewing locations of buck sign overlaid on a topo map, you will begin to see patterns.

By saving these customized maps you will be developing a valuable data base. Deer tend to follow the same patterns year after year. Every year you'll find rubs and scrapes at new random locations throughout your area. But you'll also find some places where they show up every year. Those are the places to hunt. Sure, you can keep track of all this stuff in your head, or on paper, but it's much easier and more efficient to do it electronically. The potential for other uses is limited only by your own creativity.

Indoor Ranges

Another innovation born of the marriage between computers and electronics are the indoor video ranges. Video images of animals are projected onto a screen in an indoor shooting range. In the case of archery ranges, the shooter actually fires a blunt-tipped arrow at the image. Sensors in the screen then record the location of the hit in relation to the projected image of the target, and transmit this to a computer, which calculates your score. (Firearm ranges use a laser pulse rather than a projectile to do the same thing).

The advantage here is that it offers you a chance to practice real-life shooting situations year-round. Shooting at standard targets is a good way to work on your shooting form and technique, and shooting 3-D targets helps in attaining consistent arrow placement on animals. But neither is really adequate to prepare you for actual field conditions with live animals. Electronic video ranges are as close as you can get without actually being there. The animals (or at least their images) are moving, and you have a limited time to make a clean shot. Some ranges even have hang-on tree stands you can step onto to shoot from.

These are some of the more significant tools that technology has provided bowhunters with recently. Given the rapid pace of technological evolution, there is little doubt many of these products will be improved upon or replaced in the near future and more, similar innovations will appear. While they can aid us in being more effective hunters, success still takes the right combination of woodsmanship, marksmanship, and good fortune.

Archery Manufacturers and Resources

Company Name	Mailing Address	City	State	Zip	Phone	Fax	Toll-free
Alabama							
Guns & Gear	5845 Carmichael Rd.	Montgomery,	AL	36117	334-272-9530	334-279-7148-Fax	
Summit Specialties, Inc.	PO Box 786	Decatur,	AL	35602	205-353-0634	205-353-9818-Fax	
Simmons System, Inc.	747 N Kysline Dr.	Jasper	AL	35503	205-387-7174	205-221-0866-Fax	
McPherson Archery	PO Box 327	Brewton,	AL	36426	334-867-8980	334-867-9005-Fax	
Highlander Archery Products, Inc.	PO Box 19004	Huntsville,	AL	35804	205-539-4510	205-539-9737-Fax	800-758-2346
Jerry Hill Longbow Company	515 McGowan Rd.	Wilsonville,	AL	35186	205-669-6134	205-669-0270-Fax	
Cougar Claw by T.G.M., Inc.	9559 Hickory St. South	Foley,	AL	36535	334-943-1904	334-943-1999-Fax	
Buckmaster, LTD	PO Box 244022	Montgomery,	AL	36124	334-215-3337	334-215-3535-Fax	
Arkansas							
Australian Stockman Outfitters	PO Box 351	Dermott,	AR	71638	810-538-5896	870-538-3549-Fax	
Morrell Mfg., Inc.	1721 Hwy 71 North	Alma,	AR	72921	501-632-5929	501-632-3090-Fax	800-582-7438
Knight & Hale	PO Box 1587	Ft. Smith,	AR	72901	501-782-8971	501-782-2328-Fax	

Company Name	Mailing Address	City	State	Zip	Phone	Fax	Toll-free
Gibbs Archery Gear	7781 Hwy 167 South	Sheridan,	AR	72150	870-942-4181	870-942-8798-Fax	
Arizona							
Arizona Archery Enterprises	PO Box 25387	Prescott Valley,	AZ	86312	520-772-9887	520-772-6287-Fax	
Arizona Rim Country Products, Inc.	6401 W Chandler Blvd., #A	Chandler,	AZ	85226	602-961-7995	602-961-7996-Fax	800-635-6899
Precision Shooting Equipment	PO Box 5487	Tucson,	AZ	85703	520-884-9065	520-884-1479-Fax	800-727-7789
Mar-Den, Inc.	PO Box 1037	Wilcox,	AZ	85644	520-384-3176	520-384-4891-Fax	888-620-9888
The U.S. Archer	7315 N San Anna	Tucson,	AZ	85704	520-742-5846	520-742-0027-Fax	800-742-1235
Gateway Feather Mfg.	1015 Lorenza Pkwy.	Douglas	AZ	85607	520-805-0863		
Cavalier Equipment Company	PO Box 753	Gilbert,	AZ	85233	602-497-2977	602-497-6753-Fax	
Bowman Equipment, Inc.	4838 N. 63rd Lane	Phoenix,	AZ	85033	602-848-6365	602-848-3572-Fax	
California							
NFAA	31407 Outer I-10	Redlands,	CA	92373	909-794-2133	909-794-8512-Fax	
Carbon Tech, LLC	4751 Pell, Suite #3	Sacramento,	CA	95838	916-641-8088	916-641-8087-Fax	
StormKloth Thermal Fabric Products	1831 Tapo St., Unite "B"	Simi Valley,	CA	93063	800-755-6944	805-583-0754-Fax	
Sagittarius, Inc.	9030 Carroll Way, Suite 5	San Diego,	CA	92121	619-566-6290	619-566-0501-Fax	
Rancho Safari	PO Box 691	Ramona,	CA	92065	619-789-2094	619-789-1506-Fax	
Leven Industries	11100-554 Sepulveda Blvd	Mission Hills,	CA	91345	818-700-2899	818-700-2897-Fax	
Pam Archery	2852 A Walnut	Tustin,	CA	92680	714-838-8566	714-838-0020-Fax	

Company Name	Mailing Address	City	State	Zip	Phone	Fax	Toll-free
BBC Mfg.	PO Box 3565	S. El Monte,	CA	91733	626-443-5160	626-443-3933-Fax	
Fieldline	1919 Vineburn Ave	Los Angeles,	CA	90032	323-226-0830	323-226-0831-Fax	800-438-3353
Jim Fletcher Archery Aids, Inc.	PO Box 218	Bodfish,	CA	93205	760-379-2589	760-379-5745-Fax	
Frontier Archery Co., Inc. *	9777 Business Park Dr.	Sacramento,	CA	95827	916-362-1332	916-362-2307-Fax	800-451-8307
Brookwood/BBC MFG.	1414 Samta Amota Ave.	S. El Monte,	CA	91733	626-443-5160	626-443-3933-Fax	
Bow & Arrow Hunting Magazine	265 S Anita Drive, Suite 120	Orange,	CA	92868	714-939-9991	714-939-9909-Fax	
Petersen's Bowhunting	6420 Wilshire Blvd.	Los Angeles,	CA	90069	213-782-2222	213-782-2867-Fax	

Colorado

Company Name	Mailing Address	City	State	Zip	Phone	Fax	Toll-free
Golden-Key Futura, Inc.	14090-6100 Rd.	Montrose,	CO	81401	970-249-6700	970-249-4108-Fax	800-448-7378
Bighorn Bowhunting Company	2709 W Eisenhower Blvd.	Loveland,	CO	80537	970-962-9306	970-962-9316-Fax	
Gordon Composites, Inc.	2350 Air Park Way	Montrose,	CO	81401	970-240-4460	970-240-2853-Fax	
Zebra Publishing Company	1475 Casson Court	Colorado Springs,CO		80919	719-266-6336	719-266-6330-Fax	888-373-6080
W.R.I./Vista	PO Box 70	Poncha Springs, CO		81242	719-539-1295	719-539-1293-Fax	800-525-1181
Rocky Mt Bowstrings, Inc.	PO Box 504	Meeker,	CO	81641	303-878-4300	303-878-4064-Fax	
Dart International Inc.	1390 S. Potomac St, Suite 100	Aurora,	CO	80012	303-745-1600	303-745-1666-Fax	800-745-7501
Elk Mountain Archery of Colorado, Ltd	Box 803	Aspen,	CO	81612	970-925-9342	970-925-2258-Fax	
Allen Company, Inc.	PO Box 445	Broomfield,	CO	80038	303-469-1857	303-466-7437-Fax	800-876-8600

Company Name	Mailing Address	City	State	Zip	Phone	Fax	Toll-free
Connecticut							
Power Target Inc.	65 Eastern Steel Rd.	Milford,	CT	06460	203-876-9530	203-876-9532-Fax	
Wasp Archery Products, Inc.	PO Box 303	Plymouth,	CT	06782	860-283-0246	860-283-6659-Fax	
BCY, Inc.	PO Box 466	South Lyme,	CT	06376	860-434-3126	860-434-0492-Fax	
Brownell & Co., Inc.	PO Box 362	Moodus,	CT	06469	860-873-8625	860-873-1944-Fax	800-222-4007
Florida							
Bow Maniac Stabilizers	13146 157th Ct N.	Jupiter,	FL	33478	561-747-1378		
Century International Arms Corp.	1161 Holland Dr.	Boca Raton,	FL	33487	407-998-3200	407-998-3210-Fax	800-998-4867
Bear Archery	4600 SW 41st Blvd.	Gainesville,	FL	32608	352-376-2327	352-376-6115-Fax	800-874-2327 /4603
Buckskin Industries	PO Box 512143	Punta Gorda,	FL	33951	941-639-8831	941-639-9671-Fax	800-985-5773
L.W. Looney & Son, Inc.	5795 John Givens Rd.	Crestview,	FL	32536	904-682-0293	904-689-1595-Fax	
R & R Enterprises	10003 Raymar St.	Pensacola,	FL	32534	904-857-0092	904-857-1863-Fax	800-683-1819 Pin #0386
Warren & Sweat Mfg. Co., Inc	Box 350440	Grand Island,	FL	32735	352-669-3166	352-669-7272-Fax	
NC Manufacturing, Inc.	153 Henderson Dr.	Crestview,	FL	32539	904-682-8033	904-682-3543-Fax	800-646-8933
Barnett International, Inc.	PO Box 934	Odessa,	FL	33556	813-920-2241	813-920-5400-Fax	800-237-4507
Ultra Fine Line Co.	500 S. Green Dolphin Dr.	Cape Haze,	FL	33946	941-475-8805		
Golden Eagle/Satellite Archery	1733 Gunn Highway	Odessa,	FL	33556	813-920-5407	813-920-0726-Fax	
Ultra Press	710 Amy St.	Mt. Dora,	FL	32757	352-735-1188	352-735-9644-Fax	

Georgia

Company Name	Mailing Address	City	State	Zip	Phone	Fax	Toll-free
Bull'seye Sights	1320 Pinyon Place, NE	Lawrenceville,	GA	30043	770-822-6868	770-682-9307-Fax	800-497-3755
Archery Partners, LLP	PO Box 399	Kennesaw,	GA	30144	770-795-0232	770-795-0953-Fax	
Realtree Products, Inc.	PO Box 9638	Columbus,	GA	31907	706-569-9101	706-569-0042-Fax	800-992-9968
Muzzy Products Corp	110 Beasley Rd.	Cartersville,	GA	30120	770-387-9300	770-386-1777-Fax	800-222-7769
Hesco, Inc..	2139 Greenville Rd.	LaGrange,	GA	30241	706-884-7967	706-882-4683-Fax	
Tink's by Wellington	PO Box 244	Madison,	GA	30650	706-342-4915	706-342-7830-Fax	800-624-5988
Sullivan Industries, Inc.	1472 Camp Creek Rd.	Lakemont,	GA	30552	706-782-5863	706-782-1055-Fax	

Iowa

Company Name	Mailing Address	City	State	Zip	Phone	Fax	Toll-free
Delta Industries	117 E. Kenwood St.	Reinbeck,	IA	50669	319-345-6476	319-345-2125-Fax	
Specialty Archery Products	10510 265th, PO Box 889	Clear Lake,	IA	50428	515-424-5762	515-423-2022-Fax	
Southern Archery	PO Box 1030	Spencer,	IA	51301	712-262-7213	712-262-8149-Fax	800-252-7769
North American Outdoors, Inc	603 Redbud Ridge	Mt. Pleasant,	IA	52641	319-385-3875	319-385-2855-Fax	
Waterloo Archery, Inc.	PO Box 171	Waterloo,	IA	50704	319-232-1842	319-232-6014-Fax	
Resco Inc.	PO Box 167	Everly,	IA	51338	712-834-2333	712-834-2393-Fax	
3-J Inc.	PO Box 32	Fostoria,	IA	51340	712-332-5072	712-332-5072-Fax	
Hunter's Specialtiies, Inc	PO Box 10044	Cedar Rapids,	IA	52402	319-395-0321	319-395-0326-Fax	

Idaho

Company Name	Mailing Address	City	State	Zip	Phone	Fax	Toll-free
Stacey Archery Sales, Inc.	6866 Jennifer	Idaho Falls	ID	83401	208-523-7278	208-523-7278-Fax	
Carter Enterprises	PO Box 19	St. Anthony,	ID	83445	208-624-3467	208-624-7515-Fax	

Company Name	Mailing Address	City	State	Zip	Phone	Fax	Toll-free
Scout Mountain Equipment, Inc.	1553 E. Center St, Suite D	Pocatello,	ID	83201	208-237-3315	208-238-0073-Fax	
Timberline Archery Products	PO Box 333	Lewistown,	ID	83501	208-746-2708	208-746-6997-Fax	
Saxon Archery Manufacturing	PO Box 587	Potlatch,	ID	83855	208-875-0408	208-875-0605-Fax	

Illinois

Company Name	Mailing Address	City	State	Zip	Phone	Fax	Toll-free
Pine Ridge Archery	PO Box 310	Wauconda,	IL	60084	847-526-2349	847-526-1604-Fax	
Konco Industries, Inc.	6135 W 26th St	Cicero,	IL	60804	708-652-1555	708-652-1558-Fax	
Ultra Products, Ltd	Rt 2, Box 100	Fairfield,	IL	62837	618-842-5796	618-842-5769-Fax	800-223-6858
New Archery Products	7500 Industrial Dr.	Forest Park,	IL	60130	708-488-2500	888-323-5414-Fax	800-323-1279
C.S. Gibbs Corp.	592 Quality Lane	South Beloit,	IL	61080	815-624-4130	815-624-1134-Fax	
Spence's Targets, Inc.	3056 Lincoln Hwy.	Lynwood,	IL	60411	708-758-9144	708-758-9277-Fax	800-743-4650
Merit Screw Machine Products	2910 So 17th Ave.	Broadview,	IL	60153	708-344-9170	708-344-9397-Fax	
The Old Master Crafters, Inc.	130 LeBaron St.	Waukegan,	IL	60085	847-623-2660	847-623-6948-Fax	
Foxzy Products Corp.	3240 S. Central Ave.	Cicero,	IL	60650	708-780-3927	708-780-3928	888-338-8991
Prototech Industries, Inc.	5155 Portage Lane	Gurnee,	IL	60031	847-623-2268	847-623-2096-Fax	800-523-3109
Roberts Swiss, Inc.	2135 S Frontage Rd.	DesPlaines,	IL	60018	708-298-4820	08-298-9410-Fax	
Archer's Choice	27514 N Forrest Garden	Wauconda,	IL	60084	847-526-4827	847-526-4858-Fax	
Trio Swiss Secondary, Inc.	281 E Beinoris Dr.	Wood Dale,	IL	60191	708-766-5860	708-766-5875-Fax	
Smart Sight	431 Huey St	Huey,	IL	62252	618-594-4721	618-594-4721-Fax	

Company Name	Mailing Address	City	State	Zip	Phone	Fax	Toll-free
Indiana							
American Whitetail	Rt 1 Box 244 J	Ferdinand,	IN	47538	812-937-7185	812-937-4157-Fax	888-233-1976
True Flight Arrow Company, Inc.	PO Box 746	Monticello,	IN	47860	219-583-5131	800-348-2224-Fax	800-348-2224
Indian Industries, Inc.	817 Maxwell Ave.	Evansville,	IN	47711	812-467-1200	812-467-1394-Fax	
HanDee Co.	4800 N. Happe Rd.	Evansville	IN	47720	812-963-6438	812-963-8076-Fax	
True Flight Arrow Company, Inc.	PO Box 746	Monticello,	IN	47860	219-583-5131	800-348-2224-Fax	800-348-2224
CDM, Inc.	PO Box 129	Geneva,	IN	46740	219-368-7728	219-368-7540-Fax	800-827-7128
Kansas							
Key Industries, Inc.	400 Marble Rd, Box 389	Ft. Scott,	KS	66701	316-223-200	316-223-5822-Fax	
Cover Up Products, Inc.	Rt 1, Box 66	Hill City,	KS	67642	785-421-5503	785-674-2730-Fax	800-832-5505
Bushnell Sports Optics	9200 Cody	Overland Park	KS	66214	913-752-3400	913-752-3580-Fax	800-423-3537
BPE, Inc.	890 Rd 160	Emporia,	KS	66801	316-343-3783	316-343-9151-Fax	
Precision Designed Products	Rt #4, Box 214 C	Independence,	KS	67301	316-331-0333	316-331-0333-Fax	
Magnus Archery Company	PO Box 1877	Great Bend,	KS	67530	316-793-9222	316-793-9141-Fax	800-720-5341
Zephyr Mfg., Inc.	PO Box 42	Sabetha,	KS	66534	785-284-3557	785-284-3771-Fax	
Kentucky							
Third Hand Inc.	77 W Southgate Ave.	Ft Thomas,	KY	41075	606-441-1222		
Coffey Marketing	1678 Gilead Church Rd.	Glendale,	KY	42740	502-369-7323	502-369-6244-Fax	

Company Name	Mailing Address	City	State	Zip	Phone	Fax	Toll-free
Shelter-Pro, LLC	PO Box 190	Whitley City,	KY	42653	606-376-2004	606-376-4314-Fax	
Pape's Archery, Inc.	PO Box 19889	Louisville,	KY	40229	502-955-8118	502-955-7863-Fax	800-727-3462
"AIM" Archery International Marketing	244 Beechwood	Berea,	KY	40403	606-986-4551	606-986-4551-Fax	
Jackie's Deer Lures	Rt 1, Box 306-B	Tollesboro,	KY	41189	606-798-2256	606-798-6505-Fax	
X-Ring Archery Products	700 B South Kneeneland Dr.	Richmond,	KY	40475	606-623-3660	606-625-0935-Fax	
Pape's Archery, Inc.	PO Box 19889	Louisville,	KY	40229	502-955-8118	502-955-7863-Fax	800-727-3462

Louisiana

Company Name	Mailing Address	City	State	Zip	Phone	Fax	Toll-free
Foresite	34624 Hwy 16	Denham Springs, LA		70706	225-665-7578	225-665-0405-Fax	800-284-9005
Cajun Archery, Inc.	2408 Darnell Rd.	New Iberia,	LA	70560	318-365-6653	318-365-0316-Fax	800-551-3076
Savage Systems, Inc.	110 North Front St.	Oak Grove,	LA	71263	318-428-7733	318-428-7030-Fax	800-545-4868
API Outdoors Inc.	PO Box 1432	Tallulah,	LA	71282	318-574-4903	318-574-4428-Fax	800-228-4846

Massachusetts

Company Name	Mailing Address	City	State	Zip	Phone	Fax	Toll-free
Northeast Products	PO Box 1648	Lawrence	MA	01842	978-683-5434	978-686-4753-Fax	800-262-7328
Rogers Foam Corporation	20 Vernon St.	Somerville,	MA	02145	617-623-3010	617-629-2585-Fax	
Custom Bow Equipment	38 Hickory Dr.	Dudley,	MA	01571	508-949-3500	508-949-1368-Fax	800-949-4911

Maryland

Company Name	Mailing Address	City	State	Zip	Phone	Fax	Toll-free
Buck Wear	427-B Eastern Blvd.	Baltimore,	MD	21221	410-687-3337	410-687-3331-Fax	
Precision Products, Inc.	714 Bradford Lane	Abingdon,	MD	21009	410-515-3967	410-515-3967-Fax	

Company Name	Mailing Address	City	State	Zip	Phone	Fax	Toll-free
W.L. Gore & Associates, Inc.	301 Airport Rd.	Elton,	MD	21921	410-392-3500	410-392-3849-Fax	
Michigan							
Big Buck Treestands	855 Chicago Rd.	Quincy,	MI	49082	517-639-3815	517-639-4576-Fax	
Bohning Company, Inc.	7361 N Seven Mile Rd.	Lake City,	MI	49651	616-229-4247	616-229-4615-Fax	800-253-0136
Burr and Company	3351 Claystone, SE Suite G-19	Grand Rapids,	MI	49546	616-977-7750	616-977-7755-Fax	800-878-2877
Buck Stop Lure Co.	PO Box 636	Stanton,	MI	48888	517-762-5091	517-762-5124-Fax	800-477-2368
Kwikee Kwiver Company, Inc.	PO Box 130	Acme,	MI	49610	616-938-1690	616-938-2144-Fax	800-346-7001
Lee's Pure Deer Urine Co.	2125 Miller Dr.	Niles,	MI	49120	616-683-8678	616-683-2961-Fax	800-551-3911
Bitzenburger Machine & Tool Inc.	13060 Lawson Rd.	Grand Ledge,	MI	48837	517-627-8433	517-627-8433-Fax	
Bohning Company, Ltd.	7361 N Seven Mile Rd.	Lake City,	MI	49651	616-229-4247	616-229-4615-Fax	800-253-0136
Carbon Impact	2628 Garfield Rd. N-Suite #38	Traverse City,	MI	49686	616-929-8152	616-929-8156-Fax	
Deer Quest LTD	PO Box 296	Belmont,	MI	49306	616-784-0312	616-784-7461-Fax	800-795-7581
Classic Displays	532 Cottage Grove SE	Grand Rapids,	MI	49507	616-247-6800	616-247-0309-Fax	
Darton Archery	3540 Darton Rd.	Hale,	MI	48739	517-728-4231	517-728-2410-Fax	
Stand Safe LLC	3375 Merriam Ave, Suite 103	Muskegon,	MI	49444	610-733-5560	610-733-5352-Fax	888-690-5625
Archery Center Intl., Inc.	PO Box A	Monroe,	MI	48161	313-243-3454	313-243-5710-Fax	800-822-USAV
Archery Dynamics, Inc.	2029 S Elms Rd.	Swartz Creek,	MI	48473	810-733-8766	810-733-2993-Fax	800-968-3121

Company Name	Mailing Address	City	State	Zip	Phone	Fax	Toll-free
Archery Innovations Inc.	390 East 11 Mile Rd.	Sault Ste. Marie,	MI	49783	906-635-9840	906-635-9840-Fax	
Stratton Outdoor Products	2896 Neuman Rd.	Rhodes,	MI	48652	517-879-4300	517-879-2299-Fax	
Patton Archery Mfg., Inc.	PO Box 161	Norway,	MI	49870	906-563-5990	906-563-7344-Fax	
Tailormaid Archery Products Inc.	12731-B Huron River Dr.	Romulus,	MI	48174	313-941-6611	313-941-8288-Fax	
A.L.S. Enterprises	821 W Western Ave.	Muskegon,	MI	49441	616-725-6181	616-725-7183-Fax	
Deer Crack	PO Box 245	Hartland,	MI	48353	810-632-6684	810-632-2257-Fax	
Phillips Industries, Inc.	2601 Davison Rd.	Flint,	MI	48506	810-239-4703	810-232-6698-Fax	800-416-3100
Pro Release, Inc.	33551 Giftos	Clinton Twp,	MI	48035	810-792-1410	810-792-1412-Fax	800-845-8515
Hunter's Choice Products, Inc.	PO Box 326	Romeo,	MI	48065	810-752-0046	810-752-1809-Fax	800-775-7664
Arrow Art	42093 Carriage Cove Circle	Canton,	MI	48187	734-844-1002	734-844-1745-Fax	
Arrowhead Adventures, Inc.	PO Box 5040	Muskegon,	MI	49445	888-423-4868	616-744-6428-Fax	
The Craft Agency, Inc.	PO Box 1187	Jackson,	MI	49204	517-787-0077	517-787-9356-Fax	
ArrowTrade Magazine	2285 E Newman Rd.	Lake City,	MI	49651	616-328-3006	616-328-3060-Fax	
North Starr Tree Stands	338 East Bell St.	Camden,	MI	49232	517-368-5890	517-368-5976-Fax	
Wyandotte Leather, Inc.	1811 Sixth St.	Wyandotte,	MI	48192	734-282-3403	734-282-3621-Fax	
Game Tracker, Inc.	PO Box 380	Flushing,	MI	48433	810-733-6360	810-733-2077-Fax	800-241-4833
Barnsdale Archery Manufacturing, Inc.	100 E Antoine	Iron Mountain,	MI	59801	906-774-1010	906-774-1705-Fax	
Metalmasters Target Systems	250 S. Sprague Rd.	Coldwater,	MI	49036	517-278-7475	517-278-7475-Fax	

Company Name	Mailing Address	City	State	Zip	Phone	Fax	Toll-free
Grayling Outdoor Products, Inc.	PO Box 192	Grayling,	MI	49738	517-348-2956	517-348-8628-Fax	800-426-8929
Maple Leaf Press, Inc.	1215 Beechtree St.	Grand Haven,	MI	49417	616-846-8844	616-846-6408-Fax	800-846-8847
Predator Products Co.	4030 Chilton Dr.	Muskegon,	MI	49441	616-798-3648	616-798-7060-Fax	

Minnesota

Company Name	Mailing Address	City	State	Zip	Phone	Fax	Toll-free
Detowis, Inc.	3137 Hennepin Ave. S, Ste. 104	Minneapolis,	MN	55408	612-825-2524	612-825-7102-Fax	800-438-9851
Double Bull Archery, LLC	PO Box 923	Monticello,	MN	55362	612-482-5651	612-295-2375-Fax	888-464-0409
Field Logic, Inc.	2117 Charles Ave.	St. Paul,	MN	55111	651-917-3655	651-653-3637-Fax	
Flex-Fletch Products	1840 Chandler Ave.	St. Paul,	MN	55113	651-426-4882	651-488-3344-Fax	
Great Grips Mfg., Inc.	Rt 5, Box 26	Austin,	MN	55912	507-437-4878	507-437-8564-Fax	
H & H Archery Supply	PO Box 363	Maple Lake,	MN	55358	320-963-5118	320-963-6521-Fax	800-356-2209
High Racks Inc.	PO Box 201	Staples,	MN	56479	218-894-2442	218-894-2442-Fax	
Barrie Archery	PO Box 482	Waseca,	MN	56093	507-835-3859	507-835-5097-Fax	
Archery Business	6420 Sycamore Lane	Maple Grove,	MN	55369	612-476-2200	612-476-8065-Fax	
Interregional Credit Systems, Inc.	7710 Brooklyn Blvd, Suite 103	Minneapolis,	MN	55443	612-560-1400	612-560-1900-Fax	
Robinson Laboratories	110 North Park Dr.	Cannon Falls	MN	55009	507-263-2885	507-263-5512-Fax	800-397-1927
Rocket Aerohead Corp.	PO Box 6783	Minneapolis,	MN	55406	612-722-9335	612-722-9335-Fax	800-762-0281
Ambush	PO Box 337	Shakopee,	MN	55379	612-496-0189	612-496-0204-Fax	800-944-0189

Company Name	Mailing Address	City	State	Zip	Phone	Fax	Toll-free
Wildlife Research Center, Inc.	1050 McKinley St.	Anoka,	MN	55303	612-427-3350	612-427-8354-Fax	800-873-5873
Babe Winkelman Productions	119 Smiley Rd.	Nisswa,	MN	56468	218-963-4424	218-963-7346-Fax	
Robinson Laboratories	110 North Park Dr.	Cannon Falls,	MN	55009	507-263-2885	507-263-5512-Fax	800-397-1927
USL Products	3110 Ranchview Lane	Minneapolis,	MN	55447	612-559-1052	612-559-7965-Fax	
Missouri							
Westark Pro Outdoor	3620 Arrowhead Ave.	Independence,	MO	64057	816-795-7722	816-805-4729-Fax	888-769-0183
Neet Products, Inc.	RR #2, Box 269B	Sedalia,	MO	65301	660-826-6762	800-645-7276	800-821-7196
Gran Pa Specialty Co.	3304 Woodson Rd.	St Louis,	MO	63114	314-427-0011	314-427-0011-Fax	
Visual Concepts	HCR 80 Box 170	Cuba,	MO	65453	573-885-4619	573-885-4649-Fax	
5-X Archery Products, Inc.	13208 Horseshoe Dr. W	Smithville,	MO	64089	816-532-0847	816-842-5949-Fax	
Toxonics Mfg. Inc.	1324 Wilmer Rd.	Wentzville,	MO	63385	314-639-8500	314-327-8105-Fax	800-748-8083
Sky Archery Company	11510 Natural Bridge	Bridgeton,	MO	63044	314-731-1600	314-731-1310-Fax	
American Rod & Gun	PO Box 2820	Springfield,	MO	65801	417-887-1915	417-887-9287-Fax	800-332-5377
Black Widow Bows	PO Box 2100	Nixa,	MO	65714	417-725-3113	417-725-3190-Fax	
Mississippi							
Hunting Solutions	2486 Commercial Dr.	Pearl,	MS	39208	601-932-5832	601-932-0068-Fax	
Primos, Inc.	PO Box 12785	Jackson,	MS	39236	601-366-1288	601-362-3274-Fax	800-523-2395
Blackwater Creek Treestands	PO Box 58	Marion,	MS	39342	601-484-2987	601-484-7433-Fax	
Southern Archery	PO Box 204	Louisville,	MS	39339	601-773-7956	601-773-9557-Fax	800-526-4868

Company Name	Mailing Address	City	State	Zip	Phone	Fax	Toll-free
Haas Outdoors, Inc.	PO Drawer 757	West Point,	MS	39773	601-494-8859	601-494-8742-Fax	800-331-5624
L & L Enterprises-Ol' Man Treestands	32 Raspberry Lane	Hattiesburg,	MS	39402	601-261-9410	601-261-9892-Fax	800-682-7268
Montana							
Sports, Inc.	333 2nd Ave. N	Lewistown,	MT	59457	406-538-3496	406-538-2801-Fax	
Performance Archery Products	PO Box 1002	Townsend,	MT	59644	425-335-0432		
Sight Master, Inc.	1093 Hwy 12 East	Townsend,	MT	59644	406-266-5516	406-266-5693-Fax	
Montana Black Gold	34370 Frontage Rd.	Bozeman,	MT	59715	406-586-1117	406-586-0853-Fax	800-586-0853
North Carolina							
McKenzie Supply, Inc.	PO Box 480	Granite Quarry,	NC	28072	704-279-8363	704-279-8958-Fax	888-279-7985
Carolina Archery Products	940 Sanford Rd.	Pittsboro,	NC	27312	919-542-0281	919-680-0303-Fax	
Elastic Products	PO Box 39	Marble,	NC	28905	828-837-9074	828-837-4074-Fax	
Loc On Company	111-F Gralin Rd.	Kernersville,	NC	27284	336-992-0990	336-992-0991-Fax	800-445-5799
James Greene Archery Products	2321 Yellow Banks Rd.	N. Wilkesboro,	NC	28649	336-670-2186	336-670-2149-Fax	
Nebraska							
Cabela's Inc.	812 13th Ave	Sidney,	NE	69160	308-254-5505	308-254-7809-Fax	
Saunders Archery	PO Box 476, Industrial Site	Columbus,	NE	68601	402-564-7176	402-564-3260-Fax	800-228-1408
Cornhusker Archery Company	PO Box 467	Bassett,	NE	68714	402-684-3590	402-684-2857-Fax	

Company Name	Mailing Address	City	State	Zip	Phone	Fax	Toll-free
New Hampshire							
New England School of Archery	109 School St.	Concord,	NH	03301	603-224-5768	603-224-5768-Fax	
Archers World.Com	PO Box 990	Exeter,	NH	03833	603-778-4720	603-778-7265-Fax	
New Jersey							
Wing Archery	227 Center Grove Rd.	Randolph,	NJ	07869	973-989-8957		
Original Brite-Site	34 Kentwood Rd.	Succosunna,	NJ	07876	973-584-0637	973-927-6779-Fax	
Ballistic Archery Inc.	PO Box 9	Rosemont,	NJ	08556	609-397-1990	609-397-0374-Fax	
Leica Sport Optics	156 Ludlow Ave	Northvale,	NJ	07647	770-993-8197	800-222-0118	
New York							
Deer Run Products Inc.	17 Ridgeview Terrace	Goshen,	NY	10924	914-294-9646		
Kaufman Footwear	700 Ellicott St.	Batavia,	NY	14020	519-749-3002	519-742-0034-Fax	800-265-2760
Kutmaster	820 Noyes St	Utica,	NY	13503	315-733-4663	315-733-6602-Fax	800-888-4223
Oneida Labs, Inc.	1263 County Route 54	Fulton,	NY	13069	315-668-0028	315-676-7686-Fax	800-269-6634
Sports Afield Magazine	250 West 55th St/3rd Floor	New York,	NY	10019	212-649-4300	212-581-3923-Fax	
Feather Visions, Inc.	6 Besemer Rd.	Ithaca,	NY	14850	607-539-3308	607-539-3308-Fax	
Pete Rickard, Inc.	R.D. #1, Box 292	Cobleskill,	NY	12043	518-234-3758	518-234-2454-Fax	800-282-5663
Quaker Boy, Inc.	5455 Webster Rd.	Orchard Park,	NY	14127	716-662-3979	716-662-9426-Fax	
Lansky Sharpeners	PO Box 800	Buffalo,	NY	14231	716-877-7511	716-877-6955-Fax	

Company Name	Mailing Address	City	State	Zip	Phone	Fax	Toll-free
Ohio							
Horton Manufacturing Company, Inc.	484 Tacoma Rd.	Tallmadge,	OH	44278	330-633-03053	30-633-7751-Fax	800-291-3649
Wilderness Tree Stands, Inc.	3645 Whitehouse-Spencer	Swanton,	OH	43558	419-877-0872	419-887-5051-Fax	
AcuSport Corporation	One Hunter Place	Bellefontaine,	OH	43311	937-593-7010	937-592-5625-Fax	800-543-3150
Columbus Industries, Inc.	PO Box 257	Ashville,	OH	43103	614-983-2552	614-983-4622-Fax	
Wildlife Legislative Fund of America	801 Kingsmill Parkway	Columbus,	OH	43229	614-888-4868	614-888-0326-Fax	
MTM Molded Products Co.	3370 Obco Ct.	Dayton,	OH	45414	937-890-7461	937-890-1747-Fax	800-543-0548
Horton Manufacturing Company, Inc.	484 Tacoma Rd.	Tallmadge,	OH	44278	330-633-0305	330-633-7751-Fax	800-291-3649
Hunter's Manufacturing Co.	1325 Waterloo Rd.	Suffield,	OH	44260	330-628-9245	330-628-0999-Fax	800-548-6837
Foster Manufacturing	PO Box 458	Batavia,	OH	45103	513-735-9770	513-735-9770-Fax	
Oklahoma							
Will Stop Target Co.	24808 Amah Parkway	Claremore,	OK	74017	918-343-4704	918-351-8449-Fax	800-543-8718
D.M.I., Inc.	Box 270723	Oklahoma City,	OK	73137	405-947-2191	405-947-6841-Fax	
Cobra Manufacturing Co., Inc.	PO Box 667	Bixby,	OK	74008	918-366-3634	918-366-3614-Fax	800-352-6272
Okie Manufacturing, Inc.	Rt 1, Box 234	Hendrix,	OK	74741	580-285-2270	580-285-2275-Fax	
Norman Archery Wholesale	8317 Gateway Terrace	Oklahoma City,	OK	73149	405-636-1415	405-636-1123-Fax	800-234-1811

Oregon

	Mailing Address	City	State	Zip	Phone	Fax	Toll-free
Leupold & Stevens, Inc.	14499 NW Greenbrier Parkway	Beaverton,	OR	97006	503-646-9171	503-526-1455-Fax	
Spot-Hogg Archery Products	PO Box 226	Harrisburg,	OR	97446	541-995-3702	541-995-6370-Fax	
Wilderness Sound Productions, LTD.	4015 Main St. Suite A	Springfield,	OR	97478	541-741-0263	541-741-7648-Fax	800-437-00060
Tepper Innovations, Inc.	PO Box 7	Shady Cove,	OR	97539	503-878-3113	503-878-2251-Fax	
Norway Industries	PO Box 516	Myrtle Point,	OR	97458	541-572-2950	541-572-3414-Fax	800-778-4755
Stanislawski Archery Products	7100 SE 72nd Ave.	Portland,	OR	97206	503-777-1228	503-777-0887-Fax	

Pennsylvania

	Mailing Address	City	State	Zip	Phone	Fax	Toll-free
Ideal Products, Inc.	PO Box 1006	DuBois,	PA	15801	814-371-3200	814-371-7242-Fax	800-544-3325
Bruin Industries, Inc.	1840 County Line Rd, unit 203	Hunting Valley,	PA	19006	215-357-7236	215-364-3951-Fax	
Apple Fastener's, Inc.	4698 East Trindle Rd.	Mechanicsburg,	PA	17055	717-761-8962	800-633-7916-Fax	800-704-8112
Hoyes Outdoor Products	235 Cameltown Hill Rd.	Danville,	PA	17821	717-275-1813	717-275-1813-Fax	
Kinsey's Archery Products, Inc.	1660 Steel Way Drive	Mt. Joy,	PA	17552	717-653-9074	717-653-6278-Fax	800-366-4269
Apple Archery Products, Inc.	PO Box 414	Manchester,	PA	17345	717-292-0418	717-292-0419-Fax	800-745-8190
Hi-Tek Sports Products	284 Jans Drive	Harleysville,	PA	13601	315-788-0107	315-788-0107-Fax	800-356-7285
Hunter's Valley Supply	RD 1, box 469D	Liverpool,	PA	17045	717-444-7075		
Full Adjust Archery Products	2195 A Old Phila. Pike	Lancaster,	PA	17602	717-394-7229	717-394-8635-Fax	
BuckWing Products, Inc.	2650 Lehigh St.	Whitehall,	PA	18052	610-821-5858	610-821-5808-Fax	

Company Name	Mailing Address	City	State	Zip	Phone	Fax	Toll-free
Archery Horizons	159 Elkin Ave.	Indiana,	PA	15701	724-349-9313	724-349-0698-Fax	
JoJan Sportsequip Co.	West Pointe Drive, Bldg 3	Washington,	PA	15301	724-225-5582	724-225-5582-Fax	
Woolrich, Inc.	1 Mill St.	Woolrich,	PA	17779	717-769-6464	717-769-6234-Fax	
Classic Archery Products	580 Kirks Mill Rd.	Lincoln University, PA		19352	610-869-2877	610-869-2730-Fax	
Nelsons Arrows	1181 Swede Hill Rd.	Greensburg,	PA	15601	724-837-6210	724-837-9755-Fax	
South Carolina							
Atsko/Sno Seal, Inc.	2530 Russell SE	Orangeburg,	SC	29115	802-531-1820	803-531-2139-Fax	800-845-2728
Jeffery Archery	PO Box 9625	Columbia,	SC	29290	803-776-3832	803-776-3832-Fax	
Ellett Brothers	PO Box 128	Chapin,	SC	29036	803-345-3751	803-345-1820-Fax	800-845-3711
Tiger Tuff	#3 Custom Mill Court	Greenville,	SC	29609	861-370-1500	864-370-1368-Fax	800-294-1526
Tennessee							
Archer's Choice Bowhunting Equip. LLC	PO Box 279	Dunlap,	TN	37327	423-949-4812	423-949-3119-Fax	
High Country Archery	PO Box 1269	Dunlap,	TN	37327	423-949-5000	423-949-5252-Fax	
Texas							
B & J Archery	PO Box 8461	Jacksonville,	TX	75766	903-586-0715	903-586-5496-Fax	
Hot Trails, Inc.	PO Box 460221	San Antonio,	TX	78246	210-545-4308	210-545-4308-Fax	
Longhorn Archery Systems	17585 Blanco Rd #10	San Antonio,	TX	78232	210-492-8774	210-492-4531-Fax	800-979-0915
TruGlo, Inc.	13745 Neutron Dr.	Dallas,	TX	75244	972-774-0300	972-774-0323-Fax	

	Mailing Address	City	State	Zip	Phone	Fax	Toll-free
Red Feather, Inc.	PO Box 560	Cibolo,	TX	78108	210-945-8552	210-945-8459-Fax	
Americase Inc.	PO Box 271	Waxahochie,	TX	75165	972-937-3629	972-937-8373-Fax	800-880-3629
Great Plains Traditional Bow Co.	314 W. Foster	Pampa,	TX	79065	806-665-5463	806-665-3035-Fax	
BoDoodle, Inc.	3301 US Hwy 84 North	Coleman,	TX	76834	915-625-2797	915-625-2623-Fax	800-467-8781
Grey Goose Traditional Archery	3701 Kirby Dr., Suite 1196	Houston,	TX	77098	713-521-0486	713-523-0386-Fax	
American Excelsior Company	PO Box 5067	Arlington,	TX	76005	817-640-1555	817-640-3570-Fax	800-777-7645
E.W. Bateman & Co.	PO Box 109	Fischer,	TX	78623	830-935-2255	830-935-2866-Fax	800-233-1208
Doskocil Manufacturing Company, Inc.	4209 Barnett	Arlington,	TX	76017	817-467-5116	817-472-9810-Fax	800-433-5186
Stanley Hips Targets	17585 Blanco Rd.	San Antonio,	TX	78232	210-492-4675	210-492-4531-Fax	800-325-2900

Utah

	Mailing Address	City	State	Zip	Phone	Fax	Toll-free
Sportsman's Outdoor Products	9352 S 670 W	Sandy,	UT	84070	801-562-8712	801-562-4306-Fax	
Jakes Archery	765 South Orem Blvd.	Orem,	UT	84058	801-225-0509	801-225-9509-Fax	800-225-0903
Bingham Projects, Inc.	1350 W. Hinckley Dr.	Ogden,	UT	84401	801-399-3470	801-399-3471-Fax	
Easton Technical Products, Inc.	5040 W Harold Gatty Dr.	Salt Lake City,	UT	84116	801-539-1400	801-533-9907-Fax	800-755-2117
Hoyt USA	543 N Neil Armstrong Rd.	Salt Lake City,	UT	84116	801-363-2990	801-537-1470-Fax	800-366-4698
Browning	One Browning Place	Morgan,	UT	84050	801-876-2711	801-876-3333-Fax	800-234-2045

Virginia

	Mailing Address	City	State	Zip	Phone	Fax	Toll-free
Tomorrow's Resources Unlimited, Inc.	PO Box 11529	Lynchburg,	VA	24506	804-929-2800	804-929-3864-Fax	

Company Name	Mailing Address	City	State	Zip	Phone	Fax	Toll-free
Trebark Camouflage-C.A.M.O.	3434 Buck Mountain Rd.	Roanoke,	VA	24024	540-774-9248	540-772-2790-Fax	800-843-2266
Parker Compound Bows, Inc.	PO Box 105	Mint Spring,	VA	24463	540-337-5426	540-337-0887-Fax	800-707-8149
Quality Archery Designs	PO Box 940	Madison Hts.,	VA	24572	804-847-5839	804-528-1696-Fax	

Vermont

Company Name	Mailing Address	City	State	Zip	Phone	Fax	Toll-free
Ambroid Company	PO Box 38	Springfield,	VT	05156	802-885-9244	802-885-9223-Fax	800-367-5507

Washington

Company Name	Mailing Address	City	State	Zip	Phone	Fax	Toll-free
Advanced Interactive Systems	565 Andover Park W, Suite 201	Tukwila,	WA	98188	206-575-9797	206-575-8665-Fax	800-441-4487
Fine-Line, Inc.	11220 164th St E	Puyallup,	WA	98374	253-848-4222	253-848-8671-Fax	800-445-0801
Archers-Ammo Inc.	4124 148 Ave N.E.	Redmond,	WA	98052	425-556-0492	425-556-9213-Fax	800-424-6737
Vital Sight, Inc.	9840 M.L. King Jr. Way S.	Seattle,	WA	98118	206-723-0383	206-723-7971-Fax	800-480-3496
Martin Archery, Inc.	Rt 5, Box 127	Walla Walla,	WA	99362	509-529-2554	509-529-2186-Fax	

West Virginia

Company Name	Mailing Address	City	State	Zip	Phone	Fax	Toll-free
Custom Shooting Systems, Inc.	526 10th St.	Huntington,	WV	25701	304-522-4659	304-522-4654-Fax	

Wisconsin

Company Name	Mailing Address	City	State	Zip	Phone	Fax	Toll-free
Buck Rub Archery, Inc.	157 Bank St.	Waukesha,	WI	53188	414-547-0535	414-547-0693-Fax	800-367-2182
Come-Alive Decoy Products	4916 Seton Place	Greendale,	WI	53129	414-421-2840	414-421-7671-Fax	
Mathews Inc.	919 River Rd, PO Box 367	Sparta,	WI	54656	608-269-2728	608-269-3120-Fax	
Whitewater Outdoors, Inc.	W4228 Church St.	Hingham,	WI	53031	920-564-2674	800-666-2674	

Company Name	Mailing Address	City	State	Zip	Phone	Fax	Toll-free
Del-Ma Archery /Renegade Bows	PO Box 23	Coleman,	WI	54112	920-897-2493	920-897-4568-Fax	800-659-6865
Lakewood Associates, Inc.	2905 Silver Cedar Rd.	Oconomowoc,	WI	53066	414-567-7672	414-567-7692-Fax	800-227-7672
Kolpin Mfg., Inc.	PO Box 107	Fox Lake,	WI	53933	920-928-3118	920-928-3687-Fax	800-5kolpin
K.D.L. Outdoor Products, Inc.	10438 South Young St.	Wisconsin Rapids,	WI	54494	715-325-4160	715-325-4162-Fax	
Trendsetters, Inc.	420 Sunshine Ave.	Delavan,	WI	53115	414-728-8824	414-728-9976-Fax	
Trueflight Manufacturing Co.	Box 1000	Manitowish	WI	54545	715-543-8451	715-543-2525-Fax	
BoneBuster Outdoor Inc.	Box 244	Kieler,	WI	53812	608-748-4493	608-748-4342-Fax	
Sport Climbers, Inc.	PO Box 597	Kenosha,	WI	53143	414-652-3126	414-652-3188-Fax	800-877-7025
Predator, Inc.	2605 Coulee Ave.	La Crosse,	WI	54601	608-787-0500	608-787-0667-Fax	
Little Jon's	5346 Missouri Rd.	Marshall,	WI	53559	608-655-3750	608-655-4621-Fax	800-344-4011
Tru-Fire Corporation	N7355 State St.	N. Fond Du Lac,	WI	54937	920-923-6866	920-923-4051-Fax	
Retract-O-Blade Archery Products	127 W Birch Ave.	Whitefish Bay,	WI	53217	414-961-2098	414-961-2098-Fax	
Renegade Archery Company	6316 Center Rd.	Sturgeon Bay,	WI	54235	920-746-1477	920-743-1767-Fax	888-350-2697
Forge Flite, Inc.	2860 So. 171st St	New Berlin,	WI	53151	414-789-5236	414-789-5218-Fax	

Wyoming

Company Name	Mailing Address	City	State	Zip	Phone	Fax	Toll-free
Brunton	620 E. Monroe Ave.	Riverton,	WY	82501	307-856-6559	307-856-8282-Fax	
Sims Vibration Lab.	W450 Enterprise Rd.	Shelton,	WY	98584	360-427-6031	360-427-4025-Fax	

Company Name	Mailing Address	City	State	Zip	Phone	Fax	Toll-free
Natpro Inc.	PO Box 1076	Lander,	WY	82510	307-332-3068	307-332-3089-Fax	800-824-0092
Canada							
Excalibur Crossbow, Inc.	45 Hillinger Cr., Unit #2	Kitchener, Ont.,	Canada	N2K2Z1	519-743-6890	519-743-6964-Fax	800-463-1817
Sportchief Canada	888 Chambly Rd.	Marieville, Queb.,	Canada	J3M1R2	800-567-1729	800-567-0631-Fax	
Jackson Archery Mfg., Inc.	PO Box 537	Lindsay, Ont.,	Canada	K9V4S5	705-324-4227	705-324-8366-Fax	
England							
Merlin Compound Bows	Bull in the Hollow Farm, Leicester Rd	Loughborough, England			1509233555	1509235252-Fax	
Japan							
Shibuya Archery-M. Yasui & Co., Ltd.	Yasui Bldg. 3-7-4 Ikejiri, Setagaya-ku	Tokyo,	Japan	154	011-81 3-5430 7211	011 81 3 5430 5813-Fax	
Korea							
Samick Sport Co., Ltd	610-6, Kameong Don	Kimpo, Kyungki-Do	Korea		341-983-5599	341-983-3338-Fax	
Sweden							
Bow Pro AB	Box 12016-220 12 Lund	24502 Hjarup, Sweden			01146 40 465035	01146 40 465037-Fax	

KEEP ONE STEP AHEAD

The Expert Advice of These Hunting Professionals Will Show You How!

The Deer Hunters
Tactics, Lore, Legacy and Allure of American Deer Hunting
by Patrick Durkin, Editor
Liberally illustrated in dynamic full-color, this coffee-table treasure examines effective deer hunting strategies and the mystique surrounding the magnificent white-tail. Also provides a thought-provoking look at hunting ethics in the 1990s, and the common bonds shared by hunters, the whitetail and the land.

Hardcover • 8-1/2 x 11 • 208 pages
110 color photos
BOD • $29.95

Big Bucks the Benoit Way
Secrets from America's First Family of Whitetail Hunting
by Bryce Towsley
Finally, the long-awaited second book on the tried-and-true hunting strategies of the legendary Benoit family. Although tracking and woodsmanship are emphasized, hunters of all ages, no matter where they hunt, will gain the knowledge needed to bag trophy bucks.

Hardcover • 8-1/2 x 11 • 208 pages
150 b&w photos • 16-page color section
HBB • $24.95

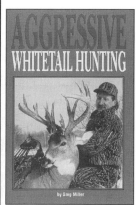

Aggressive Whitetail Hunting
by Greg Miller
Answers any hunter's questions on how to hunt trophy bucks in public forests and farmlands, as well as in exclusive hunting lands. It's the perfect approach for gun and bow hunters who don't have the time or finances to hunt exotic locales.

Softcover • 6 x 9 • 208 pages
80 b&w photos
AWH01 • $14.95

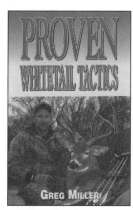

Proven Whitetail Tactics
by Greg Miller
Both entertaining and educational, this volume, from one of America's premier deer hunters, explains effective strategies for scouting, calling and stalking white-tailed deer in the close-to-home locales available to most hunters. Packed with tips and tactics that spell deer hunting success.

Softcover • 6 x 9 • 224 pages
100 b&w photos
AWH02 • $19.95

Hunting Mature Bucks
by Larry Weishuhn
Special focus on the awesome old buck and incredible tips from North America's top whitetail deer authorities sets the pace for hunting those big, elusive bucks. Learn about proven hunting methods and herd management techniques.

Softcover • 6 x 9 • 213 pages
80 b&w photos
HMB01 • $14.95

Mule Deer: Hunting Today's Trophies
by Tom Carpenter and Jim Van Norman
Monster mule deer lead hunters into the toughest territory around, but Jim Van Norman & Tom Carpenter show how to bring back "one for the wall." From the art of spotting mule deer before they spot you to the delicate job of stalking for the perfect shot, this book puts you right in the middle of mule deer action.

Softcover • 8-1/2 x 11 • 256 pages
150 b&w photos • 16 color pages
HTMD • $19.95

OWN A WORLD CLASS
HUNTING LIBRARY

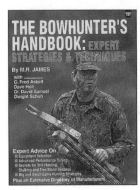